CIAO OUSMANE

HSIAO-HUNG PAI

Ciao Ousmane

The Hidden Exploitation of Italy's
Migrant Workers

HURST & COMPANY, LONDON

First published in the United Kingdom in 2021 by
C. Hurst & Co. (Publishers) Ltd.,
41 Great Russell Street, London, WC1B 3PL

Distributed in the United States, Canada and Latin America by
Oxford University Press, 198 Madison Avenue, New York, NY 10016,
United States of America.

A Cataloguing-in-Publication data record for this book
is available from the British Library.

ISBN: 9781787384699

www.hurstpublishers.com

Printed in Great Britain by Bell and Bain Ltd, Glasgow

For the unbeatable Dave, with all my love

All workers' names have been changed.

CONTENTS

Southern Italy

FOREWORD

As I write, in late March 2020, a new infectious disease, for which there is as yet no vaccine or effective treatment, is spreading in multiple countries around the world. While mortalities in Italy are the highest in Europe, surpassing China, other countries are fast catching up. For many weeks now, those of us Europeans whose work is desk-bound have had the luxury of packing up our offices and working from home. It goes without saying that workers in the emergency services and other key sectors simply cannot recreate the working day in their living rooms. Not just the doctors, nurses, ambulance drivers, paramedics, pharmacists, care workers and teachers, but also the caterers, cleaners, those employed in warehousing, sanitation, dairy farming, the slaughtering and processing of livestock, fisheries, cockle-picking, vegetable and fruit harvesting, and general food distribution: they cannot go to 'war on the virus' (British prime minister Boris Johnson's favourite phrase) through social distancing strategies and self-isolation.

Maybe, just maybe, we will emerge from this global pandemic with a heightened awareness of the *omertà* about suffering that Hsiao-Hung Pai identifies as scarring the lives of our fellow human beings living in Europe in abandoned farmhouses and shack-and-tent cities. They labour in Italian fields—an estimated 405,000 of them—in subhuman conditions, imprisoned within a cynical quasi-legal system designed to keep them 'out of sight, out of mind.' If the current situation on the Aegean island of Lesvos is anything to go by, Africans in places like

Sicily, and the doctors who attend them, could soon find themselves vilified by the Far Right as the carriers of Covid-19.

In agri-food production and distribution, globalisation has long since opened up a global food market, but the fruit and vegetable pickers who are the lynchpin of Italy's food supply-chain are invisible, as the state is forever 'diluting their presence by pushing them further underground.' They harvest the asparagus, mandarins, grapes, olives, and tomatoes (the last two known as 'black gold' and 'red gold' respectively) in Italy. In the 'Made in Italy' context, it is no longer Italians (once emigrants themselves), but postcolonial subjects, mainly from sub-Saharan Africa, who are doing the making—often having escaped torture, forced labour and detention in Libya and risking the perilous journey across the Mediterranean Sea. These Africans are not the invading scroungers of popular myth. They are men and women of immense courage, with coping mechanisms and inner resources that many of us 'settled' Europeans could only dream of. They left their homes in, say, Senegal, Nigeria, Gambia or Mali because of a mixture of IMF and World Bank imposed Stabilisation and Structural Adjustment Programmes, climate change, and neoliberal cuts to public spending and public services. This gave them no choice but to sacrifice themselves, for the good of their families, by seeking a livelihood elsewhere.

But how is this sacrifice rewarded? Instead of valuing their contribution to society, Europe passes laws and policies that dehumanise and disenfranchise them. Confined to segregated agricultural spaces, and rendered collectively homeless in a field, they are usually unable to find work in other sectors because this would bring them in contact with the Italian public. 'They were labourers in the fields and customers in the shops, and nothing else,' records Hsiao-Hung Pai, in this breathtaking, hard-hitting take on the lives of agri-workers in Italy. Her anger may be controlled, but it is palpable when she writes of Mohammed, 'No local person would even look him in the eye; it was as if he had no soul.'

The first step taken is to imprison migrants within an asylum and residence permit system that is designed to enforce economic exploitation and racial exclusion, a form of 'violence by design'. Here, housing, or rather the lack of it, is the key instrument for maintaining the conditions of super-exploitation: in the Catch-22 world of migration law, an offer of a work contract requires a residence permit, but a residence permit requires an address. It would seem that international law and indeed the country's own constitution have no jurisdiction in Italy. The 1948 UN Declaration of Human Rights and the 1966 International Covenant on Economic Social and Cultural Rights (ICESCR) both recognise the human right to adequate housing for oneself and one's family. And the revised Italian Constitution (2001) acknowledges minimum state provision of housing as a core component of human dignity.

In the context of the Covid-19 pandemic, when we are constantly being told that, in this war on the virus, 'we are all in it together,' the lack of housing perhaps foreshadows worse to come. In centuries past, plagues and epidemics would be quickly followed by mass famines. Though we do not expect anything on this catastrophic scale today, Covid-19 has already been accompanied by food scarcity. In London, as I write, several emergency food aid charities have been forced to close, finding it impossible to replenish stocks, even as thousands more people are turning to them for help. The rich may not be protected from disease, but they do not live amongst the marginalised; they have no idea what existence is like in tents and shacks where every day is a fight for survival against hunger, hypothermia, and homelessness. For, as Giorgio Agamben has written, the camp, where people are defined as having lives not worth living and are vulnerable to early death and state killings, long preceded the Holocaust.[1]

And as Hsiao-Hung Pai, who provides chapter and verse on EU policies, knows only too well the treatment of migrant agricultural workers in Italy and the use of the law to set exploitation in situ are not exceptions—either in Europe or globally. The plastic greenhouses for tomatoes, cucumbers and peppers of the Costa del Sol are worth €2 billion a year to supermarkets, profits made on the backs of migrant workers from Morocco, West Africa and Eastern Europe. In California, the labour of Mixteco migrants from the mountain villages of Oaxaca ensures not only that American consumers eat strawberries all year round, but also that producers and distributors such as Driscoll's and Walmart, reap incredible profits.[2] After the first Palestinian intifada in 1987, and restrictions on the number of

Palestinians allowed to work, Israel looked to the western provinces of Thailand for migrant workers to grow vegetables, fruits, seeds, plants and field crops. Disturbing patterns of 'sudden nocturnal death syndrome' were soon reported, most likely due to long hours without rest, leading to heat exhaustion and heat stroke.[3] In Queensland, Australia, the deplorable treatment of migrant citrus pickers from nine Pacific islands and Timor-Leste has been compared to the nineteenth-century practice of 'blackbirding' whereby traders transported more than 62,000 people from the South Sea Islands to the Australian continent as 'sugar slaves.'[4]

But what is exceptional about the Italian context is the way in which this racial super-exploitation echoes the country's colonial and fascist history, and its denial of that history.

In the mid-nineteenth century, the peninsula now known as Italy was made up of city states, republics, and other independent entities, some under the Austrian Habsburg yoke. The Kingdom of Italy only emerged in 1861. Being a relative latecomer to Europe's colonial and imperialist extraction of Africa's resources, Italy's leaders were eager to catch up and, from the start, the kingdom's acquisition of colonies became closely linked to the forging of a national identity. Garibaldi himself spoke 'in favour of loading on Africans the chains of servitude that Italy had struck from itself.'[5] In this way, the colonisation of parts of Africa was seen as a rendezvous with history, aimed at reliving the glories of the Roman Empire, in what the fascist leader Benito Mussolini later came to define as *Africa Orientale Italiana*. By the end of the nineteenth century, Italy had acquired Eritrea and Somalia and, in 1912, it finally succeeded in conquering Libya (which it regarded as the 'Fourth Shore' of Italy) in a lengthy and brutal war. Humiliated by its defeat by the Ethiopian army at the Battle of Adwa in 1896, Italy reasserted itself during the fascist period, invading and occupying Ethiopia. At the end of the Second World War, many Italian war criminals escaped prosecution by the skin of their teeth, with the duplicitous game played by the British at the UN War Crimes Commission ensuring that the crimes committed by Mussolini's forces in Ethiopia were treated as an acceptable feature of modern warfare.[6]

Italy's record of colonial crimes, terror and extermination includes, in Libya, the imprisonment and extermination (through starvation and disease) of at least 80,000 people in a network of concentration camps, and the bombing of its cities with poison gas; and in Ethiopia, during the invasion of 1936, the use of 280 kilograms of mustard gas to bomb Ethiopian villages and Red Cross camps. Appearing at the League of Nations, emperor-in-exile Haile Selassie described how vaporisers for mustard gas were attached to planes so that the deadly poisonous gas could be dispersed over a wide area in a 'never-ending rain of death.'[7] Also in Ethiopia, the Graziani Massacre in Addis Ababa (named after General Graziani, Viceroy of Italian East Africa who ordered the killings after an attempt on his life), saw at least 19,000 but perhaps as many as 30,000 men, women and children slaughtered over three days by Blackshirts armed with rifles, pistols, bombs and flamethrowers.

Although Mussolini's crimes in Africa are well known there has been no real calling to account—though, in one cynical move in 2008, Prime Minister Silvio Berlusconi signed a cooperation treaty with Gaddafi, whereby Italy paid $5 billion to Libya as compensation for its former military occupation, with Libya in return taking measures to combat illegal immigration from Libya and boosting investments in Italian companies. In this way, Italy became complicit in both Libyan human rights abuses including torture, and EU necropolitics in the Mediterranean Sea.

Ciao Ousmane tells the most graphic tale of what happens to Africans who make it to Italy—how they live, work, and, most importantly, resist. Just as John Steinbeck turned his dispatches to the *San Francisco News* into the gripping novel *The Grapes of Wrath*, after travelling westward through the dustbowl of the late 1930s with the poverty-stricken pickers, so it does Hsiao-Hung Pai turn her life on the frontline with African migrant workers into a harrowing panorama of life today amongst those she describes as Italy's 'necessary outcasts.'

Principled journalist, dedicated anthropologist, insurgent sociologist with a depth of imagination comparable to C. Wright Mills himself, Hsiao-Hung Pai is a compelling teller of truth. She has lived alongside migrants and has been attentive to every detail of their daily lives and their suffering. She is a weaver of tapestries—the weft lies in the storytelling, while the warp, the invisible threads, is the political analysis. The layers of deceit that our European societies are built on are peeled back in *Ciao Ousmane*, forcing us to confront the nature of a European civilisation that confines Africans displaced by neoliberal globalisation to subordinate spaces and leaves them vulnerable to early death.

Her conclusion is inescapable. We need to collapse and overthrow all social relations determined by structural racism.

Liz Fekete,
Director of the Institute of Race Relations (IRR), London

OMERTÀ

4:45 am. The small Sicilian town was yet to stir on this autumn Sunday morning. The streets were deserted; not a soul to be seen but a few stray dogs. The shuttered windows of rows of identical post-war houses were tightly fastened. There were no women chattering across the balconies of apartments along the narrow lanes. The sleepy silence was like the night before, and the night before that—slumber that this 400-year-old town would always fall into. Even its Roman name, Campobello di Mazara, or simply Campobello, the Handsome Fields, had a drowsy tone. On the edge of town, only a few metres away from the empty streets, a mass of white rocks stood on a hill where dozens of sheep would soon be grazing. In front of the hill stood fresh groves of dark green olives, soaked in the early morning dew. They looked heavy, their leaves weighed down, the green and black fruits waiting to be picked. The fields stretched out handsomely for many miles until they reached the sea.

In the middle distance, hidden well behind the thick olive groves, were dozens of tents and shacks. The area was called Erbe Bianche, or White Grass. You could tell by the way the tents and shacks were built so close together that there were more than a few hundred people living there. While the town still slept, many of them had already got up and were dressed and ready for the start of the day's work in the fields. They had come from countries thousands of miles away, across the Mediterranean Sea: Senegal, Gambia, Mali and elsewhere in West Africa. It was not their choice to have found shelter here, in an encampment that bore no resemblance to the concrete-built Italian farming town not so far away. Tacked on to the edge of Campobello, the place was an unwanted secret, kept locked away. The *omertà* of the town.

To the right of the encampment were a couple of derelict farmhouses that had been occupied by several farm workers. Ousmane was living in one of them. Dotted around as part of the furniture of the rural landscape, these farmhouses embodied many untold tales that had been buried with the past of the forsaken.

At a couple of minutes to 5:00 am, Ousmane opened and rubbed his eyes, probably disturbed by the chirping of the birds, or one of his co-workers turning over in a bed a few metres away. In this abandoned farmhouse where they slept, sounds came from everywhere. Ousmane sat up. He was not sure whether the sun had risen yet. It was pitch-dark inside the farmhouse, daybreak or not, because the windows had been bricked up years before. He looked for a match to light a candle, not noticing the smell from a gas cylinder that had started leaking during his sleep. Only half awake, he struck a match.

The gas cylinder exploded in front of him, the sound reverberating across the fields. Before Ousmane was even able to scream, he had been burned terribly. He lost consciousness. His fellow workers, utterly shaken, phoned for an ambulance. They explained the situation in broken Italian, telling the emergency services their location—White Grass. The help came too late. Upon arrival, the paramedics decided that Ousmane's condition was too severe for the local hospital. Sixty per cent of his body was severely burned and the hospital in Campobello was not equipped to help him. He had to be sent to the civic hospital in Palermo, more than three hours away. That morning, when he eventually arrived in the city, he passed away. It was 20 October 2013.

At the hospital, it was learned that his full name was Ousmane Diallo. He was twenty-six years old and came from Senegal. Sadly, apart from his age and country of origin, very little seemed to be known about him. Perhaps it was because Ousmane was a quiet, unassuming person, who simply committed himself to working and did not stand out in a crowd. What was clear was that, like his fellow countrymen who started arriving in 2008 and 2009, Ousmane had every reason to be in Campobello.

As a young man who felt responsible for his family, Ousmane had been compelled to leave his home to seek a secure livelihood several months before he met his death. He was not alone. In the old days, Senegal had been a key destination where many Africans would go to find better means of making a living. By the mid-1970s, however, Senegal's external debt increased so sharply that the government had to turn to the International Monetary Fund (IMF) and the World Bank. Things went rapidly downhill from there. From the early 1980s to the 1990s, the IMF and the World Bank had dominated economic and public policies in Senegal—and other sub-Saharan African countries—with their Stabilisation Programmes and Structural Adjustment Programmes (SAPs). These meant cuts to public spending, dismantling of the public sector, and the privatisation of state enterprises and public services. The economic liberalisation under these institutions led to the collapse of Senegal's industries and agriculture. It had, in fact, exacerbated Senegal's debt problems and pushed the country into permanent poverty.

Ordinary people bore the brunt of this intensified crisis as their livelihoods and basic security were taken away. Small farmers and peasants found it hard to survive in the face of competition from subsidised imports from developed countries. Young people like Ousmane had found it increasingly difficult to find work in both the private and public sectors, with competition being fierce for the very few jobs they had left. It became clear that prospects for Ousmane were slim. The young people of Senegal could not wait to pack their bags and leave home to search for opportunities in the outside world. Senegal had become what they call a 'migrant-sending' country—a country from which to emigrate.

As most young and able Senegalese would say: 'It is a necessity to leave home to improve your lot.' Not only the Senegalese, but every other sub-Saharan African who happened to be on this journey, would tell you exactly the same thing. Those who are able to overcome the difficulties and ordeals of the journey and manage to succeed in improving their lot by working abroad are given the utmost respect at home. They are the ones setting an example for others who want to follow in their footsteps. They are seen as heroes whose struggles—and remittances—lead to their families, their communities and their home countries being rebuilt. They are seen as the role models for future generations.

Ousmane did not choose to come to Italy. He simply followed the path that was available to him. In the past, France, being Senegal's coloniser until 1960, was where the Senegalese would go. French cities such as Marseille had seen large Senegalese communities build up over the decades. But when France introduced a visa system for Senegal in 1985 to keep out the unwanted, Senegalese people started looking for other destinations. Since laws regularising undocumented migrants were passed in Italy in 1990 and 1994, just as Senegal's economic crisis was worsening, it became the most popular country in Europe for Senegalese people to emigrate to.

Ousmane did not stand out in his endeavour to improve the life of his family back home. He was one of tens of thousands. He kept his head down and endured the most extreme hardships in Libya, before saving enough cash to afford an unsafe boat ride to Europe. He was what Europeans called a refugee or a migrant. The Europeans, being the former colonisers of African countries, looked at him in an entirely different way from how his fellow countrymen viewed him. They did not see him as a hardworking man who was prepared to take risks for his family's future. Rather, he was a foreigner—a *clandestine*, as the Italians would usually call him—albeit a fit and working-age foreigner who was harvesting olives in the fields and making profits for local agriculture. Even when he died, he became a lifeless name in the newspapers, and nothing more.

Ousmane's life was cut short, his dreams left unrealised, his family back in Senegal devastated. Harvesting olives was not all that he had wanted to do with his life. Campobello was only supposed to be a stop on his journey, a place to come only during harvests. He wanted to go much further, beyond farming in Campobello and Sicily. Had he saved enough to afford to rent a room somewhere, and been permitted to do so, he would not have looked back at his life in the deserted farmhouse. He would have moved to a bigger town, or even another country, like many fellow Senegalese did to embrace new opportunities. But his life did not go beyond the time in that derelict farmhouse.

Not many people outside of African communities heard about Ousmane's tragic death. In fact, few Sicilians outside of Campobello ever knew of it. Even fewer knew about the existence of Senegalese people in White Grass between 2008 and 2013. Only a couple of Italian newspapers mentioned Ousmane's death—and even then, they literally only mentioned it. A couple of lines were all that he seemed to deserve. His twenty-six years of life were reduced to a paragraph about his death. It was as if there was a deliberate muting of the news. Perhaps anything more would have provoked thoughts about what kind of society had enabled this to happen. It would have rocked the boat— and few in the Italian media would feel it in their interest to do that. But instead of something conspiratorial, their silence was a habit.

The truth was that African workers had kept this olive region going for two decades. When Ousmane died, there were already more than 25,000 men and women from outside the country toiling on Sicilian farms, pumping life into agriculture and keeping it prosperous. With around 5,000 olive growers,[1] Campobello had always been one of the most important stops in the cycle of seasonal labour in Sicily. It had always been known for its Nocellara del Belice olives[2]—dubbed by British celebrity chef Jamie Oliver as 'the world's best olives'— which are specifically and uniquely produced in this region. Ninety per cent of olive growers in Campobello had small farms with areas of no more than two hectares,[3] and these family farms had gradually started employing workers from outside the area by the early 1990s. This was mainly because there was insufficient local labour to do the strenuous and increasingly on-demand, flexible work. Subsequently, between September and December each year, around 3,000 African workers, the majority from Sub-Saharan Africa, had come to work on the farms here. Their presence had guaranteed the harvesting of the olives across the region. Not only that—the workforce that came into the area during harvests had also given a visible boost to the local shops and businesses. The town simply could not survive without them.

Few mourned Ousmane's death in Campobello, although it could never have been kept a secret in this rural town, which, with a population of just over 11,000, felt more like a village. A horrific accident of this kind was unheard of in Campobello—certainly one involving an olive harvest worker. It would have been unthinkable for this to have happened to a local worker, who would never have found themselves in similar circumstances. 'A black man, a *clandestine*, was killed in an explosion,' local residents said, passing on the news, each time adding a bit of colour of their own. They did not even need to have talked to an African worker to be able to hear or picture what had happened. The story took on a life of its own.

But what is a *clandestine*? The use of this word has always been derogatory, much like the way the word 'wop' (derived from the word *guappo*, meaning 'dandy' or 'ruffian' in Italian) was used by white Americans to refer to Italian migrants to the US, particularly the undocumented, in the early twentieth century. The term *clandestine* became a much more meaningful word in Italy in July 2002, when Silvio Berlusconi's government passed legislation known as the Bossi Fini law.[4] The law built on the 1998 Consolidated Act on immigration, which had been introduced by the centre-left government of Romano Prodi, the founder of the Democratic Party (PD) and its first president in 2007. Prodi's law introduced holding centres[5] for migrants who were unable to provide proof of their identity and immigration status. The Bossi Fini law consolidated these existing measures and brought in criminal sanctions for people who entered Italy without permission and made them targets for deportation. Under this law, a formal employment contract was required to obtain or renew a two-year residence permit (*permesso di soggiorno*), which tied a migrant's immigration status (the right to stay) to a job, making them dependent on their employers to remain. It therefore exposed migrant workers to a far greater risk of exploitation.

Then, in May 2008, the Berlusconi government announced the Security Package (*Pacchetto Sicurezza*) which aimed to fight 'widespread illegality' linked to migration. The Package, spearheaded by Manuela Del Lago of what was then the Northern League, introduced the criminal offence of 'illegal entry and stay within the territory of the state.' The bill became law in 2009 and formally criminalised entering or living in Italy without permission.[6]

These policies defined the *clandestine* and helped create an underclass of undocumented or status-less workers in Italy. Meanwhile, unrealistic quotas were set for migrant workers[7]—so unrealistic that they resulted in five regularisation programmes for a total of 1.4 million irregular migrants from 1986 to 2012. However, quotas for seasonal workers have been nearly cut in half, from 35,000 in 2012 to 18,000 in 2019,[8] while at the time of writing in 2020 the last regularisation programme was in 2012. It is as if the creation and maintenance of an underclass of African workers through the asylum reception system—particularly since 2011, when the Western military intervention in Libya led many people to flee to Europe—have enabled the authorities and the agricultural sector not to worry about granting an amnesty.

Clandestine simply became part of the day-to-day Italian vocabulary. In the public mind, consciously or subconsciously, the meaning of the word had expanded beyond an immigration status and come to connote blackness. Irrespective of whether he had documents, Ousmane was viewed by Italian locals as a *clandestine*, signalling his belonging to a racialised and segregated category.

This was the context in which Ousmane lost his life. He was but one of tens of thousands of workers who leave Africa for Europe, fleeing chronic poverty, persecution and conflict in countries once ruined by colonialism and still ravaged by institutions of the West in the decades since. Those who escape forced labour, torture and death in Libya and survive the dangerous sea journey in the middle of the Mediterranean, arrive in Italy only to find themselves exploited and marginalised in their new country and continent.

Ousmane is the embodiment of the most racialised Other in Europe. He was neither the first nor the last African worker to be forsaken by an advanced capitalist EU country that has human rights in its charters.

The aim of *Ciao Ousmane* is to document and expose the segregation and subjugation of people whom Italy and Europe have demonised as a burden and society's gravest problem, all while exploiting their labour. The book tells the story of how state and society create and keep the secret of its 'necessary outcasts.' The vilification of migrants serves a clear purpose, just as the colonial European powers racialised those over whom they ruled and thereby justified their expropriation and domination of other continents.

The death of Ousmane and the stories of other migrant workers reveal this secret. This is for you, Ousmane.

1

OLIVE COUNTRY

By the time of Ousmane's death, migrant workers had been toiling in the fields of the region for over fifteen years. Whatever their migratory status, they had one common goal: to survive and work to support their families back home.

Local people in Campobello had seen African men and young boys walking around town for a long time, but a conversation with them was rare. Most people preferred to keep their distance from 'the blacks.' Those who had any contact with the Africans—in shops when topping up mobile phone credit, or when buying food in a supermarket— would always keep interactions to a minimum. The Africans were kept out of sight in their encampment on the edge of town. In this way, the town had created an enclave for African workers—economically, socially, culturally and emotionally.

What was visible was the power relationship between the town and the ghetto. As Loïc Wacquant would put it:[1] it had always been 'us' (the townspeople) setting the rules and making plans for 'them' (the 'foreigners,' 'the blacks'). The power relationship meant that the ghetto was distinguished from the town by its desolation, as in Wacquant's reaction when he first saw the ghettoes of Chicago: 'I remember thinking: "It's like Beirut. Or Dresden after the war."'[2]

Local residents in Campobello had little knowledge about what went on in the ghetto and what happened to the African workers in the fields. Even the day after Ousmane died, the townsfolk did not know who he was. As it turned out, Ousmane was not quite a *clandestine*, as he was described. He had received his documents and had been given the disused farmhouse to sleep in by the farmer for whom he was working. Derelict as it was, a bed in that building was a step up from sleeping out in the fields. It was the 'boss's house', as his co-workers called it. Ousmane died on the premises of the farm and was therefore the responsibility of the farmer, the boss.

Even after his death, townsfolk in Campobello did nothing for Ousmane. It was the Senegalese from other parts of Sicily who travelled to Campobello to show solidarity, organising an angry protest against the conditions that had caused his death. Activists from the Palermo Anti-Racist Forum arranged to return Ousmane's body to his family in Senegal. Other associations and NGOs from across the province of Trapani also came to Campobello and took part in attempts to uncover the circumstances that led to Ousmane's death.

Among the activists was Alberto Biondo, who had been working for Borderline Sicilia to monitor reception camps in the province over the previous decade. Back then, he had observed that more and more Africans were coming to work on farms and realised that there was a reality outside the reception camps with which Italians were not familiar. They started to see that there were tents and shacks next to the reception camps. He realised there was something else going on. Since Ousmane's death, Alberto and his colleagues have discovered more about the situation in White Grass. For him, Ousmane's death was not an accident. He died as a result of political choices. There was a hidden history of blood and violence behind the crops that the country produced and lived on. '*Sangue nostrum*,' some activists started to call it. Our blood.

What was the world really like at White Grass? What was allowed to happen? The immediate cause of the tragedy was clear to see: the farmers were not abiding by the rules.[3] From the day African workers came to work in the Campobello area—and across the entire country—they had never been provided with suitable housing, however temporary. But what made the community and wider society blind to the situation all these years? How did it remain hidden and stay unchallenged for so long?

* * *

Sanji, from Gambia, was one of the longest-serving workers in Campobello. He was among the 700 Africans who were working in the olive fields at the time of Ousmane's death. Sanji was then twenty-one. He stood out, with a relaxed smile and his short Rasta dreadlocks hanging above his shoulders. His calm demeanour seemed to contrast with the extremely precarious environment in which he found himself. The living space that he shared with fellow African workers was in the open area of White Grass, demarcated by a metal gate, the area surrounded by nothing but piles of waste with no method of disposal. Through the metal gate stood a makeshift camp of more than fifty self-built shacks and tents, each a couple of square metres wide and covered with plastic tarpaulins to fend off the wind and rain. There was no electricity, no water supply, other than a pipe from a nearby farm, and no toilets. People collected wood from the area to set up a fire, allowing them to stay warm and boil water with which they could wash. They also relied on liquid petroleum gas (LPG) canisters for cooking, which weren't always safe. This self-maintained ghetto sat right next to the derelict farmhouse where Ousmane lived.

A few months before Ousmane's death, Sanji had come from Basse in Gambia. He would always proudly tell people about his hometown, the easternmost market town on the south bank of the River Gambia. Basse, with a population of around 18,000, was almost the same size as Campobello, and it had a similar kind of simplicity about it. Sanji was called 'Santiago' by many close to him, named after a good friend of his father from Mexico, whom his father met during his working years in Spain. His father was a linguist, as Sanji liked to tell people. He had inherited father's talent, speaking four tribal languages from Gambia as well as Senegalese and Malian languages, alongside English. Sanji talked about his father a lot. Sadly he died when Sanji was seven. Sanji's uncle married his mother and took over the compound owned by his father, promising to take over the care of Sanji and his siblings. But Sanji was later left to find his own means to pay for school fees.

He worked as an engineer for an electricity company. He only got the job because of his passion for football: he played for the company football team, helping them to win a cup. They rewarded him with a job. If there was anything that he was truly mad about in life, it was football. He had always been a great fan of Manchester United, like many Gambians. However, the electrician's job did not pay enough. Sanji then tried to make use of his language skills and worked as a guide in Gambia's tourism industry. The wages were low and he depended on tips from tourists. He met a tourist from Holland who was kind enough to offer to pay for his school fees. But, in the long term, a reasonable and steady income was hard to come by. He was unable to bring in money during the off-peak season. He couldn't find any other employment that would enable him to support his mother, brother and younger sister. He also had a newborn baby daughter to support, but he couldn't afford to marry his daughter's mother, who then married someone else.

Sanji was, however, determined to look after his family. He was close to his mother, who had suffered from poor health for a long time. Apart from taking care of his baby daughter, he also felt the moral duty, as the eldest brother, to look after his sister and provide for her as she was growing up. He always referred to her as 'my little sister;' she was then only fourteen years old. When Sanji finally left the country during the rule of dictator Yahya Jammeh, his mother's health deteriorated and she began to suffer from high blood pressure.

Sanji went on the work-seeking journey that tens of thousands of other Gambians had taken before him. For months, he made money selling pancakes in the streets of Mali, Burkina Faso, and other countries. The earnings he made in each country then went towards paying for the fare to the next country. Eventually, he decided to go to Libya as everyone said there was plenty of work there. When he arrived in Agadez, the largest city in central Niger and the connection point on the way to Libya, his nightmares began. He and fellow travellers were kidnapped and taken to a compound where their documents and belongings were confiscated. They had no idea how it would end. This was the first time on the journey that Sanji actually feared for his life.

The kidnappers told him at gun point to hand over all the cash he had. As he believed that he was about to be shot dead, he simply replied, looking up at the gunman, that 'I have no money and my family have no money. I'm a poor man. Let me pray and you can shoot me.' They decided to keep him alive to work. He was then kept in a compound with many others.

One day, during the detainment, a frustrated detainee started talking loudly. On hearing it, a military guard came in, asking, 'Who's mouthing off?' The man pointed to Sanji who stood out with his long dreadlocks. 'It's him.' The guard then took Sanji into a room. To his surprise, the guard didn't do anything to Sanji but asked him to pretend to be beaten whilst the guard repeatedly hit a piece of wood against the wall. Sanji did what he was told. This had the purpose of intimidating everyone else. A day later, the same guard came in and took Sanji out at gun point. Now everyone thought that this time he was going to be shot. Sanji was confused and terrified and thought that maybe he really would be killed this time. But the guard took him to a building site and got him to work. 'You look like you're a good worker,' the man said. So, Sanji started working there and was fed well for a while. By this point, he had seen that there were no rules in this sadistic anarchy. Whether he died or not was completely in the hands of those who controlled him.

Sanji planned his escape. One night, he attempted to break out with a Malian man he had befriended in the compound. They had to first climb over a fence. The Malian let Sanji climb the fence first, helping him up with his shoulder. When it was the Malian man's turn and Sanji tried to pull him over, the man was shot dead by a guard right as he got to the top of the fence. Frightened for his life, Sanji ran into the trees and sand dunes, and hid in the dark for several hours. All he could hear was the guard shooting bullets into the desert from a distance and his own heartbeat.

Sanji was one of the lucky few who succeeded in running away. But his kidnappers went looking for him around town, using the picture on his confiscated ID. Sanji cut off his dreadlocks, fearing that they would give him away. But he couldn't get rid of a small birthmark on his left cheek. The kidnappers found him in the street a day later. They held the ID up next to his face, recognising the birthmark, and said, 'It is you, isn't it?'

'No, no, that's not me,' said Sanji, pointing to his birthmark. 'This is just a tattoo.' He got away.

Libya was waiting for him, with yet more nightmares. By the time Sanji got there, he had spent around €10,000 transporting himself from Gambia through various other countries. In Libya, he lived in fear, not knowing whether he would survive to see the following day. Someone also robbed him of his gold earring given to him by his mother when he was a child. 'They're not real Muslims,' he summarised Libya to his friends. When he finally escaped and got on a boat to Europe, Sanji was prepared for just as much danger ahead. However, he was now accustomed to the permanent threat to his life and was no longer fearful.

On his boat journey across the Mediterranean, there were many more passengers than the inflatable vessel could take. The plywood floor of the boat soon broke. They were barely afloat, and everyone feared that the worst would come before long, when they saw a boat in the distance. However, they had not been at sea long enough to have travelled far, and some on board didn't want to signal to the boat fearing they would be returned to Libya. Arguments broke out about what to do. Their boat was about to sink, and something had to be done. Sanji happened to be sitting near the boat's inflation point and he told everyone that he would let the air out if they refused to signal and be rescued. They decided to signal and, luckily, the boat was heading to Italy. A day later, they all disembarked in Syracuse, the capital of the province of Syracuse in southeastern Sicily. Sanji and some others were sent to an emergency camp, where he stayed for a month.

He thanked God for sending him to Syracuse, which felt like a kind place to him. This 2,700-year-old city impressed and charmed him with its ancient buildings, amphitheatres and relaxed atmosphere. During that month, he took numerous walks around town and tried to talk with anyone he happened to meet. It felt like therapy. It felt like his life was coming back to him. Once, he tried to buy food in a market and didn't have enough cash. A local woman came up and paid for him. Ten euros. He always remembered that. A stranger who wanted to help him. She treated him with kindness, and they met to talk several times after that. Like many young people in Syracuse, she had worked abroad before. Young Italians would go to London or other western European cities to work and look for better opportunities.

Later, Sanji heard about people being transferred to reception camps for minors. He was worried that he could be mistaken for one, as he had a small frame and looked young. If that happened, he feared he would not be able to work. To avoid being sent to a minors' shelter, he pretended to be five years older, telling the authorities that he was born in 1990. Soon enough, Sanji was transferred to the province of Trapani on the other side of Sicily to a shelter in a town called Castelvetrano. It seemed a lifeless, dull little place, with nothing much happening except the farming of olives and grapes on the outskirts. Most Africans in the shelter were working in the fields. They told Sanji about a place called Campobello, where there was a lot more work. He realised that they all went to Campobello to work during the olive harvest. He was excited. He joined the others straight away. Thus started his working life in the olive town.

Mohammad, also from Gambia, was an old-timer in Campobello who knew the area and region like the back of his hand. He was thirty-five years old, and only arrived in Italy a few months before Ousmane died. Mohammad stood out for being tall, neat and well-dressed. His hair was shaved, and he often put on a clean, well-ironed white shirt and a pair of casual slacks like a European man going out on a Friday night. He sometimes even wore these clothes to pick olives, his smart dress making him no less productive in his work.

Back in Gambia, Mohammad had an eight-year-old son who was being looked after by his mother and two sisters. He used to run a food store in Brikama Ba, his hometown in central Gambia with a population of around 5,000 people, where he would sell couscous and other dried products. The store hadn't been doing well enough and he wasn't able to support his family with his small income. Then a friend of his in Libya told him there was plenty of work to be had in Tripoli and asked Mohammad to join him.

Mohammad had heard about the things that happened to Gambians who worked in Libya, but he stuck to the idea that it was some people's bad luck that got them into bad situations. He had no idea that the abuses people were reporting back were commonplace rather than the exception. He desperately wanted to improve his lot and do something with his life and, in doing that, make a difference to the lives of his family. However, his wife objected to his plan and threatened divorce. Mohammad was insistent, even at the expense of their marriage. He and his wife broke up before his departure.

Seeing was believing, and it was only when Mohammad spent time in Tripoli himself that he understood the reality in Libya. He counted himself lucky, and happened to find work in a shop for a while. But he never stopped fearing for his safety on a daily basis. Mohammad planned an escape from Libya, but when he got on the boat, he had no idea where he would land. He had never planned to come to Italy. He believed that it was destiny that had brought him here. The sea journey was the only moment in his life that would make his eyes well up to recall. When he was rescued, he was sent to an over-crowded emergency camp in Trapani. He was there for a short while before being transferred to a CAS (*Centro di Accoglienza Straordinaria*, Extraordinary Reception Centre) in a small town called Castellammare in the same province.

Castellammare had a population of just over 15,000, similar in size to Campobello. It was a quaint little country town that the young had deserted for more opportunities and better prospects in the outside world. On the surface, it seemed like a backwater that was not made for a long stay. But just like the rest of Sicily, things were never quite what they seemed to be. Castellammare was notorious for having been the birthplace of various US mafias. The town was the origin of the Castellamarese War, fought between the Masseria and Maranzano clans in the early 1930s for control of the Italian mafia in New York. As a new arrival, Mohammad had no idea of the extent to which the local mafia still controlled businesses there and across Sicily. All that he cared about was the lack of work in and around the town. Before he had time to plan ahead, the next transfer brought him to another CAS shelter—this time on Via Roma in Campobello, where he was to find plenty of work waiting for him in the surrounding olive fields.

* * *

Campobello, as Sanji arrived, looked as if it had been painted in various shades of yellow earth. There was a dusty feel to it. As he walked through the lanes named 'Via A,' 'Via B'—as if they had run out of street names—he saw numerous houses with courtyards serving as family compounds, some of them converted from old convents. Several tractors drove past. The sunset flooded the town with a golden orange glow.

Sanji had been told that all the African workers were living in a place called White Grass. Instead of returning to his reception camp in Castelvetrano every evening and coming out again in the early morning for the farm work, he needed to sleep over in White Grass. He and two friends shared a wooden shack in the middle of the makeshift encampment. All they had inside were a couple of old mattresses. Outside their shack stood a pile of rubbish and a shopping trolley, which was used as storage space for water containers and cooking utensils.

Sanji's shack was in the field next to the disused farmhouse where Ousmane was killed. When the news came in the late morning that he had passed away in hospital, it shocked and saddened Sanji. Throughout his journey to Europe via Libya, the deaths of strangers had made him emotional. He knew of Ousmane but, as they didn't share the same living space, they never exchanged words. He would, however, nod to Ousmane when walking past him in the fields. He could only imagine what it must be like for Ousmane's family. There was a lot of anxiety among his fellow workers, as they did not know what to expect in the aftermath of his death. What were the authorities going to do? Sanji was worried, too. He was still trying to get used to the tough pace of work and the over-crowding in White Grass.

He got up at 5:00 am and walked with fellow workers to the centre of town, to be selected by farmers for the harvest work. The farmers would shout out to them what they would pay per crate for the harvested olives, usually starting as low as €2. Most Africans here would accept the rate of €3 per crate. When the farmers reached an agreement with the workers about the pay, they would then drive those who had been chosen to the allocated olive grove to start work. There were numerous plants built to process the local olives, *Nocellara del Belice*. There is a distinct, mouth-watering flavour to *Nocellara del Belice* that pulls merchants into Sicily from hundreds of miles away. Every summer and autumn, businessmen would visit town from as far as Naples to get *Nocellara del Belice* olives and olive oil.

At 6:00 am, as workers arrived at the piece of land they were to work on, the day's labour started. Each person would choose a line of olive trees to work on as if they were conveyor belts in a factory. Sanji picked his line, put on a plastic harvesting box with webbing straps fed through the handles on each side and started picking straight

9

away. Hand harvesting, called *brucatura,* is the norm here and across the region. It is the most traditional way of picking olives, preventing bruising which can increase acidity.[4] Good-quality olives and olive oil required intensive labour.

Everyone in the team was picking as fast as they could, with olives tumbling into their boxes. From a distance, it sounded like the first rumble of thunder as a storm approached. These plastic boxes became full quickly and pushed into their chests, with the straps digging into their skin and leaving marks on their necks. Sanji didn't stop. He worked his way up the thick trees, layer by layer. When he reached a point too high for him, he got a ladder, placed it against the thick branches and climbed up to pick the olives at the top.

During the one-hour unpaid lunch break, Sanji took off his T-shirt, soaked with sweat, and let it dry in the midday sun. He then stretched his back, which ached after hours of standing and bending. He looked out into the vast olive fields and thought about how magnificent the olive country was. He could not see the end of the fields, which seemed to stretch out to surrounding towns and villages, like a long green belt along the coast and into the interior. In the distance he could see the olive oil processing factories dotted around the landscape. This region truly lived and thrived on olive production. Four more hours of work followed the break.

Then came four o'clock, and Sanji and others finished work for the day. The fast workers earned the most, as work was paid at a piece rate. It was an illegal practice for piecework rates to constitute a worker's only pay in Italy. However, it was also a prevalent practice in the country's agriculture. On most days, everyone received €3–€3.50 per fifteen-kilogram crate of olives. One crate usually took about an hour to harvest for someone with an average amount of experience. Sanji was new to the job and only managed to harvest an average of ten crates per day in the first two weeks, earning him around €35 for each eight-hour day. His fellow workers seemed to be working at a similar speed. This was the rate of pay at harvest. The normal rate for Africans outside of harvest season would be a little over *half* that amount. The wage arrangement was made completely on 'trust,' as there was no contract. The farmer kept hold of the wages for between a week and a month before paying.

Sanji worked on. Over time, he became accustomed to the way things worked in the fields as well as inside the makeshift encampment at White Grass. He got used to having his water boiled in a giant metal pot over a wood stove—the only way he could have hot water for a shower. He got used to being half-full after a meal. And he got used to being in a pitch-dark shack without any lighting. Sanji was popular among his fellow workers in the communal living space, as he was sociable and always had time for others. There was a certain charisma about him. His laid-back manner made people feel comfortable in his presence. They liked the way he talked and the way he cited little proverbs from home. Even though he had not been around that long, he gathered a group of Gambian boys around him. They simply liked hanging out with him. He also got along with the Senegalese and Malian boys. Perhaps it was also something to do with his humour, his ability to see above things, crack a joke and lift people's spirits. Sometimes that was what people needed in these extremely difficult circumstances.

At the same time, inside White Grass, African workers were still waiting for the local authorities to take action to improve their living conditions. So far, no proposals for a solution had been heard, let alone delivered.

2

BUILDING BABYLON

Seasonal workers were arriving from outside of Sicily. Many of them worked from crop to crop, region to region, across the country. Alsane, a thirty-five-year-old from Senegal, was one of them. He was easily recognisable because he always wore the same anorak and jeans all year round. He was soft-spoken and approachable, and was the kind of person who could blend into any crowd and get on with most people. He would adapt to new situations and find ways to get around difficulties instead of confronting them. His laid-back approach probably had something to do with his years of experience working in different countries and having to adapt to their various socio-cultural environments.

Alsane went to Spain as a farm worker back in 2006 and was one of the tens of thousands of undocumented Senegalese workers who harvested fruits and vegetables in the vast 30 miles of greenhouses, known as the 'sea of plastic,' south of El Portus in Almería. Throughout the 2000s, more than 100,000 workers from Morocco and West Africa were toiling in these greenhouses, producing 3 million tonnes of fruit and vegetables for export to Britain and other northern European countries every year.

According to Francesco Caruso, a professor of sociology, 70% of Almería's agricultural production is absorbed by a handful of multinationals, in which process 'labour cost reduction is often the only strategy through which farmers are able to protect their profit margins.' 'Migrant farmworkers—mainly Moroccans—usually accept informal, underpaid, intermittent, temporary jobs, which are also dangerous due to the constant risk of chemical poisoning in greenhouses,' Caruso has written. 'The official union wage for this province is €50 a day for a 6-hour shift, while the actual daily wages in the region is around €30 for a daily shift of 8 to 9 hours.'[1] In many cases, it was even lower. On top of all this, appallingly, migrant workers also lived in makeshift shacks that lacked even the most basic of facilities.

Back then, in 2010, Alsane's friend living near Venice invited him to join him there, so that became his first stop in Italy when he arrived that year. He travelled light—wherever he moved, he had only a small rucksack and a plastic shopping bag. He did not want to be weighed down with too many belongings. In Venice, Alsane learned about fishing from his friend and made a living from it for a while. Following that, he travelled to Florence where he joined another friend, also from Senegal, and stayed with him at his lodging in the poorer suburbs. There, Alsane's friend worked on a sewing machine in a local Italian-run factory. He was earning €35–€40 per day. He didn't want to do the same job in a Chinese-run factory of which there were many, because there he would earn just €30 for a ten-hour day. Alsane did not know how to use a sewing machine and therefore could not get a job with his friend. Instead, he found a new type of work for himself from the Chinese residents he came across in town: he bulk-bought handbags and hats from the people who manufactured them in the local Chinese factories. He started selling them to tourists and townsfolk in the streets of Florence. In the summer, sales were quite good, and he could live on the earnings for a while. He also travelled to Verona, Padua, Trieste and Lido di Jesolo where tourism was the main source of income, and carried on with his street sales. Living in these towns and cities was expensive, however, and Alsane found it hard to keep up with the costs.

Therefore, when his friends living in Foggia, in the Puglia region in the south, called and invited him to join them, he took up the offer straight away. There, deep in the countryside around Foggia, Alsane started working on the tomato and asparagus fields in the spring.

During that time he lived in a makeshift camp called Borgo Mezzanone. It was his first time living in a ghetto in Italy—a place he saw as only for the 'blacks.' Thereafter, whenever he mentioned the word 'ghetto', he would naturally point to his arm and the colour of his skin, as if indicating a necessary link between 'ghetto' and 'being black.'

After that, he would go to the surrounding areas of Rignano Garganico and San Severo for more asparagus harvesting, following which he would travel up north to Turin for work on the apple farms on the outskirts of the city. When apple season was over, he would then move on to Saluzzo in the north-west, to pick fruit for a while. Subsequently, in the autumn, he would travel back south to work in the province of Foggia, in the olive groves in Carpino, for two months, where he would earn €35 a day, or travel all the way south to Campobello for the olive harvest, as he had done this time. Alsane joked to everyone that he was running up and down the country 'like a tourist.'

* * *

The same month Ousmane lost his life, a Gambian man named Benjamin arrived in Syracuse, after being rescued at sea. 'Italians saved my life,' he told his mother on the phone. He had escaped hell in Libya and headed to Europe on a boat, like tens of thousands before and after him. For the Italian coastguards, he was another rescued migrant. But for Benjamin, who turned thirty-five that year, a new life was about to begin. It was a sunny day when he arrived at the emergency camp in Syracuse, the same camp in which Sanji had been placed a few months beforehand. Benjamin looked thin and frail after his time in Libya, but he felt grateful for being alive.

Soon enough, he was transferred to a 260-bed CARA camp (*Centri di Accoglienza per Richiedenti Asilo*, hosting centre for asylum seekers) in Salinagrande, a village a few kilometres west of Trapani in west Sicily. The camp was opened in 2005 and was apparently considered a 'showpiece' by the Ministry of Interior. In August 2010, its management was taken over by a social cooperative called Badia Grande, founded in 2007 by the notorious Don Sergio Librizzi, the former director of the Catholic charity Caritas of Trapani, who was arrested in June 2014 on charges of extortion and sexual abuse. He was sentenced to 9 years imprisonment in 2015, but had his condemnation overturned on appeal in 2017; he had been accused of sexual harassment of migrants in exchange for residence permits. Under Badia Grande's management, the Salinagrande camp earned a bad name through its poor sanitary conditions, lack of hot water and heating, and the absence of basic healthcare services for its residents. The place was described by an EU delegation as 'hell' and a 'concentration camp.'

However, a nasty reputation was not going to stop Badia Grande from making its' money. It was a major player in the profitable business of Italy's asylum reception system. It also ran a 200-bed CIE camp (*Centri di Identificazione ed Espulsione*, identification and expulsion centre) in Milo, 4 kilometres outside of Trapani, which it converted into a hotspot in 2015 with a turnover of almost €10 million in 2016 and €5 million in 2017. It was converted into a CPR (*Centri di Permanenza per il Rimpatrio*, centre for residence and repatriation) in October 2018. For those who ran these camps, someone of Benjamin's background was just another number, another bed, with which to justify funding. In their eyes, he was just another African to bring in revenue from the state.

Benjamin came from a village called Mbankam in Gambia. He was the youngest of three brothers and a sister. Back then, Benjamin made a living as a driver for hotels. He used to brush his hair back and put on his one smart suit, which made him look like a handsome city lawyer. He would drive tourists to-and-fro between the airport and hotels. Sometimes he caught a few interested glances from white female tourists. He picked up some English from British tourists over the years—even learning a few phrases in cockney. 'Alright, mate?' he would repeat cheekily to any English-speaking person he met. He would tell his friends, 'There is this place in London where people speak a funny language called "cock-ney".' There was a lot of work during the summer and it was good while it lasted. But the tourist season was only half a year and Benjamin had his mother, wife and then two-year-old son to support. When there was little income from tourism, Benjamin had to find all kinds of odd jobs to keep money coming in for the family. At one point, he found a vacancy at a bakery and trained as a baker, low paid as it was. He had also done some fishing work, having been taught by his father who was a fisherman on Jinack Island (known as 'Coconut Island') his whole life.

Later on, Benjamin got a job working as a driver for a well-known Gambian imam, Bakawsu Fofana, after being introduced by his close friend, the imam's brother. The imam became a big part of his life: not only did Benjamin work for him, but he also went to listen to his preaching. Bakawsu Fofana said to Benjamin: 'I can't pay you much, but I can pray for you.' Benjamin felt he could not afford to lose the job, even though it was not well paid. The real insecurity of the job for Benjamin was that the imam took a more hard-line approach to religion than the then dictator, Yahya Jammeh, and was constantly critical of the government's policies. At one point, the imam was arrested and imprisoned for nine days, during which time he was badly beaten. When he was eventually released, the imam carried on preaching and it was predictable that something would happen to him. And indeed, one day, the imam got a tip-off that his life was in danger and that leaving Gambia was the only way out. He asked Benjamin to drive him to the border of Gambia and Senegal, where they changed car and drove on into Senegal. Now Benjamin was an accomplice aiding in the imam's escape. There was no returning home. At that time, his son was only three.

When in Senegal, Benjamin's family told him over the phone not to return to Gambia for the time being. They believed that the imam would be killed in prison if he returned. Benjamin's life would be in danger too. The two parted company in Senegal. Benjamin then decided to join his friend Yugo who had also left Gambia, and travelled on, from Senegal to Libya, working along the way to pay for the trip.

At that time, Benjamin's mother was in her eighties. She had no pension and could hardly cope with supporting the family. His wife had fallen ill as well. He needed to work so he could send money to them. For him, Libya was the obvious choice. When he and Yugo reached Tripoli, they lived in a compound and were driven to work when there was some. Sometimes they were paid, other times not at all. They began to see the reality of work in Tripoli and the imminent danger inherent in everyday living. Benjamin started to fear walking home from work—many sub-Saharan Africans had been kidnapped and killed on their way back at night. But staying inside the compound was not safe, either. Once, their compound was shot at, randomly, by a gang. Everyone ran. Gangs could come in to take them away, either to shoot at for fun or force to work as slaves.

His traumatic experiences in Libya—and witnessing the experience of others—shook him to the core. He still shook every time he described being there, and is still recovering. For the first few weeks in Italy, he could not help feeling vengeful whenever he came across any Libyans in the reception camps.

The one thing Benjamin rarely spoke of to anyone was that his wife had died when he was in Libya. Her health had deteriorated since he left home. He felt immense guilt as was clearly shown through his silence. Since then, he talked to his young son regularly by phone. As there was no internet access at his mother's home, he saved up money to call and chat with his family each month. During the calls, his young son always asked for a bike and shoes. His school fees were €100 per year, which Benjamin paid.

When Italian coastguards saved his life, Benjamin thought that all was going to be fine in Italy. Life inside the overcrowded camp in Salinagrande was the first thing that changed his perception. The way he was dealt with by the Italian authorities also disillusioned him. Fleeing from the risk of persecution could have guaranteed him refugee status in Italy, but the authorities did not believe his story. He waited nearly a year for a commission interview, which would determine the outcome of his asylum application. Once he had attended the interview, his wait began for the decision on his claim. He had no idea how long he might have to wait and, judging by the experiences of others, it would usually take up to two years for a decision to be made. He had to start finding ways to spend his time more constructively, instead of simply waiting. There were no language lessons provided at the camp, and, as a result, he started to spend a lot of his time wandering around the surrounding area.

Benjamin felt guilty for doing nothing. He needed an income, as his family was waiting for his support. Local tomato farmers knew the score. They knew that Africans inside these reception camps were all eager to work. They also knew that these men were mostly waiting for decisions on their asylum claims and that their insecure status guaranteed an inferior wage bargaining position. Why pay €40 when you can get away with as low as €15 a day? This was indeed the way local farmers were thinking. New arrivals like Benjamin would not have the slightest idea about the normal wage level in Italian agriculture.

Although there was no national minimum wage in Italy, minimum wage levels were set by collective bargaining via trade unions across different sectors: Italy's agricultural minimum wage was €7.13 per hour. Benjamin was unaware of this, but he was beginning to see his position in the supply chain.

* * *

When tomato farmers came to the CARA camp to recruit workers, they selected the cheapest labour possible. They felt the pressures on the price of their products, which were imposed on them by the multinational supermarket chains.[2] According to Italian journalist Antonello Mangano,[3] there was fierce competition to keep prices of agricultural produce as low as possible, and the mechanism that focused on quantity affected producers caught up in the cut-throat global competition.

Italy's tomato production accounted for 50% of tomato production in the EU. According to the European Commission, Italy exported €38 billion worth of agricultural products in 2016. Sicily was Europe's third largest producer of vegetables. Cost-cutting had always been key to sustaining the profitability of agriculture, and migrant workers, positioned at the bottom of the supply chain, paid the price.

Around half of the workforce employed in Italian agriculture—around 405,000 out of a total of 843,000 workers—were migrant workers, according to official data in 2015. Also, among the 430,000 agricultural workers in Italy who were irregularly employed (i.e. without contracts) in Italy, 80% (around 344,000 people) were migrant workers. Of them, at least 100,000 suffered extreme exploitation and high risk, according to an Observatory Placido Rizzotto investigation into working conditions in agriculture. It had always been considered acceptable to squeeze these *stranieri* (foreigners) like Sicilian lemons.

As farmers felt the economic squeeze from higher up the chain, they began to see the 'exploitability' of migrant workers, back when they started to arrive in the southern regions in the 1970s. Workers came from around the world: southeast Europe, Tunisia and Morocco, Bangladesh, and sub-Saharan Africa. Since the 1990s, demand for labour in seasonal agriculture has been met mainly by migrant workers. Farmers across the country stratified migrant workers according to the worth of their labour as a commodity. Cultural and linguistic affinity and skin colour all came to play a part in employers' assessments of them. Many of the Tunisian workers, for example, had been around for decades and spoke Italian, with some closely connected to the existing Italian-Tunisian community. They were paid, on average, €30–€35 per working day. The Romanians were the largest migrant worker population in Italy, having EU entitlement to freedom of movement to their advantage. Many were temporary visitors and would return to their home country or go to other parts of Europe when the harvest season was over. They received as little as €25 per day, due to their lack of an organisational bargaining position. And then came the sub-Saharan Africans, most of whom had been through the asylum reception system and were nicknamed the 'CAS people,' after the *Centro di Accoglienza Straordinaria* (Extraordinary Reception Centre). Sub-Saharan African workers were at the bottom of the hierarchy: they were usually paid between €15 and €20 on average.

This labour stratification had deviously created a situation where workers from different countries and with different migratory statuses would have to compete with one another, making it doubly difficult to organise them for collective action against their employers. The regime of segregating workers had also created fertile ground for the *caporali* (gangmasters, middlemen; many workers call them *capo*, meaning 'boss') who thrived on the vulnerability of the workers. The *caporali* system perfectly served the requirements of 'just in time' production, with its seasonality and need for flexibility (workers' ability to move from one harvest to the next), which meant that suppliers had a high demand for casual farm labour. Labour stratification seemed to benefit every party in the chain except the workers.

The majority of tomato farms in Italy were small and labour-intensive (tomatoes were harvested by hand) and mostly concentrated in the south—and it was here that migrant workers suffered most from exploitation by *caporali*. The *caporali* recruited workers, organised their transport (and sometimes accommodation), supervised their work, took charge of wage distribution and deducted a broker's fee and transportation costs from their pay. Each could manage 3,000 to 4,000 farm workers, earning €10–€15 a day per worker under their management. Meanwhile, a worker employed by *caporali* earned €3–

€4 for every 300 kilograms of tomatoes picked, wages which were paid through piecework. They were usually paid 50% less than the industry's legal wage level, and normally worked eight to twelve hours a shift, despite legal working hours of six and a half hours a day.

Benjamin was yet to learn that the tomatoes he harvested would be processed into *pelati* (peeled canned tomatoes) and would eventually end up being sold by supermarket chains across Europe. He was just pleased to be working. The reward in cash, a meagre €20 per full day's work, was all that mattered to him. He felt good when he was able to send cash home.

At the same time, from his first day toiling in the fields, he never told his family that he was doing farm work. They wouldn't be able to understand how he could end up working in agriculture in Europe. Most likely, someone in the family would say to him, 'you might as well be back home.' He didn't want to feel the shame.

When the harvest season ended, the wait for documents became much more wearing for everyone in the camp in Salinagrande. There was less farm work around and nothing else to do. Despite this, Benjamin didn't run away from the camp. He was not tempted to go to Germany or France for work like many fellow Gambians. He felt somehow loyal to Italy because, as he kept saying to his mother, 'Italy saved my life at sea.' He would never forget that.

3

FIRES AND A MODEL WORKER

One day, the reception shelter in Castelvetrano suddenly announced its closure—possibly due to poor management, or other reasons unknown to its residents. Sanji was transferred, just like that, to another reception camp, this time in Campobello, which coincidentally suited his need for work perfectly. Had luck come his way this time? 'Man proposes, God disposes,' he said, and this felt like God's good will.

Sanji and his fellow residents from the shelter arrived in Campobello through the country lanes on their second-hand bikes. They stopped at a square in the centre of town to take a break and ask for directions to their new shelter. The square had a memorial to local men who died during the First and Second World Wars. US forces fought their way into Campobello as part of the Allied invasion of Sicily in July 1943, a few weeks before Mussolini was toppled from power. Decaying bunkers could still be seen in various places on the outskirts of the town. Sanji and his friends were unaware of the history of the town just as the town was oblivious to theirs. They walked with their bikes down the main street, which was dotted with run-down cafés with plastic tables outside on the pavement. At the top of the street, they turned the corner onto Via Roma, where the reception camp was located. It was a narrow street like all the others but with a few more shops. There was a pizza takeaway on the road, with a massive smiling fiberglass chef fixed to the side of the building.

At the other end of Via Roma was a popular Chinese shop, which sold clothes and all sorts of household utensils. It was one of the hundreds of downmarket Chinese superstores that catered to low-income shoppers in all Italian towns. African boys from the reception shelter often visited the shop for cheap items, such as made-in-China battery-powered lights and fan heaters. The Gambian boys, in particular, were familiar with the sight of Chinese shops. Back home, the Chinese presence was always associated with incoming international investment and, in some eyes, the encroachment of international capital. There was even a village in Gambia called Sabu which was inhabited only by Chinese people who had come to Gambia to work on various infrastructure projects.

In Campobello, the middle-aged couple who ran the shop, Mr and Mrs Li, were from Wenzhou, a city in southern China known for its traditional textile industry. The industry had been imported to Italy by the Wenzhou men and women who pioneered Chinese migration to the country in the 1920s. The Li family were among those who followed suit in the 1960s and 1970s. Many of them were initially employed in the Chinese garment industry across Italy, with some later becoming entrepreneurs themselves. Among them were many who managed to take up the *pronto moda* (ready-to-wear fashion) business of the Italians, bringing cheap garments from China to sell in Italy. Some of the successful Chinese businesses became subcontractors for big Italian brands, using cheaper Chinese materials and hiring lower-paid Chinese workers in sweatshops in Italian towns and cities. They tended to be concentrated in larger cities, like Florence, Prato, Milan and Rome.

The high visibility of the Chinese traders in Italy made Mr and Mrs Li's modest shop in modest-looking Campobello look quite peculiar. How did they end up here? As it turned out, there were only two Chinese shops, both family businesses, in town. They were in fact the entire 'Chinese community.' They had both come to Campobello to join relatives ten years ago, having decided that competition among Chinese traders in mainland Italian cities was too fierce. Even Palermo, the capital of Sicily, was too big and busy for them as there were already more than a dozen Chinese trading firms and catering businesses competing with one another. 'There are just too many people in the city,' Mr Li told the rest of the family back in Milan and Wenzhou when they asked for the reason behind his choice of going to live in a country town on an island, which the family saw as remote and impoverished or, in their words, 'a place where birds don't lay eggs.' In their eyes, the couple's settlement in rural Sicily was, in effect, self-exile, which would create a lot of gossip. Mr Li did not seem to mind being talked about; all he wanted was some peace of mind. Besides, the warm weather here was like the climate back home in Wenzhou, and what could be better than that?

Despite it being their own choice to be here in Campobello, the Li family were nevertheless socially isolated, as it was not the local custom to welcome new arrivals. Ten years went by, and the couple was just as alone as before. They were simply seen by locals as 'the polite Chinese immigrant traders.' Perhaps this explained Mrs Li's quietness, as if she had adopted it from the town. Every day, she would sit behind the shop counter and nod, shake her head or point with her hand, without saying a word, when someone came in and asked her a question about the products they sold. It was as if she were mute.

* * *

The place that every African here called 'the camp on Via Roma' was a two-storey building, painted in the same yellow earth colour as the rest of the town, albeit half peeled off, and with its front windows sealed with metal bars. It was hard to see that this was once a hotel. Now, it more resembled an old factory warehouse than a reception centre for asylum seekers. It was the kind of place that made your heart sink at first sight. And that was exactly how Sanji felt.

As it turned out, the management style of the centre was entirely compatible with the unwelcoming appearance of the building. The staff member who showed Sanji in was also in charge of the residents' care. The new arrivals were puzzled about where the manager was. As weeks went past, it became more puzzling as to why the manager didn't show up. Perhaps he had another business elsewhere? Later, Sanji had the opportunity to bump into him as he came into the office. What was his name? Sanji didn't know. He was literally an absentee manager.

Just like an absentee landlord. The manager felt it sufficient to take the cash from the state without actually being there. The young Africans were left to look after themselves. To top it all, it was an open secret that he was associated with the local mafia, although people preferred to keep quiet about that. With this, the camp had a reputation with the Africans in the area, not least those who had lived there before. However, as asylum camps were independent in terms of how they were managed, and there were rarely any inspections or monitoring, the local entrepreneurs, who saw reception centres as nothing more than a new profit-making venture, were able to run these places like cheap hostels without having to be on site themselves.

It was overcrowded, and the food was stale and often inedible. Most young residents would try to make complaints to the staff every now and then. But not Mohammad, who had been transferred from Castellammare. During his time here, Mohammad did not make a single complaint about the poor conditions. When his fellow residents asked him to join them in their protests, he chose not to take part. He stayed quiet. He said to the others, 'If you want to talk about problems, there is always Libya back there.' He adopted the attitude that he should avoid conflict in these asylum camps in Italy as it had not been easy to escape from the hell of Libya and land in Europe. His days in Libya had truly haunted him. His heart ached for those who still remained there. He would constantly compare the horrific treatment of sub-Saharan Africans in Libya with their miserable experiences inside these reception camps in Italy. The latter was always more favourable. Even now, as he sat outside a café on the streets of Campobello, he thought back to those days in Tripoli, where to do likewise would be unthinkable. 'Blacks' didn't get to sit in cafes in Libya. He would have been arrested and beaten by the police if he dared—simply because they could.

Mohammad tried to tolerate things inside the Via Roma camp. He distracted himself by going out and spending time looking for work from the first week of his arrival. Back then, he was unable to speak Italian. While sitting outside a café one day, a farmer approached him asking if he wanted to work. He did not understand. 'No,' he said, his usual response when he couldn't understand people. Then, fortunately, a passer-by explained to him what the farmer meant. Mohammad was thrilled, and immediately said yes. To start with, he worked a week for him, unable even to communicate about wages and not knowing how much he was to be paid. But he knew that he had to give it his best shot. He went to work and picked olives every day. He worked as hard and fast as he possibly could. At the end of the week, Mohammad waited and hoped for his wages. The farmer eventually turned up at his camp on Via Roma and passed Mohammad's wages for the week to the staff in the camp. Subsequently, as work increased, gradually he learned to speak and understand more Italian, from farmers and supervisors. Bit by bit, within a year, he became capable of basic social interaction in the language.

From Libya to Italy and to where he was now in Campobello, Mohammad had lost a lot of weight. He had been a well-built man weighing 120 kilograms, but now he was only eighty-five kilograms. When his sisters saw him on WhatsApp video calls, they screamed, 'You're not OK, brother! You're not OK!' To which he replied, with a cheeky smile, 'I'm working like a donkey for you.' Mohammad was close to his sisters and loved them dearly. They were looking after his child and he was grateful to them. He often looked at family pictures to keep his spirits up and keep himself going. Hearing their voices gave him strength. He video called them a lot. He would sometimes walk along the country lanes and call his younger sister, showing her the rural landscape as he walked.

Mohammad carried on ignoring things that went on inside his shelter and concentrated on work. But things got worse. The two-storey building had no fire prevention equipment. It was as if there was no awareness of such an eventuality. The place was set up without even the minimum standard of health and safety protection in place.

The absentee management and the lack of care had serious consequences. It led to two major fires, each of which almost destroyed the building. People might have been killed if the fires had not woken them up. On both occasions the fire started at 3:00 am by the front door. There were around fifty residents inside. Both fires were so severe that residents woke up choking from the thick smoke and had to run out of the building in the middle of the night, gasping for air. Sanji and Mohammad ran out with the others. The panic continued to overwhelm Mohammad, even after he had reached the street. He struggled to get his breath back. The fire was suspected to be arson, the obvious sign being a burning car tyre left near the door on both occasions. But the police never caught anyone and didn't even have a suspect. Several residents were so frightened that they ran away immediately after the first fire.

Mohammad contemplated leaving the camp. For the first time, he realised what those metal bars outside their windows meant. He had not really paid attention to them before. The bars would prevent people from escaping in a fire. Why were they there? It was symbolic of the entrapment of Africans and institutional negligence. It was as if those bars were there to keep them in. And, this time, it was not only symbolic—the bars could have killed them.

Mohammad wanted to ditch the life he was living in an unprotected environment inside the asylum camp. He had just qualified for humanitarian protection and received his documents. As such, he was one of the very few fortunate Gambians who did not go through a lengthy waiting period. He had started to look forward to a fuller working life here. Safety risks in the camp were the last thing he needed. Sanji, however, felt that he had fewer options. He wanted to wait for things to improve after the first fire. He felt he could not afford to act too fast. Both decided to stay put for now. A sufficient number of people remained, which kept the camp going. Their presence justified the funding that the camp continued to receive.

However, nothing was said or done regarding fire prevention. After the second fire broke out, Sanji felt certain that their lives were at risk and their safety was not the concern of those in charge. He had to follow the others and get out of the camp straight away. For the African residents, enough was enough. There could be a third fire. No one took responsibility and the management's contempt for the residents was obvious. Still no arrests were made. Sanji would rather sleep rough than risk a further fire. He and Mohammad had followed similar paths after reaching Europe. Their lives were about to move in different directions after the second fire.

* * *

Life went on, and had to go on, for the migrant workers at White Grass, after Ousmane's death. In the absence of any action from the authorities, activists from a variety of NGOs tried to intervene. Salvatore Inguì, provincial coordinator of the national anti-mafia organisation, Libera, and many of his colleagues in Libera and other groups, saw that the people of White Grass were totally abandoned. They started to find ways to try to improve their conditions. First, they brought blankets, shoes, vests and sleeping bags to the 500 workers there.

As the year went on, these activist groups began to ask what they could do next. Salvatore and his colleagues searched for all the properties confiscated from the mafia in the area. There were plenty, as Campobello was close to Castelvetrano, home of the Cosa Nostra boss, Matteo Messina Denaro, nicknamed 'Diabolik.' Denaro had been on the run since 1993, and the police had been unable to capture him. The area had been infested with the mafia for years. Salvatore and his colleagues identified a former olive oil processing factory, under the company name Golden Fountain (*Fontane d'Oro SAS*), on Via Rosario, a road parallel to White Grass. The factory had been confiscated from the Indelicato brothers, Franco and Giuseppe, who acted as the front for the Campobello mafioso Francesco Luppino. Luppino was the owner of the factory, but through the artificial sale of branches of the company to the Indelicato brothers, he registered the company under their names. It allowed Luppino and his wife to be the tenants of Golden Fountain while they continued to administer the company and receive the profits. His assets were seized by the police when he was arrested in 2013.

Salvatore Inguì said to me that he believed in taking mafia-owned assets and giving them back to the community. For him, housing seasonal workers in this location would give olive production back to Campobello. Salvatore made a proposal on the use of the Golden Fountain site to the associations with which he was collaborating, the local collective Libertaria and Libero FUTURO. Together, they brought the proposal to the prefect of Trapani, Leopoldo Falco. Finally, as a result of the proposal, and continuous pressure from activists on the local authorities to improve things, it was announced that a living space was to be created at Golden Fountain to accommodate the seasonal workers in Campobello.

That was just the beginning for Salvatore. The culture of the mafia ran deep in this part of Sicily. In Campobello, it was not unusual for mafia leaders to be implicitly accepted and sometimes even protected by local residents. The first obstacle that Salvatore and his colleagues found was that members of the mafia family were still living inside the Golden Fountain site, despite it having been confiscated. They had the confidence to carry on occupying the property partly as a result of quiet local complicity. Salvatore and his colleagues visited them and asked for their departure. They refused. Salvatore therefore had to ask for the intervention of the police to evict them the following day. When the air was finally cleared, Salvatore and colleagues started working to clean up the site and set up showers and toilets. That autumn, in September 2014, as workers began to arrive in White Grass for the harvest, Salvatore and the volunteers started inviting them to the Golden Fountain site, which they informally re-named the 'Ciao Ousmane' hospitality centre.

Inside, much of the voluntary work was organised by Libera, Libertaria, Libero FUTURO and other groups. Libera, in particular, had launched a campaign for the collection of blankets, clothing and food. Donations came from many places, like those collected by the community association Archè Onlus, which included stocks of foods such as pasta, milk and tuna from Marsala.

Temporary medical assistance was also provided, for a few hours a day, in and around the Golden Fountain site by the Red Cross. When people started moving onto the site and setting up tents, makeshift shops and a mosque were also spontaneously set up. A new camp was coming into shape. Volunteers were on site to serve the needs of the residents. That autumn, Salvatore and his colleagues, who looked after the conditions inside, began to get to know some of the people who came to stay, listened to their stories and spent a lot of time with them. For Salvatore, at least, it was a year of exceptional solidarity.

In October 2015, the prefect of Trapani, Leopoldo Falco, came to the area, along with the mayor of Campobello, Giuseppe Castiglione, to formally mark the setting up of the Golden Fountain site as a living space. Giuseppe Castiglione had been elected mayor of Campobello in November 2014 following years of mafia infiltration, which resulted in the dissolution of the local council. Back then, according to local press, Castiglione promised 'the rebirth of Campobello' and that he would 'return the smile to the town' and 'lead our town to become a reference point and flagship of the whole province in the sectors of agriculture, tourism and culture.' Thus, in the town's much-delayed response to the death of Ousmane, Castiglione suddenly appeared to be among those offering a solution. The site was formally named the Ciao Ousmane camp. It was jointly managed by Libera and charity organisations including the San Vito Onlus Foundation and Caritas.

According to the 2018 report 'Ghettos and Camps: The Institutional Production of Marginality in Sicilian Rural Areas' (*'Dal Ghetto al Campo: La Produzione Istituzionale di Marginalità Abitativa nelle Campagne Siciliane'*), by Martina Lo Cascio and Valeria Piro,[1] the housing situation of the migrant workers in Campobello had changed over time, 'from the total invisibility and absence of institutional interventions, up to the institutional management of the only spaces made visible and acceptable.' Those involved in these processes, said Martina Lo Cascio and Valeria Piro, are 'the representatives of the institutions, initially absent but then gradually more and more present; and volunteers and activists, ... with the workers always present as the main "beneficiaries" of the interventions but who are in fact without a voice.'

The optimism of the statements issued by the institutions did not reflect the picture on the ground. Although there were lights around the clock and water was available for showers and toilets at the Golden Fountain site, these were the most basic improvements. Living conditions remained substandard inside the Ciao Ousmane camp. With only €5,000 available from Campobello's prefectural commissioners, the fifteen chemical toilets and eight showers set up by the 'health station' were nowhere near sufficient for the hundreds of workers. As Salvatore noted, volunteers were on their own when sorting out any day-to-day difficulties that arose inside the site, with limited resources or backup. Outside institutions and society did not want to know. Indeed, according to Cascio and Piro, during the 'semi-institutional' and 'semi-formal' management that lasted for three harvest seasons, from 2014 to 2016, the presence of volunteers and associations led to 'an almost total lack of responsibility from local institutions.'[2]

The problems certainly worsened when the number of workers increased. The site's capacity was stretched to the maximum. It simply could not accommodate the majority of workers, and, as a result, large numbers of them continued to live out in tents and shacks at White

Grass. While some activists were hoping that the Ciao Ousmane site was going to be the best example of housing for the workers, African workers themselves knew that this was not the case.

Meanwhile, local attitudes in Campobello remained largely hostile. A Facebook page was set up shortly after the establishment of the Ciao Ousmane camp. It was called, 'Let's defend Campobello; let's send them home.' Salvatore told me he tried to encourage local residents to come to the site to take a look and learn that 'there's nothing scary about these people.' However, most local residents chose to keep themselves well away from the 'foreign' presence.

* * *

A year had passed, and Benjamin had done a substantial amount of farm work in the Trapani area. He was still at the CARA camp in Salinagrande. Then, one day, his long-awaited asylum decision arrived: negative. He was told by the lawyer that his appeal would start soon. Shortly afterwards, without explanation, Benjamin was notified of his transfer to another asylum camp, in a village named Pianosinatico, in the affluent Tuscany region of northern Italy, hundreds of miles away from Sicily. It came as a shock to him. He had to say goodbye to all the people he had befriended over the past year—and with so little time. He had to leave his hard-earned social networks and work contacts all behind. The departure traumatised him. He felt that the transfer to the mainland was a decision made without considering his interests and well-being.

Benjamin knew nothing about Tuscany, except what he had been told by a fellow resident in the Salinagrande camp. Apparently, it was a much wealthier part of Italy, not far from Florence, and it produced lots and lots of wine. Chianti, Vino Nobile di Montepulciano, Morellino di Scansano, Brunello di Montalcino—you name it. Before he arrived, Benjamin had already heard about the mass of vineyards for which Africans were recruited to work.

The camp in Tuscany was a CAS reception shelter hosting no more than two dozen people. Benjamin was looking forward to starting work in the vineyards. Before long, he was picked by farmers and joined other Africans from the reception camps to be sent to work a few miles away. Acres and acres of vineyards spread out in front of him.

Along with others, Benjamin did hard eight-hour shifts almost every day throughout August and September.

In order to travel fast to the fields, Benjamin spent a few euros and got himself an old bike. Riding a bike in the hills was strenuous enough, but the traffic made it worse. One day, like every other day, Benjamin woke up early and got on his bike to work. On one of the hilly roads, a car drove towards Benjamin, not braking in time to avoid hitting him. Benjamin's bike fell to the side, throwing him onto the road. He felt a sharp pain in his right leg and ankle. He sat still on the ground, unable to move, his first thought being that it was lucky that he didn't land on his head. The car had not stopped.

Then he saw the blood pouring out of his leg. He panicked. He needed to get help, but what was the number for the ambulance service? He had no idea. He had never asked about it and no one had ever told him. At times like this, he wished he had been prepared. Quickly, he took out his mobile phone and dialled his friend in the camp, a fellow Gambian who seemed much more informed about such things. Eventually, Benjamin got the number. The ambulance was coming. He sighed with relief, dragged himself to the roadside, and waited.

When Benjamin arrived at the hospital, the doctor told him straight away that he had to stay there overnight for the injury. His heart sank. He knew that his reception camp did not allow residents to stay elsewhere overnight. Like in some other camps in the country, residents, particularly those under eighteen, were not permitted under any circumstances to leave the site overnight. Benjamin did not think through the severity of the rule. Besides, he was well over eighteen. Surely, he thought, they could not control his movements like this. He was lying in a hospital bed, in pain, looking at his swollen leg in a plaster cast. At this moment, adhering to a curfew should have been the last thing on his mind. He called his friend, asking him to tell the staff in the camp about his bike accident and his injury, and to pass on the message that he could not return that evening.

But the curfew rule was upheld. Benjamin was discharged from the hospital the following afternoon and headed back to the reception camp, but the staff shut the doors on him. 'No, you cannot stay here anymore,' a staff member said to him, firmly. 'You didn't come back last night.' She handed him his belongings in two plastic bags and told him never to return. 'This can't be happening!' Benjamin shouted. He was being thrown out of the camp because he had been hospitalised. This could not be right. Didn't they see that his leg was in a plaster cast? How could they turn him away? He screamed and screamed outside the door. But no one listened; no one cared.

Benjamin felt utterly distraught and helpless. He kept banging on the door of the camp until he had no more energy left in him. Then he sat down in a corner next to the camp building, thinking about what the hell he was going to do now. He was still in need of further treatment, but he had to find a place to stay first. Call your friend in Rome, a voice inside told him. Yes, a fellow Gambian who was living in a shelter in Rome. He would probably be able to find Benjamin a bed for a while.

'Come to Rome,' his friend said to him sympathetically over the phone. 'I'll sort you out.' And so, Benjamin spent some of his savings from the farm work to get himself a train ticket to the capital. He was hoping that things would stabilise from there.

In Rome, Benjamin's friend managed to sneak him into the asylum shelter where he was living and put him up for a couple of days. The staff never paid much attention to the residents, making it easier for people to provide a temporary sleeping space for their friends in transit. As Rome was a hub for many Africans passing through on their way north, Benjamin's friend often had people coming to stay a couple of nights before they moved on.

Things didn't go as planned in Rome, though. When his friend took him to a local hospital for further treatment on his leg, the medical staff told Benjamin that they 'wouldn't be able to help.' They couldn't—or wouldn't—give him the treatment he needed. He was told that he should seek help in a German hospital instead. He did not speak enough Italian to be able to fully understand the instructions. It was the first time in his life that he ever had to cross a border to seek medical treatment. His friend told him that this was quite normal; a lot of Africans had this experience and sought medical treatment in Germany. Sometimes it was because the Italian hospitals could not cope; other times it was because the African patients could not afford the treatment.

So this was how Benjamin's life took a bizarre turn after his bike accident on the way to work in the vineyards. Nowhere to live, with no medical treatment, he felt utterly desperate. But he thought back to those months in Libya, to hell on earth. He knew that the bad times right now were small misfortunes compared to Libya. He knew he had to put on a brave face and deal with whatever difficulties destiny presented him. Fortunately, he had his best friend, Yugo, in Stuttgart, to help him. Yugo and Benjamin had spent their entire time in Libya together and escaped on the same boat to Europe. When you had gone through that journey together, you were friends for life. After their landing in Sicily, they were sent to Syracuse together and had the same lawyer to process their asylum claims. Yugo decided to leave the reception camp in Sicily a year earlier and went to Germany to find work. On hearing Benjamin's news, he offered to help immediately. He reassured Benjamin that he would have a bed to sleep in when he got there. So off he went on a train to Milan and then a coach to Germany.

In Stuttgart, Benjamin got his medical treatment and managed to get by working as a casual labourer on building sites, without documents. Soon, he was advised to claim asylum in Heidelberg and was sent to live in a reception camp there. He took up cleaning work at the same time and was able to send a little cash home whenever he was given work.

One day, Benjamin called his Palermo-based lawyer on WhatsApp to get an update on his asylum case in Italy. The lawyer informed him that his appeal for humanitarian protection had been accepted and that he would receive a two-year residence permit. This was the very news for which he had been waiting for years, and Benjamin did not hesitate to head back to Sicily. On the long coach trip back, he went through all the possible scenarios of how his life would turn out from this moment on. Perhaps, from now, he would be able to get more work and do so in the open. He really hoped so.

* * *

For the townsfolk, life carried on quietly as usual in Campobello. Most working days here felt like a Sunday, with streets nearly empty. It was as if the sound of the town had been switched off. There was no news and no one to pass it on. Except something was going on along Via Roma. Out of the blue, in summer 2015, the reception camp on that street—the only shelter in town for adult asylum seekers—announced its closure. It had been coming, due to poor management and the safety risks highlighted by the two fires. Crucially, almost half of its residents had fled since the second fire. The shelter could no longer justify receiving funding.

By now, Mohammad was well acquainted with a local olive farmer named Salvatore, who liked his pace of work, saw him as a fit, excellent worker, and had given him a great deal of work to do in the fields. In the eyes of many farmers, Mohammad was one of the best workers in Campobello. Not only did he look the type, with his solid build and bulky arm muscles, he also demonstrated high productivity for his employers in the way that he worked. He stood in the fields with sweat dripping down his forehead in the fierce sun and still carried on working—and working extremely fast. He spent much less time taking a lunch break than other workers. On average, from 6:00 am to 4:00 pm, he was able to harvest twenty crates of olives per day, which, according to his harvest rate of €3–€3.40 per fifteen-kilogram crate of olives, was earning him €60–€68 a day. His productivity was enviable to his fellow African workers. They looked at him, shaking their heads in amazement. This was why Mohammad also got a lot of work even during the off-peak season.

The amicable relationship that he had established with Salvatore made it easier for him to ask for help when the time came. Following the second fire at the asylum camp on Via Roma, Mohammad politely inquired whether Salvatore could offer him a place to stay. It just so happened that Salvatore had a house on Via Roma, but he wasn't going to offer it to Mohammad. Instead, he said that the garage was empty, if Mohammad wanted to rent it. With the wages he was earning from Salvatore, Mohammad was able to pay the rent of €70 per month. He was not the type who would want to negotiate and bargain with his employers. He felt that 'kicking up a fuss' would bring him nothing good at this stage. He was content that he was given a garage space to live in while fellow Gambians in the Via Roma camp had only their own very limited personal networks to fall back on, and many had to resort to living in the shacks and tents in the open fields of White

Grass. Mohammad knew his situation was unique, and he was not going to demand more and risk losing what he had. He moved into the twenty-square-metre garage on Via Roma, where he was to live for 2 years. He did everything possible to make it look like a home, collecting second-hand lampshades, chairs and a dining table, to make a living space for himself, or at least a place he wanted to come back to at the end of a long day at work.

On his days off, Mohammad often walked about in town on his food shopping trips. He would see fellow Africans walking about too. In the way they walked and talked, he saw himself and his place in this society. Like him, they were always excluded from the daily life of the town. They were not seen as part of the community and were never treated as such. They tried not to tread on the toes of the locals. They were labourers in the fields and customers in the shops, and nothing else. No local person would even look Mohammad in the eye, as if he had no soul. He felt alienated, as much as his fellow Africans did— even though he had a roof over his head and a real bed to sleep in. He wanted to stop feeling this way. He did not want to be seen as a permanent foreigner and endure inferior treatment for the rest of his life.

He asked himself the question: if local farmers saw him as a 'model worker,' what was stopping local society from seeing him as a fellow resident? He did not want to feel like a commodity to be used when needed and discarded when not. He longed for human contact in the town. He felt in need of some recognition that he was just like them: human. He longed to be able to live like the local people and be part of Campobello.

Deep down, however, he knew that doing that would be a long-term project; a wish that for many would only be an unrealistic dream. For the moment, he had to do what was needed and what was possible. He took up as much work as he was offered. He gave his utmost in the fields each and every time. In reward, he received more work.

As hardworking as he was, Mohammad had never received a real work contract, a contract that said what he actually did, because contracts were only for the benefit of the farmers. Holding a valid residence permit did not guarantee protection of labour rights. Without a real work contract, he could never open a bank account in Italy, because he feared that at any time the authorities could close down the account and confiscate his money if they found out that the contract was not real. This was the reason Africans working in agriculture didn't hold bank accounts here or anywhere else in Italy. Mohammad was paid in cash once or twice a week, sometimes once a month, depending on how the farmers liked to do it. He would always transfer money home as soon as he received it from his employers.

It gave Mohammad tremendous peace of mind to be able to send cash home regularly to support his parents. His mission had always been supporting his family. He was the eldest and the only breadwinner. His father had been out of work for a long time, and as his parents reached retirement age, their pension was minimal. Therefore, they had depended on his help, which gave him ongoing pressure to carry on working hard. Since he had started working in the fields of Sicily, he sent €40 to each family member every month for their living expenses. He also sent home €85 each year for his son's school fees. Meanwhile, he took on the duty of paying for his siblings' college education: €240 each per year, for his brother and two sisters. That amounted to €720 per year, just for their tuition fees. This much-needed regular support for his family was a heavy weight on his shoulders, although he wouldn't be who he was without these responsibilities.

Each call from his mother was a reminder to Mohammad of his commitments. 'How is life in Italy?' was all she had to say. He never told her about the problems that he had. What was the point of worrying her? He believed that he was capable of coping on his own. 'I am fine, Mum, I'm fine,' he always replied.

4

IN AND OUT OF CAMPS

Soon after the second fire, which finally led to the closure of the reception camp on Via Roma in Campobello, Sanji had been transferred, yet again. This time it was to a shelter in Castellammare, the same one in which Mohammad had stayed before him. As Sanji got to know later, the name Castellammare originated from the Arab occupation in the early part of the ninth century, when it was called 'Al-Madarij,' meaning 'the steps', due to the hilly streets from the harbour to the fortified bastion. Since then, he had become interested in the names of Sicilian towns, which always involved a history of conquerors, among which the Arabs left a strong imprint. He believed that the history and destiny of Sicilians were closely tied with those of the Arabs—all the way to the relationship in modern times between Libya and Italy.

Sanji felt more anxious living in Castellammare from the first day, despite its tranquillity, and because of it. Castellammare was a rural town to him, cut off from the world, and had nothing going for it except fishing and some tourism in the summer. As time went on, he felt increasingly isolated.

Sanji returned to Campobello and continued working in the olive fields. He started to search for a better place to stay. He heard about the Ciao Ousmane camp at the Golden Fountain site, but he didn't go there because he was not sure if he could trust those who were running it. There were numerous abandoned farmhouses and barns around the area, but no farmers were willing to make them available or equip them with basic facilities for African workers. As Sanji walked up and down White Grass, he happened to see a disused factory storage unit. It was filled with rubbish and looked like it had been deserted for years. Yet, compared with the tents and shacks in the fields, this was a slight improvement—at least there was a concrete roof instead of plastic sheets. He stopped hesitating and moved in.

Soon enough, Sanji began to have problems with his reception shelter in Castellammare. The management had ruled that people were not permitted to stay outside the camp for more than three days. When the staff summoned him to return to the camp, Sanji pleaded, 'I can't just sit here [in Castellammare] doing nothing and waiting for the €75 monthly allowance anymore. My family needs my support. I must work.' Who could blame him? Sanji asked for fifteen days away from the camp each time he was offered work, but the request was refused. He wasn't prepared to back down. He had a mission to provide support for his family. Nothing was going to stop him fulfilling his duty. Therefore, he defied the reception camp's rules and stayed out, working in Campobello, during which time the shelter management in Castellammare didn't give him a penny of his allowance and pocketed it all. This was apparently the way it was in many reception camps across the country, as Sanji knew too well from the experiences of fellow Gambians. A while later, the shelter was closed down due to inadequate management, and its residents were dispersed across the region. Sanji no longer had to concern himself about reporting to the shelter about his whereabouts.

* * *

By this time, the conditions inside the Ciao Ousmane camp site, which had been set up just a year before, were deteriorating. Few people seemed to be looking after it. In the years 2015 and 2016, 'The initial collective began to fall apart, and only a few members remained in the camp, receiving in exchange a small economic compensation from the municipality of Campobello. At the same time, the number of workers present in the [Ciao Ousmane] camp is growing, following the arrival of many migrants from reception centres in the area.'[1]

Before the harvest season approached in 2016, the Ciao Ousmane camp had been completely deserted by the authorities. The showers and toilets were dirty and without water. Piles of mattresses were lying about the place. The entire building was empty, with the gate closed. Then, adding insult to injury, it was reported in *Mazara News* in mid-September that the municipality of Campobello was to receive €60,000 from the Ministry of Interior 'for expenses incurred in relation to the reception of migrants.'

As harvest time neared, more people came into the area and the number at the derelict farmhouses and outbuildings was growing. Some workers came to the Golden Fountain site to pick things up, like mattresses, which they could use for their tents and shacks at White Grass. Activists demanded the re-opening of the site. In Trapani, a delegation of organisations and volunteers met, where it was agreed that the authorities would reopen the site, install six light points, and start the boiler working to provide hot water.

When the Golden Fountain site was officially reopened on 1 October 2016 for the harvest, basic facilities were still not available for days. The showers and toilets weren't ready for use, and there was still no hot water provided. Beyond everyone's belief, the boiler wasn't to be fixed this harvest season. As a result, several people resorted to heating up water in metal containers and selling it for a few cents per bucket.

Not all the charities and associations that had previously been involved in managing the site were there in autumn 2016. For one, the Italian Red Cross wasn't present at first. The provision of workers' food and blankets couldn't meet the demand because of the dwindling amount of donations received. Farmers often paid workers at the end of the harvest, which meant that many workers didn't have cash on them to spend on food. Then, the Italian Red Cross appeared again, and its staff helped out for four hours a day, although their presence could not solve the problems of the lack of basic provisions.

As time went on, the Ciao Ousmane site became dangerously overcrowded as more and more people tried to find space to sleep inside the camp, simply because there was not enough space outside.

Some were sleeping on cardboard. Salvatore Inguì, coordinator of Libera, saw the number of workers rising to more than 1,500 within a month in 2016. The space and facilities were no longer adequate and might also pose high health and safety risks. Given the huge amount of responsibility placed on volunteers, Salvatore and his colleagues decided to inform the new prefect of the province that the volunteer groups alone no longer had sufficient capacity to manage the camp under these worsening conditions. 'We did what little we could, but we did it all. There was now a need for more intensive intervention by the institutions. They need to take up the rest of the work,' Salvatore said to me.

However, instead of improving facilities and capacity to suit the needs of a larger number of workers, the response of the authorities was to turn away and leave it to rot. There was a lot of confusion among workers as to what was going on. One thing was certain: the authorities no longer dared to refer to the site as the Ciao Ousmane camp. It would have been the most humiliating mockery to do so.

This year, as with every other year, the vast majority of workers set up tents and shacks across the open fields of White Grass. No electricity, no water, no toilets. The same inhumane conditions that had preceded Ousmane's death three years earlier.

* * *

Sanji travelled in and out of Campobello as seasons changed—each time following a phone call with a friend. As July 2017 approached, he received a call from a friend of his who was living in an asylum shelter in Alcamo, the fourth largest town in the province of Trapani and four times bigger than Campobello. 'You want to come here for the harvest, brother?' It sounded like a promising idea, and Sanji jumped at the opportunity. He would be able to work in the vineyards on the outskirts of Alcamo and stay with his friend in the shelter, with a roof—a concrete roof—over his head for several months, until the end of September.

The vast stretch of land between Alcamo and Segesta, one of the historic towns once inhabited by the ancient indigenous Elymian people, was filled with vast vineyards that went all the way to the coast. Alcamo was built on its vineyard agriculture and the wine industry, which brought the town affluence. It sat on a hill with quaint, narrow cobblestone streets, well-maintained, pretty churches and more than a few antique shops. Almost a perfect pensioners' paradise, until you walk down the hill to the edge of the town and reach a Jack the Ripper-themed pizzeria, with a bowling alley, in a converted warehouse. Otherwise, the town remained tranquil throughout the year until August. Then, thousands of African workers would arrive for the grape harvest. In fact, workers of the world—Tunisians, Romanians and, later, West and East Africans—have over the years injected new life into this place,[2] making its agriculture a growing source of wealth.

Despite the town's need for them to provide indispensable farm labour, farmers in the area around Alcamo, like everywhere else, refused to provide housing to migrant workers. The local council did not address migrant workers' housing needs but instead came up with a temporary accommodation project in a gym hall. Every year, it tendered a contract for the hosting of seventy migrant workers in the gym. The workers were permitted to come in to the gym hall to stay for the night on the condition that they paid €2 per visit and had a residence permit and work contract. These conditions would have ruled out the majority of incoming workers. Over the entire vineyard harvest season, between August and September, only around fifty people out of thousands chose to stay in the gym. Then, after a bidding process, the management of the gym was handed over to Badia Grande, who subsequently managed the project with the Red Cross, Caritas and ANPAS as partners—the usual parties in the 'migrant management' business.

Across the province of Trapani, sixteen institutions managed twenty-two large CAS camps—with just three institutions controlling nearly half of all places in the province's asylum reception system. These three were the social cooperative *L'Arca*, *Vivere Con* and Badia Grande. *L'Arca*, founded in 2010, earned more than €3.5 million for managing CASs in 2017. *Vivere Con*, established in 1997, managed two out of eighty CASs and 120 beds, earning around €2 million in 2017.

Most workers who spent the harvest season in Alcamo had to make do sleeping in the streets next to the piazza in the town centre. They curled up in their sleeping bags and tried to get a night's sleep while tourists walked to-and-fro between the restaurants. Many of them also squatted in disused buildings.

In the early evenings, Sanji and his friend would often come into the town centre for a stroll around. Everyone, families and couples, would be out for their *passeggiata* (evening stroll). People would gather in the square, chatting and looking happy and part of a community. Children would run around, playing with balloons and drums, and eating the candy floss that was always on sale at the little stalls. At times, Sanji would run into one of the religious processions that gathered hundreds of local residents at the centre of the square. He and his friend never knew what each procession was for, apart from that they were Catholic. People were simply parading in an orderly manner, holding up banners and wooden statues of saints. They would stand quietly to take part in a mass that ended as late as 9:00 pm. Sometimes the crowd got so big that it looked like the whole town had joined in.

When the summer ended, many of the African boys and children who had been working in Alcamo travelled to Campobello for the autumn harvest. The minors, between sixteen and eighteen years of age, came from reception shelters in Palermo, Trapani, Marsala and Mazara del Vallo in west Sicily. They travelled to work on different crops across the region.

Many children from shelters in Palermo ended up going to work in agriculture in towns such as Balestrate and Partinico. Balestrate, a commune about twenty-five kilometres southwest of Palermo, was an agricultural centre known for the production of vegetables, olives and citrus fruits. Partinico, slightly further away from Palermo, was another commune and centre of agriculture, known for its production of grapes and wine as well as greenhouse-grown vegetables and fruits.

Living conditions back at the makeshift camp in White Grass had remained the same all this time. Despite the autumn harvest, there remained no facilities on site. As for the Golden Fountain site, where the Ciao Ousmane camp was, the authorities were reluctant to re-open it for the harvest. Since January 2017, a roundtable working group of the prefecture had been dealing with these issues alongside the associations involved. For the first time, workers' unions, such as Flai-CGIL, farmers' representatives, the Labour Office in Trapani and the local authorities of Campobello all took part in the debate. As before, migrant workers were missing and had no say in the process. Those involved came up with a memorandum of understanding stating that 'the objective is to implement Law L.199 of 29 October 2016, 'Provisions on the fight against the phenomena of undeclared work and the exploitation of labour in agriculture,' and the Protocol of 27 May 2016, 'Care-Legality-Exit from the ghetto,' in order to combat the phenomenon of illicit labour brokering in agriculture…that restores the main foundations of legality, democracy and civilisation…'

'Legality, democracy and civilisation,' the institutional key words for combatting undeclared work and exploitation, were therefore consistent with a municipal ordinance against the migrant encampment, which defined migrant workers' informal settlements as 'illegal.' (It was equivalent to saying that to crack down on unauthorised work, they should crack down on unauthorised workers). As a result, the encampment at White Grass was declared 'illegal,' with the *carabinieri* patrolling the site much more often.

According to sociologist Loïc Wacquant, the political nature of a 'ghetto' is a racialised space produced by a combined absence and presence of the state.[3] From total abandonment to criminalisation, this is truly the story of how Italy forms and maintains ghettoes for its migrant workers.

Shamefully, the institutions and parties involved in the roundtable working group concluded that the maximum reception capacity of the Golden Fountain site would be only 250 people, as a SPRAR (*Il Sistema di Protezione per Richiedenti Asilo e Rifugiati*, or the Protection System for Asylum Seekers and Refugees, a secondary reception centre) was apparently to be opened within the site that September. For this reason, the municipality of Campobello stopped utilising the Golden Fountain site as a harvest workers' camp as it had done for the past three years.

The authorities' shabby plan to provide 250 beds—for those with work contracts and residence permits and able to pay €2 a day—at the Golden Fountain site was certainly not going to work, as the number of harvest workers reached 1,500 that October. The low capacity and the criteria for entry made it impossible to offer it as even a temporary housing solution for the workers. Therefore, as the harvest began in 2017, the Golden Fountain site remained empty. No one would go in. More than 1,000 workers were, as usual, staying at the old makeshift camp in the fields of White Grass, where conditions remained as intolerable as ever. The authorities had not even attempted to improve basic conditions, such as installing regular water supply and basic washing facilities.

'From White Grass to Golden Fountain and then back again,' Salvatore Inguì said to me sarcastically. He would like to ask the citizens of Campobello 'to open their homes without fear' and rent their rooms to migrants. Unfortunately, this idea would have been treated with contempt by local residents.

By this time, across the country, Interior Minister Marco Minniti, whose tenure, under the PD government, lasted from December 2016 to June 2018, put in place a series of extremely repressive measures to stem the flow of migration and to further restrict rights for migrants in and outside the reception system. On 2 February 2017, supported by the EU, Minniti signed a Memorandum of Understanding with factions and militias in Libya, which sealed the border to the south of Europe. This came to be known as Minniti's Signature Policy, under which Italy would supply Libya with technical support for the Libyan coastguard and secure the Libyan shores. Also under Minniti, a restrictive Code of Conduct was imposed on NGO search and rescue activities in the Mediterranean, under which NGOs would not be allowed in Libyan waters. This was Italy's unprecedented step towards the criminalisation of NGOs.

Furthermore, in April 2017, the Minniti-Orlando decree came into effect, with the aim of curtailing 'illegal immigration' and speeding up deportations through the signing of bilateral agreements with migrants' countries of origin and transit. By establishing only two judicial levels, instead of three, for asylum appeals, the decree practically removed the possibility of rejected asylum seekers winning appeals. Worse still, courts for assessing these appeals would no longer be obliged to hear asylum seekers, therefore permitting judges' decisions to be based on video recordings of the asylum seekers' interviews with the Territorial Commission. This utterly violated asylum seekers' right to defence. Meanwhile, under the Minniti-Orlando decree, detention facilities were expanded: the number of CIEs, renamed CPRs, had since expanded from four to twenty, each with a larger capacity of 1,600 people.

* * *

At this time, Benjamin knew nothing about Palermo nor anyone there. It was the first time he had come back to Sicily after being away for nearly two years. He felt totally alone, coming all the way from Milan, on a twenty-two-hour coach ride, into the not-so-glamorous coach station of Palermo, carrying his belongings in a small bag, looking around to get his bearings. He had to be here for his documents because this was where his lawyer happened to be based.

As Benjamin walked out of the coach terminal, he carefully zigzagged through a row of Bangladeshi street stalls selling mobile phone covers and all manner of cheap electronic appliances. He felt anxious, not knowing the directions to the lawyer's office, whose address he kept on a piece of paper. He had to ask someone.

Palermo seemed to be greeting Benjamin with its winter sunshine. He had long heard about this city and how lively and vibrant it was; a cosmopolitan place that never ceased to stimulate and excite. It was filled with ancient magnificence and modern contradictions. Tourism-generated affluence and visible abject poverty contrasted with each other on adjacent streets—and, at times, on the same street. A few blocks away from the Pretoria fountain square, with its sculptures from Florence and horse carriages lined up on the roadside waiting for tourists, there were alleyways filled with rundown canteens serving the not-so-well-to-do communities of Senegalese and other Africans. Behind that, lay the hustling and bustling area of Ballarò, the under-maintained historic quarter, where many new arrivals from Africa and Asia tended to live.

Palermo was known as Balarm in Arabic under Islamic rule from 831 to 1072 CE. During that time, an Arab-Byzantine culture developed, the origin of Sicily's evolving multi-religious culture. The city was divided into quarters through its markets, each with distinct character. Ballarò and its market offered one of the most important traces of Arabic heritage in Palermo.

After the bombing of the Second World War, Ballarò was left to crumble. Between the 1950s and 1980s, many Palermitans moved to the new edges of the city while the mafia ravaged much of Palermo's architectural heritage (known as 'the sack of Palermo') and built new apartment buildings, many of an inferior construction quality. Some of Ballarò's dilapidated appearance, with unfinished concrete structures and scaffoldings left unattended for years, was a result of this development.

From the late 1980s, migrants from Bangladesh started to move into this abandoned part of town, as they looked for low-cost housing. Africans followed suit soon afterwards, trying to make it their home. They all brought life to this poor quarter, which had no basic services and survived on its own limited resources. In the 2000s, many migrants had settled in neighbourhoods around the market and began to trade in it. This was while many local young people had migrated out of Palermo to seek better opportunities in the north and abroad. At least 29,000 citizens of Palermo had left town.

Today, there are more than 30,000 migrants in Palermo, most of them living in Ballarò. It is still very much the 'market of the people' (il mercato del popolo), its residents consisting of low-income families, migrants and students.

At this moment, Benjamin desperately needed to drink some water. He had not had a drop to drink since he left Rome. Then, in front of him, an African man was walking in his direction down the street.

'Excuse me, brother,' Benjamin had to stop him, pleading. 'I'm sorry to trouble you. Is there a place to sit down and have some water around here?'

'Ah, of course!' the man responded warmly. 'Follow me, there's a good place in Ballarò and you can take a rest there.'

The man introduced himself as from Nigeria. He walked up Via Maqueda, which was dotted with several Tunisian stores and bakeries. Benjamin followed right behind him, curiously looking at the window displays of Tunisian pastries and sweets. Then the man turned a corner into a lane lined with African barbers. At the top of the lane, through some random, permanent scaffolding, was the lively outdoor market that had survived more than a thousand years. This was the heart of Ballarò, the man said to Benjamin. Its ancient market remained the 'theatre of abundance', in the words of Sergio Bonanzinga.[4] You could hear it before you could see it: the market vendors were loud and clear, literally singing Abbanniari,[5] their anthem, which was the art of shouting out in rhyming dialect, about the quality and fair price of their products—fresh vegetables, cheese, and all kinds of fish and meat. Each one of them had their own dramatic lines and tones, advertising their goods without embarrassment: '*Veru è, beddù!*' ('Truly beautiful, beautiful!')

Most of the vendors' shops had been there for at least three generations. They certainly shouted as if this was their territory. They were accompanied by several shops selling household goods and cheap electrical items, set up by later immigrants from Asia, and a few hairdressers run by Africans. Sicilian olives and pistachio products were displayed right next to a great variety of Asian spices. From 7:00 am to 7:00 pm, Monday to Sunday, these vendors and shopkeepers kept on going, every single day of the year.

The Nigerian man turned into a narrow alleyway. Benjamin followed him until they reached a small café, its doors wide open. 'This is it, the Nigerian bar,' the man turned to him, 'You can sit down for a rest now.'

The man went in and got the barman to bring over a glass of water. He seemed to know the staff well and warmly exchanged pleasantries with them.

Within two seconds, Benjamin had gulped down the water given to him, then quickly said, 'Thank you, brother!' It had been a long trip and this was a much-needed little break.

When he regained his breath, Benjamin sat back for a minute, immersing himself in the hip-hop playing in the background. He then took out from his wallet the piece of paper with the address of the lawyer and asked the Nigerian man for directions. It happened to be just five minutes away. As they got out of the café, Benjamin followed the man once again, down one alleyway and into another.

* * *

Benjamin walked alongside the Nigerian man, past a busy betting shop in front of which local men gathered to watch football on the big screen, and then turned into a narrow cobblestone lane. They had to keep to the side to avoid several scooters veering left and right through the lane. At the top of it was a café with posters on the wall depicting anti-racist demonstrations. It was called Moltivolti—Many Faces, one of the 'migrant-friendly' venues in town. Its chef, Shapoor Safari, had come to Italy from Kabul two decades ago. Safari had done all kinds of manual work, including picking olives and tomatoes. He and his teammates from Sardinia, Senegal and Iraq were known to be able to cook all kinds of cuisine, from Sicilian and Tunisian to Middle Eastern and West African dishes.

At the back of Moltivolti, Benjamin followed the Nigerian man again, past the Senegalese Association where men gathered to play chess, talk and drink tea, then down a lane that led to a square. The man pointed to a building ahead, 'This is the office you're looking for.'

'You've done more than enough for me, brother,' Benjamin said, embracing him. He waved *ciao* to the man and walked into the lawyer's office.

Immigration lawyers have many ways of letting people down. Many Africans thought of them as sadistic 'bloodsuckers' who exploit people's misery. As soon as Benjamin sat down, his lawyer told him that he would 'have to wait'. 'Wait for what?' Benjamin was puzzled. As far as he understood it, he had finally been granted his humanitarian protection.

'Be patient,' the lawyer said. The past two years had been spent in patience.

'What happened?' he asked anxiously.

'Nothing happened,' replied the lawyer. 'You'll just have to wait for them to issue the residence permit card.'

Benjamin sat there, trying to process this information. He knew that, without the permit card, the official letter that his lawyer received notifying him of the positive decision was not much use. He couldn't use it to get a work contract. But why was he asked to come all the way back to Sicily?

'How long will I have to wait this time?' Benjamin asked.

'I've no idea,' the lawyer said, looking distracted. 'I'll let you know.' Benjamin had to leave.

Confused and dispirited, he sat on a bench outside, thinking about who he could call and talk to. Had he misunderstood something in that office? He hadn't the slightest idea what was going on. No idea where his life was going, or even where he would spend the night. The uncertain nature of events had always meant that he could not really plan things far in advance. Everything was left to the last minute, as if fate would take its own course. Just as Benjamin was pondering his next move, he received a phone call from his hometown friend Alieu, who had been working in Campobello for a year.

Alieu had been in Italy for four years, and he used to be placed in an asylum shelter in Caltanissetta, a central Sicilian town. He was told by the staff that his time in the shelter was up and was asked to leave. Having nowhere to go and no bed to sleep on, he came to White Grass in Campobello where he knew other Gambians were living together. This became a place for people to go when their situations turned desperate. Many had travelled from towns across the province of Trapani, where thirty CAS shelters and camps were based. These accommodated around 2,000 people in total and were far from adequate as reception places for asylum seekers.

CASs, like other levels of shelters and camps, were run by private business people and controlled by the prefectures. The residents' length of stay ranged from six months to four years, depending on the assessments of the people who ran them. Many African youths had left these CAS facilities, either running away from the terrible conditions or, like Alieu and many others, being asked to leave—because they had reached eighteen, their asylum application decision was negative or because they had made demands and wanted improvements to their conditions. Often, they were not even given an official explanation for their removal. In some cases, people had to leave the reception shelters because they were being closed down, as had happened to Sanji and Mohammad. These adolescents and adult men would have to rely on their own social networks to find a place to go to. They were nicknamed the 'CAS people' and would often end up working in agriculture, living in conditions that should best be described as destitute. The situation of the CAS people in the province of Trapani wasn't unique; it reflected a similar picture seen across Italy. The CAS people are a big part of the army of agricultural labour in Italy.

'You can come here if you have nowhere else to go,' Alieu said to Benjamin, who was just about to ask the 'May I join you?' question himself.

'Yes, of course,' Benjamin said to him. Beggars can't be choosers. He decided to join Alieu in the fields in Campobello.

So Benjamin caught the next bus to Campobello. He was exhausted but couldn't get to sleep. The unknown prospect of his destination kept him awake and thinking. He looked out the window. When he was 70 kilometres away from Palermo, the magnificent sight of the

Greek temple of Segesta stood out in the distance. He wondered about the mystery of this beautiful land. It was a two-hour trip southwest, across Sicilian fields on the Salemi route. In the summer, it would be a landscape of vineyards followed by acres and acres of olive groves. Right now, in early winter, the fields were young and dry. At this moment, for Benjamin, there could only be hope that there would be some work to last the winter and that the harvest season would come soon enough. There was hope of a new beginning.

5

YOUNG LABOUR AND 'INTEGRATION'

In Palermo, the 'CAS people' were a reservoir of casual, flexible manual workers, particularly in agriculture. There were also the 'SPRAR people'[1] as well as the under-aged from the minors' centres. The farmers in the areas surrounding the capital had always been able to recruit young people and children from the asylum reception system to pick fruit and vegetables in the fields. While Benjamin was sitting on a bench outside his lawyer's office in central Palermo wondering where his life was leading, seventeen-year-old Samuel from Gambia was sent to harvest tomatoes just outside the city.

Samuel came from a village called Banping in Gambia where his parents were farmers and grew mangoes and other fruit. He used to help out on their farm. When it became clear that the family's earnings were insufficient to give them a reasonable level of subsistence, Samuel left the country with a friend and headed to work abroad. During their transportation from one connection house to the next, he got separated from his friend, whom he never saw again. Samuel had to carry on with his journey. When he reached Tripoli, he realised the stories that he had heard about Libya were no exaggeration. He knew of fellow Gambians who were being imprisoned, beaten and killed. His mother was so worried about him that she cried every time she spoke to him on the phone. The circumstances in Libya forced him onto a boat bound for Europe—but even when he boarded the boat, he had no idea he was to arrive in Italy.

When Samuel and the others on the boat were rescued, they landed in Palermo in 2016 and were sent to Casa Marconi, a notorious mafia-controlled emergency camp with appalling living conditions. As Samuel bitterly joked with friends, Casa Marconi was his new nightmare after Libya. During his time there, he was recruited by a farmer to work in his tomato greenhouses near Palermo. The temperatures were unbearably high in the greenhouses, up to 40°C in the summer.

As time went on, Samuel learned ways to deal with the staff and 'cowboy' management at Casa Marconi. He would always warn new arrivals that 'you've got to be tough, or you'll get chucked out when you reach eighteen.' The idea was that if you didn't make a noise about things, they would be sure to treat you like dirt. Samuel had stayed there for one and a half years, and when he was approaching eighteen, the camp was about to send him out. Where was he supposed to go? The camp was all that he knew. Samuel was not going to leave without a fight. He knew that the only way to survive in the wild world of reception camps—where decisions were often made randomly—was to 'bargain' and fight for his entitlements. He complained forcefully against their decision to throw him out. He said to the centre management, 'if you make me homeless, I will be sure to knock on your door every single day.' He also gathered a lot of support from other residents there, who would eventually share the same fate when they reached eighteen. As a result, the management decided to send Samuel to a SPRAR shelter for adults, instead of leaving him out in the street.

* * *

The shelter for adults was located near Renzo Barbero stadium, home to FC Palermo, and accommodated nineteen young men. To Samuel's surprise, not only were the rules tough about curfew times, there were also unreasonable house rules forbidding the boiling of water on the stove to make tea. Samuel couldn't do without his green tea. He spent 35 cents on each cup of green tea, and it cost him €2.50 per week—not a small amount for him, considering that he only received an allowance of €30 per month. But to him it was indispensable; he only felt energised after drinking green tea and that was how he always started his day, every day. To get around the rules, Samuel got himself a cheap electric hob from the Ballarò market, hid it under his bed and used it when no staff were looking.

At times, it was really tough—like when the shelter staff refused to change meal times to sunset to suit Ramadan. Often, he tried to be helpful to the staff, doing cleaning and other chores for them, to keep on the right side of them. This meant that sometimes the staff would back down and accede to his demands.

Not only did Samuel go to work on farms, he was also sent by the shelter to work with disabled children. His job was to put the children into their seats in the buses every morning, for which he earned €2 for three hours' work. For the money, it was hardly worth his while, but he did not want to upset the staff at the SPRAR. His fellow residents were all engaged in this kind of low-paid work in town as well as agricultural work outside. As activists from Borderline Sicilia observed, these young Africans were exploited twice: as a source of income for the shelters and as the cheapest labour outside.

These SPRAR shelters spoke of 'integration' as one of their aims, justifying state funding. In reality, many of them acted as a reservoir for cheap labour while the 'integration' training programmes often functioned as forums to recruit free labour among young Africans.

In the town of Ciminna, forty minutes outside Palermo, a priest from Caritas was running a programme with the stated aim of 'offering agricultural work skills to migrants' and had been hailed as providing 'a model for long-term integration.' There, teams of asylum seekers—most of whom were waiting for their asylum claims to be processed—were trained to produce olive oil, as much as 5,000 litres per year for export, and pick fruit and vegetables. Their labour was totally free.

'Integration' had been a dominant ideological component in the reception system. It has been part of the 'common sense,' fund-securing phraseology that has been operating in the profit-making business of welcoming new arrivals for at least a decade.

The word 'integration' asks those targeted to be invisible, according to Pierre Tevanian, French essayist, and Saïd Bouamama, Algerian sociologist, as inequality and domination always require the social invisibility of dominated groups.[2] This 'invisibilisation' has been reproduced in the sphere of migration, where migrants are reduced to an 'indebted position' (*position d'obligés*) vis-à-vis the host society.[3]

In the name of 'integration,' dozens of municipalities in northern and central Italy had been setting up volunteer projects in the years since 2011. These projects openly organised asylum seekers to do unpaid work. With help from the media, it was presented as a way to 'integrate' migrants into the local community and for them 'to give something back to Italy' for receiving them. The popular media were good at circulating these ideas, which were easy to sell, because most of the general public had already bought into the belief that asylum seekers were like 'parasites.' Getting them to do free work was seen as a good thing: street cleaning, gardening in public areas, or even harvesting fruit for church charities.

In Acate, a small agricultural working town near Vittoria, eastern Sicily, the San Giovanni Battista Foundation, which managed the 'Biscari' SPRAR came up with the idea that young asylum seekers should give their to the town for free, to alleviate the hostility from the local community to their presence. They cleaned the town's sports pitch. The SPRAR management claimed that the voluntary scheme aimed to 'prevent conflict and transform problems into resources, and to create opportunities for growth and integration.' The newspapers said it was 'evidence of their belonging and civilisation.'[4]

The idea that Africans and other migrants could be put to work for free came from the deep-seated racism that permeates Italian society. The idea was that migrants must contribute economically—or work for free in these programmes—to become 'deserving.' This racism impacts deeply on every migrant's life here, in all aspects, from employment to housing, to their everyday interactions with communities.

The Italian state went further in its integration programmes when the then PD government announced their plan on immigration and asylum in September 2017. It was a plan largely based on thinking about national security and the idea that 'it is safer to integrate migrants.' The plan specifically listed 'voluntary work for asylum seekers' as one of the top items, along with the speeding up of forced returns and extension of the detention system. The then interior minister, Marco Minniti, said that during the 'empty wait' (referring to the desperate limbo in which asylum seekers waited for decisions), they could carry out 'public utility works.'

The reality for those living in reception shelters was the racism they experienced day-to-day. In truth, Palermo meant so many different things to different people. It was all about where you were on the social ladder and in the racial hierarchy. If you were African and an asylum seeker, safety would be one of the biggest issues for you. Samuel had found it dangerous to walk around town in the evening, even walking in pairs. And he didn't use the word 'dangerous' lightly. He knew what danger meant—in Libya, when he walked in the streets under threat of kidnap, and in the building where leeches sucked his blood while waiting for a dinghy, and then on the sea that might have swallowed him up at any time.

Samuel used the word 'dangerous' to describe the streets of Palermo because he had been physically threatened several times. Once, he was pushed around and shouted at by a local man, a complete stranger. He didn't know what the man wanted from him, but he recognised the aggression. He didn't talk back, but just walked on, thinking that if he had responded in any way, other white people would join in attacking him. As far as he could see, risks were everywhere, and he had to be on his guard all the time.

* * *

Unlike the African and Bangladeshi youths who had been rescued and docked in Palermo and had little idea where this place was, there were also young people from all parts of the world who were fortunate enough to choose to come here on student visas. The University of Palermo was one place where these global youth gathered. Minh had such a background and was one of thirty students from Vietnam. She had fantasised about studying in Italy, having fallen in love with Leonardo da Vinci (as opposed to Leonardo DiCaprio) at the age of seventeen. Barely twenty-two at the time of enrolment, she was eager to qualify herself in Education in the city's leading institution of higher education.

At this point, Minh was relatively carefree, and she enjoyed her student life to the fullest. Her plans to return to Vietnam after her studies started to diminish as her fascination with life in Italy grew.

And then she met a young Italian man who was studying film at the university. They wanted to be together. Eventually Minh had to break the news to her mother, who was counting the days to her beloved daughter's homecoming. For weeks her mother cried at the thought of her absence. Minh felt so guilty for causing her sorrow and could not get over it. After her decision to stay and start a new life in Italy, her parents would not accept her offer to support them. It felt like a silent punishment: her punishment for leaving the family behind was that she would no longer have the comfort of supporting them in their old age.

After graduation, Minh went to live with her partner in his hometown of Mazara, to the southwest of Palermo. The town, with a population of around 50,000, lived on its agriculture and the fishing industry. Minh tried to adapt to a new life there. As she learned, Mazara had the highest proportion of non-Italian-born residents among towns and cities in Italy, with more than 3,500 registered immigrants, the majority of them from Tunisia, as well as from sub-Saharan Africa. Many of the Tunisians came to work in fishing.

Marco, the brother of Minh's partner—and now fiancé—was setting up a social cooperative that aimed to manage asylum shelters for minors in Mazara. This was his first job; he had no experience in working with asylum seekers and adopted the attitude that this was a business—and essentially, a family business. For some time, it had been tough for him to find a suitable location for the shelter in Mazara. The town had many mafia connections and they monopolised much of the profitable business of asylum shelters. Marco had no such connections to secure himself a site. He was basically cut out of 'sharing the pie.' Eventually, his cooperative had to make do and set up within an apartment building that he came across in the adjacent town of Campobello. The cooperative brought all of its staff from Mazara. Minh was hired to work as a cultural mediator from the day the centre opened in 2016. Their new workplace was the only minors' camp in Campobello, although for the children this would probably be the last place in Italy they would want to be sent.

At work, Minh's Italian family ties had ensnared her: her fiancé's brother Marco was the shelter owner and the boss and the source of her livelihood. He could be arrogant, she thought, but she had to put up with it. It was family. It was work. It was all she had. Her wages did not allow her to rent an apartment outside her fiancé's family home, and her fiancé was only starting to build up his work as a videographer, which meant that they couldn't just move away. As a result, Minh had to live with her future mother-in-law and experience her particular ways. At times she made offensive comments. 'You eat dogs, don't you?' 'You all eat dogs. Is that true?'

The new shelter was named 'Futuro,' although as months went by, it became a running joke for the adolescents living there who saw it as representing the exact opposite, 'no future.' The landlord of this three-storey building—which had three bedrooms with four persons in each and a terrace on the third floor—was the vice-president of the local council.

Minh committed most of her time to this shelter and wanted to take pride in what she did. Despite coming from a different background, she had an affinity with the minors with whom she was working. She felt that she learned a lot from them—especially when it came to working with people of different cultural origins. She was a Buddhist, and did not see any difficulty in getting along with the boys, most of whom were Muslims, as well as the staff who were all Catholics. Minh respected other faiths; for her, that was the true essence of being a Buddhist. Her favourite time in the shelter was Ramadan when the boys tried to cook for themselves. She enjoyed helping them and being a part of it.

The shelter hired four educators and cultural mediators. The one who Minh thought most highly of was Mouhamadou, from Senegal, whom she always referred to as the person in charge of cultural mediation. 'Commander', she called him. Being thirty-six and older than Minh, Mouhamadou was not as excitable and impressionable as her. He had a calmness about him, which people found reassuring. His laid-back way of being was an asset in an easily stressful place like this. Mouhamadou came from a poorer, lower-working-class family. He worked as a carpenter for years in Senegal, but as the economy wasn't doing well, he decided that he had to leave home to improve life for his parents and his son. He came to Italy from Senegal via Libya in 2013. He talked to his family, especially his son, on the phone every day since arriving in Europe. Their voices constantly motivated him to work hard and keep working hard.

During his first two years in Italy, Mouhamadou was placed in the CARA camp in Salinagrande near Trapani, where Benjamin had stayed. They knew of each other but weren't sharing the same room. While he was in the CARA, he travelled down to Campobello, following the footsteps of so many Senegalese people before him, to work in the olive harvest. For two months, Mouhamadou worked his hardest, and managed to send most of his wages back home to his family.

His situation took a turn for the better when he received his documents at the end of two long years of waiting. He felt free to go wherever he wanted and decided to join his brother who was working in Florence. Mouhamadou's life changed, one day in Florence, when he received news from a friend who knew Marco. 'They have a vacancy for a Senegalese cultural mediator in the camp here in Mazara', his friend told him on the phone. Mouhamadou was thrilled. Through this friend, he got the job offer. At that point, he wasn't given much information, except that the job was based in Mazara. He didn't care about the details. He took the opportunity straight away.

However, upon his arrival, Mouhamadou discovered that there was no job in Mazara. The cultural mediator job was actually based in the minors' shelter in Campobello. Campobello! He sighed at the thought. He had never liked the town.

When Mouhamadou started his job, it became clear why they would consider employing him. This type of work was usually the protected territory of white Italians. Institutions would prefer low-qualified white Italians over well-educated migrant applicants. Only very occasionally would migrant people be considered—and rarely would Africans get the chance. Mouhamadou soon discovered that the shelter staff could not work properly with the African adolescents without an African mediator, who would help 'smooth things over' between the boys and management. Mouhamadou was mainly being employed for the purpose of conflict management. However, he treated his work as a cultural mediator seriously and devoted his time helping the boys adjust to life in Italy.

Despite Mouhamadou's suitability for the job and his being good at it, he found out, sadly, that he was the lowest paid member of staff in the shelter—and his wages would not increase at all over the next two years. There were seven staff members in total, among whom there was a clear racial hierarchy. Mouhamadou was being paid €600 per month working full-time, as compared to Minh, on €700 per month, who was doing the same job, part-time. The two white Italian Campobello-based cultural mediators were also paid more than him for doing the same job: one of them €1,000 per month working full-time, the other €500 per month for working part-time (three days a week).

In addition to this, Mouhamadou was requested to do live-in work, which was not in his job description. The manager needed someone to look after the shelter in the evening but didn't want to spend money to hire anyone. For the extra evening work, Mouhamadou was not even paid. He became trapped in the job from the start; he could not go out and leave the premises at the end of the day and had to devote all his time, day and night, to this job. Every day, he watched his colleagues leaving work at dusk or earlier, going home to their families. He stayed behind, holding the fort, thinking how blatantly unjust his treatment was. He was the one who was made to work for free at night, through the night, when everyone was fully aware that he was not even paid for it. He was deeply hurt by this situation but didn't feel he could talk about it with the management. He knew that he might lose the job, just like that, if he made a complaint. Getting such a job wasn't easy for an African, he reminded himself. He recognised how fortunate he was, to be able to find employment outside of agriculture. This was not an opportunity that would come by again. He would have to remain silent about the differentiated wages and conditions and stay in the job as long as they wanted to keep him.

* * *

As time went by, Mouhamadou realised that Minh was in a terrible position, too. Apparently, she had been given a written contract by the shelter which said that her monthly wages would be €1,200–€1,400 per month. However, each month when she received her pay cheque in her bank account, her employer Marco would then ask her to withdraw several hundred euros from her account and return it to him by hand in cash, which brought her actual monthly wages down to €700. As it went on and she regretted accepting this practice, she found it impossible to stop it. Also, Marco had cunningly asked her to withdraw money in different amounts each time, so as not to cause any suspicion. He was so good at it that there was not a single trace of illegal conduct. Besides, with him being 'family,' Minh did not feel she could do anything except talk to her fiancé about it over and over again. Most frighteningly, all the staff members had consented to this practice.

Despite all this corruption in the workplace, Mouhamadou remained quiet, kept his head down and worked as hard as he could. Coming from the same country as some of the minors here and being older than them, Mouhamadou was well respected. They looked up to him as an advisor with a huge amount of life experience and always having their interests at heart. They trusted him. They would come and seek advice and help from him. When they had problems with receiving the weekly allowance of €10 from the shelter, they would report to him. When they needed improvement in the food provision, they would tell him. Minh admired him, too. She often came to him to ask for advice on the type of food the boys liked when she helped with the cooking. Any variety in food was enormously desirable, and so she tried to make pasta dishes with an 'African flavour', following Mouhamadou's advice on what ingredients she needed to make the food nicer for the boys. She experimented with putting everything in a blender to make a tasty sauce for the pasta.

However, those who controlled the budget—Marco and his aunt— had made sure that as little as possible was spent on providing food and other facilities for the children. Like other reception shelters, cost-saving was always key here. To save costs, they used a great deal of tomato sauce as the base for daily meals. Most meals were just tomato sauce with pasta. The boys were given meat in their diet twice a week—chicken and rice on Wednesday and meatballs on Sunday. The boys saw Sunday as the best day in the week, not only because Minh was the one on duty and she was quite lax with them in terms of discipline, but also because they had meatballs, although only a small amount to share among them. Minh was given the task of cooking and often saw that the food provisions were inadequate. She would then take the opportunity, when none of her superiors were around, to improve the boys' diet by adding carrots, onions and bread crumbs to the meatball stew, to bulk up the portions and make it taste nicer.

During the week, sometimes Marco came to check food preparation when Minh was helping with cooking. When he saw her adding an extra fifteen grams of rice into the cooker, he took the extra rice out and told her off. It upset Minh, but she found it impossible to express her views to Marco, whose management style was, at best, authoritarian.

Marco argued that they had to cut costs to survive as a business. The shelter had only eleven minors living there, less than the fifteen required, and therefore only received funding for eleven people. At the same time, the number of staff remained the same. Why other shelters didn't transfer minors to this shelter in Campobello was a mystery. This smelt of corruption among the shelter managers, as far as Minh could see—when Marco and his colleagues visited a shelter in Castelvetrano to discuss the possible transfers of minors, the owner said that they were transferring the minors to a shelter in Catania on the other side of the island, which was very odd. As a rule, shelters and camps transferred children within the province.

For the adolescents here, food provisions and their crowded shared bedrooms weren't the only issues. They also did not feel that they were respected or listened to by those responsible for their care. They did not have any confidence in the manager, a severe-looking woman in her thirties, who was Marco's fiancé, who they believed didn't care about their well-being. She seemed reluctant to communicate even when there were major issues that concerned them. For one thing, there was a rule that if anyone failed to return to the shelter to sleep, half of their weekly allowance of €10 would be taken away from them. The boys saw this as impinging on their rights to the already meagre allowance. They felt that the shelter manager was behaving like the exploitative employers in Libya and cheating them out of their money.

The fundamental problem for the boys was Campobello itself and what it could offer them. 'Well, there's nothing in Campobello,' was a common saying among them. The boys wandered around the town to explore what lay behind this nothing-happening place. They started to wander further away, to Castelvetrano, if they knew someone living in a shelter there, or to Mazara, for the day. Being five times larger than Campobello, Mazara seemed to offer more. They would get on the train and, unable to afford a ticket, would hide in between the seats, or go from one carriage to the next to avoid the conductor.

Often the conductor would chase after them through the carriage aisles. Sometimes, to keep them from moving between carriages, the conductor would lock all the doors just before departure and check through all the carriages.

When the boys were lucky enough to get through and get to Mazara, they would wander around the busier streets and the labyrinth of alleys inside the Kasbah and spend time there. After a wander, they would often go and hang out with friends they had in the shelters across town. They would hang around for the entire day and evening and catch the last train home. Sometimes, they would be caught by the train conductors for not carrying tickets with them and got sent back to Mazara. What luck! Then they would have to give up returning to the shelter in Campobello and try to stay the night with their friends. The next day when they returned, they would then expect the punishment of having their weekly allowance cut. So it continued—they were sure that they would not to be able to afford a train ticket the next time they travelled to Mazara and would have to do the cat-and-mouse chase with the conductors again.

Mouhamadou recognised that the biggest issue for the boys was the long wait in this rural town, more than a year and with not much to do in their lives. Their having too much time and too little to do, combined with the issue of their meagre weekly allowance, led to them having to find work in the area. Ever since the Futuro had been set up, teenagers here had always tried to work on the farms nearby, especially during the harvest. Here, outside the shelter, several farmers would come to ask whether the boys wanted to work for them harvesting olives or oranges. They were seen as good workers. Some travelled further afield to work on different crops in different towns—they would leave early on the day, on a bike, and return around 6:00 pm. Little pay as it was, for them it was better than what was given in the shelter. When paid wages, they could then spend the cash on buying cheap clothes or shoes for themselves.

Gradually, as the boys worked on farms, they met and developed friendships with the Gambian and Senegalese men living in the shacks of White Grass, many of whom were not much older than them. When there wasn't much to keep the boys' minds occupied, they preferred spending time with the adults from their own countries, like

Sanji. The boys would help Sanji and his friends charge up their mobile phones in the shelter. Two of the boys, in particular, came to talk with Sanji a lot. He was an approachable adult to them and always listened to their problems in the shelter and with school.

One of them was Omar. He had large expressive eyes and an innocent cheeky face. A proper teenager, he had started paying attention to his looks and groomed his hair in baby dreads and talked like a rap star. It was obvious that he thought of Sanji as one of the 'coolest' adults. He liked hanging out with him and saw him as a big brother. He confided in Sanji that learning Italian at school was pointless, as it wasn't aimed at full literacy. 'These language classes are not preparing us for life in society—and certainly not to prepare us to become government ministers!' he said to Sanji, with a bitter laugh. 'They just teach us to speak some Italian, to get by on a basic level.' He felt that he would be learning a lot more in the streets—and at work in the fields.

When the boys in Futuro reached eighteen, they would, in theory, be transferred to SPRAR shelters in the province. But clearly the destination was never their own choice and the decision did not take their needs into account. The unlucky ones got sent to places in remote areas where they knew no one. In the worst case, when teenagers reached eighteen, they would simply be thrown out of the shelter to fend for themselves and not be transferred anywhere.

Most of the boys at Futuro wanted to leave Campobello straight away when they reached eighteen—not to a place arranged by the shelter, but to a place where they could find good enough employment. Some of the boys did not wait until reaching the age of consent—they chose to run away, to go to Germany or France. Every time a boy ran away, it saddened Minh, because she had known them for a while and befriended them. She believed that they treasured her friendship as she had treasured it. When they left without a note, it felt like her efforts to make them happier had been rejected.

One boy who had run away was constantly on Minh's mind. A day before he left the shelter, he volunteered to help her with cooking, and she had to push him away. 'Don't worry, it's not your job to cook!' she said to him, laughing. After the meal, he helped with clearing the table. Looking back, Minh could see that this was his last gesture of good will before his departure. The next day, when Minh came to work and saw that he had gone, she burst into tears. Children who ran away would most likely end up in another town, or another country. The chances of ever seeing him again in her life were minimal.

Thinking clearly, though, Minh knew that she could not and should not blame them. She understood why they had to leave. The life in the shelter presented little hope for their future. How could they possibly want to stay? Besides, she knew that some of them had families in other countries and they wanted to join them.

For the boys, what went on inside the confines of the shelters was not the only aspect of life that they might find difficult. The toughest thing for them in adjusting themselves to life in Italy was that, fundamentally, they were not accepted by society. The racism was the harshest thing with which they were confronted day-to-day. They heard of the racial violence that occurred across Italy and of the injuries and deaths that were caused to other Africans. Hearing about these was a constant reminder of where they sat in Italian society. As they grew older and had to involve themselves in the world, these boys were going to understand how deep racism ran, in all aspects of their lives, from housing to employment to the basic forging of relations in society. For the time being, when the boys were still living in the shelter, they sometimes came to talk to Minh about their personal experiences in Campobello, about how local residents talked to them in a disrespectful way. This was only the first lesson in racism they learned in their lives here.

What was the future for the Futuro boys—and thousands of African adolescents like them in Italy? Racism was built into the system, which prevented Africans from lifting themselves out of their situation and from being able to progress in life. Many of them arrived in Europe unaccompanied, with no resources and few social networks. After a few years in Italy's shelters, most remained illiterate in Italian and did not know the alphabet, as Minh observed, even though they went to school here. The so-called school. It was designed for migrants, which meant the lessons weren't meant to teach them systematically. Most language teachers for migrants were not even qualified. The boys were already seventeen when they started school, much later than everyone else. The three-hour language lessons per week were simply insufficient. It kept them permanently behind Italian children.

Therefore in most cases it was unthinkable for them to go to college or university. And most of them wanted to be able to work as soon as possible. Having battled with the system for many years to get documents, they simply could not afford to waste more time and therefore tended not to choose to go into higher education even if given the chance. It was a vicious cycle that meant their opportunities in life would in turn be limited by their lack of educational qualifications. When they reached their early twenties, they would then find that few employers outside agriculture would accept them. Racism was indeed what made agriculture one of the few work options for Africans.

Minh was frustrated to see this happening, but there was little she could do apart from trying to encourage the Futuro boys to do as much as they could and take part in learning activities. The majority of the boys she had worked with in the shelter, however, went on to do farm or menial industrial work.

6

JOINING THE HARVEST IN CALABRIA

Benjamin reached his destination at dusk, after travelling past yet more fields which had now all been harvested. When the narrow, dusty streets came into view, he knew that it must be Campobello. It looked like a village, just as Alieu had described it. He felt a little anxious about what awaited him here.

The sight of Alieu and his warm hug reassured him. At least, from now on, for better or for worse, Benjamin wouldn't be on his own. As Alieu walked with him in the direction of White Grass, he started preparing Benjamin for the actual situation there. As he had told him on the phone, the autumn olive harvest had come to an end. Nearly 2,000 people had left the olive fields and moved elsewhere for work. All of a sudden, the large ghetto shrank to a small encampment. Those who had decided to stay on and stay put had fewer social networks outside of Campobello. They preferred to carry on here, finding whatever work was available and try to make ends meet throughout the winter.

It had been a long day travelling and hunger and thirst had weakened Benjamin's voice. What was more, his mobile phone battery was dead as he had not had access to an electric socket for two days. 'Can I charge my phone somewhere?' was the first bit of help he asked of Alieu. As there was no electricity supply in the encampment, everyone including Alieu had relied on regular visits to town and pleading with any shopkeeper to let them recharge their phones. Several people who knew the boys in the Futuro camp, where Minh worked, would be let in and allowed to charge their phones. But Alieu didn't know anyone there.

'How about the train station? Might they let me?' asked Benjamin.

'No, I'm afraid not,' Alieu shook his head. 'They don't allow us, even if we beg. They don't like us.'

Benjamin didn't need to ask why. He got it. For the time being, he had to put the dead phone aside. He followed Alieu, walking south through town. They came to the high street when they reached the top of the narrow lane; it appeared to be the centre of the town, lined with little cafés, cars and convenience stores. Benjamin looked around curiously. The town hall, a two-storey building with colourful Sicilian and EU flags on the balcony, stood in the distance like the sheriff's office in the Wild West. Several local residents walked past them looking expressionless, emotionless, in their own world. There was a curious silence about the place that could easily make a newcomer uncomfortable—it certainly did Benjamin. At one corner of the high street was a café bar where the local men hung out. There were a few stares as the two walked past. Alieu, as a habit, said *ciao* to people he met. But there was no response from these men. Alieu and Benjamin turned the corner into Via Roma, which led towards the edge of town.

As they left the town behind, there was no longer anyone about on foot, but the occasional tractors that drove past, coming back from the fields to park in the family compound. It was almost a relief for Benjamin to be away from those silent stares. He looked to their right and saw rows of young olive trees, spindly branches swaying in the early winter breeze. To the side of the road was a dusty path which they walked down to get to White Grass. As they walked through the gate and came into the makeshift camp, the first sight was an immediate shock to Benjamin. He had never seen a place like this before. Since his arrival in Italy he had lived in an emergency camp and a number of shelters. Despite the poor conditions, he had always had a roof over his head. When Alieu showed him to his shack, Benjamin could not even see inside because there was no light. He put down his luggage, in the pitch-dark. There was the stink of stale bedding from its previous occupants. Plastic water containers were everywhere—people used them to collect water from the only tap nearby. Piles and piles of rubbish were scattered around. The sight overwhelmed him. 'How am I going to last this?' he kept thinking.

Benjamin and Alieu had not the faintest inkling of the plans being set in place, which would soon make things a lot worse for them. A local councillor, by the name of Tommaso di Maria, of the Five Star Movement (M5S) in Campobello, had been asking for the eviction of Africans from the 'Archaeological site of White Grass' from as early as November 2017. Five Star, the name being a reference to its key policy issues—public water, sustainable transport, sustainable development, right to internet access, and environmentalism—was founded by Beppe Grillo, a right-wing comedian and blogger, in October 2009. He referred to Five Star as a 'populist' movement, but in essence it was a right-wing, anti-immigrant political force which had managed to shed itself of that image with help from the media, which had from the start framed it as 'anti-establishment,' putting the emphasis on its social reform and green policy pledges. Since the 2014 European Parliament elections, Five Star had been part of the Europe of Freedom and Direct Democracy (EFDD) group in the European Parliament, alongside the British right-wing anti-EU and anti-immigrant United Kingdom Independence Party (UKIP).

Tommaso di Maria's eviction request had been made in the middle of the olive harvest and no worker was aware of it. Di Maria, a shrewd local politician, knew how to make his request sound as politically neutral as possible, quite like the 'not right, not left' electoral approach of Five Star. He announced that he had conducted inspections in November along with an archaeologist, Annibale Cerrati. Following an excavation in the 1990s, bronze weapons dating back 3,500 years had been found in the area. The finds had been housed in Selinunte, 4 kilometres away, waiting to be relocated to a museum. Despite Di Maria's attempt to de-politicise his eviction request in the name of archaeology, it was clear that the request could not have been made at a more politically sensitive time. It was in line with the local authorities' policy direction to make the encampment illegal.

This was a time when local politics in Sicily were shifting rapidly to the right. In the local elections in the same month as Di Maria's eviction request, the centre-right candidate Nello Musumeci was elected to become Sicily's new governor, with the backing of three of Italy's most prominent parties on the right: Berlusconi's Go Italy (Forza Italia), Brothers of Italy (FDL), and the League (La Lega). Matteo Renzi's PD was kicked out of power, dropping to third place behind Five Star, which became Sicily's largest single party.

In his eviction request, Tommaso di Maria claimed that 'non-EU citizens illegally occupy this piece of land [and] practice commercial economic activities without a license.' He requested an 'immediate eviction' in order to clear the archaeological area. He did not, at any point, talk about alternative housing for the African workers when they were to be moved out of White Grass. This clearly was not his concern. His request helped pave the way for what was to come. At this point, the fates of Benjamin, Alieu and everyone else living at White Grass, had already been sealed.

For those who were staying in the encampment, this was their escape from homelessness. Benjamin knew that Alieu only meant to help. But the conditions here made it only a small step up from being individually homeless on the streets—it was now being collectively homeless in a field.

At the same time, people would always seek out information about the possibility of work elsewhere. On the morning after Benjamin arrived, a Gambian friend called him from a place called Rosarno.

'Many people come to Rosarno to work,' said the man who had been staying there for several months.

'Where is Rosarno?' Benjamin asked.

'It's in Calabria, just next to Sicily. It'll take you around ten hours to get here.' Then the man added: 'There's much more work in Rosarno in the winter than where you are.'

Indeed, in Rosarno winter was the harvest time for oranges, mandarins and lemons, and many seasonal migrant workers were heading there.

His friend told him more: 'Here, you'll be able to get a residence permit easily.'

'Really?' Benjamin couldn't quite believe it. 'How come?'

'Well, the local government here gave people the permission to use the address of the *tendopoli* [tent city], to apply for a residence permit.'

A postal address was always required in order to apply for a residence permit. And indeed, during this period, Africans inside the *tendopoli* were allowed to use the address of the encampment. By doing this, the local authorities were able to keep migrants in the encampment and well out of sight.

Benjamin was intrigued. Could this sort out his status once and for all? He wanted to give it a try in Rosarno and asked Alieu to join him. As there wasn't much work around, it didn't take Alieu much time to consider it—he had two daughters and a son waiting for his support. He decided to go with Benjamin—and they asked six other people to join them. For the team of eight, leaving was not an impulsive act but a survival instinct. Benjamin ignored the fact that he had only just arrived in Campobello. The following day, the team of them jumped on a bus in the early morning and reached Rosarno, in the northeast of the Calabria region some twelve hours later.

* * *

The moment Benjamin, Alieu and their team walked out of Rosarno station, it truly felt like they had arrived in a deserted town in the Deep South of Italy. The street going uphill to the left of them, which would take them into town, was lined with empty buildings, and the pavements were scattered with litter. A couple of Moroccan men approached passers-by, begging for a few coins. They must have come here for work but ended up in the streets. To the right of the station was an underpass where graffiti was sprayed across countless cracked concrete walls. Broken promises were commemorated here by the angry left-behind. 'Europe dictates,' someone wrote here, with a euro sign in black paint next to the words. Was this the dystopia of Europe?

Benjamin's only friend here came to meet them. The team followed him, going to get some food provisions for the next few days. Five minutes up the hill, he stopped at Mama Africa. It was a busy food store run by a woman named Eva, from Burkina Faso, who had come all the way from Milan where her family lived and had been running this shop in Rosarno for four years. Most of her customers came from the *tendopoli* of San Ferdinando, 2 kilometres outside Rosarno town. Eva was like a friendly auntie with whom you could always have a chat. Everyone liked her. Here, you could get the ingredients you needed for any African dish. Gambian boys liked coming here to buy the peanut paste for their favourite dish *Domoda*—the Gambian dish made of the paste cooked with meat and chilli powder. They also needed palm oil and okra. They could get carrots and onions here, too, which they would often need for a typical home stew. Along the street outside Mama Africa, there was nothing except several Chinese garment stores. The red of their lanterns was barely visible as they were covered in dust and bleached by the sun. A couple of watermelon stalls were set up on the pavement.

The team followed Benjamin's friend until they reached the centre of town at the top of the hill. There was a peculiar sense of quiet. People were leisurely chatting in groups and looking around curiously, as if waiting for something to happen. Dozens of men, mostly in their forties and fifties, talked in low voices sitting around in their vests on the benches inside the town square. Many of them looked tanned and unshaven—or were they just covered in dust too? There were few new faces in town. Any stranger walking through the square would catch their attention straight away, like a stone being thrown into a still pond, causing ripples to spread out. The middle-aged men in vests would turn around and take a thorough look at the new person. Their stares were sharper than their murmuring. Familiar, suspicious stares. They were like warnings, for strangers to hurry up and leave their sight. If you were unlucky, sometimes you could even receive a rude hand gesture indicating that you should leave the area immediately.

Benjamin was to learn that this was a town where a stranger would never receive a greeting. If anything, you had to watch your back at all times. As he walked along, he could not help noticing that there were more than a few Africans on bikes, riding against the setting sun. They too were on their food shopping trips.

Rosarno was slightly bigger than Campobello, with a population of nearly 15,000. Its bleak appearance did not indicate its history; it had once been the ancient Greek city of Medma. What was visible were the shallow natural terraces filled with olive groves and vineyards on the left bank of Mesima river overlooking the Gioia Tauro plain. Agriculture was all that this town had lived on, with its production of citrus fruits, olive oil and wine. Apart from its crops, Rosarno seemed to have little going for it. You could look for traces of past glories and be puzzled that they were not there. It was as if the place had a damaged soul.

* * *

There was a long story behind the state of affairs in Calabria, and one thing that stood out was the absence of the young. Mirco Mungari, a thirty-six-year-old musician, archaeologist and teacher from Calabria, knew all about it. He was one of the young people who had emigrated from their impoverished hometowns and out of the region in the past two decades.

Mirco came from a middle-class family in Crotone, an ancient city of Magna Graecia on the eastern coast of Calabria, 170 kilometres from Rosarno. Their family house, built by his grandfather who owned some land, was located near the Sant'Anna airport 7 miles from Crotone, and from there he was able to see the sea from a small hill. Opposite that airport, a CARA was built after he had left, on the site of the former NATO base, and it was also called Sant'Anna. Mirco grew up learning from his grandparents how to grow crops and breed cattle. But he felt lonely as an introverted child, which didn't impress his grandfather who had hoped to have strong male offspring to carry on earning a secure livelihood for the family. Mirco spent most of his childhood fighting against his grandfather's anger. He found escape in studying and practising music.

Mirco would always remember the smell of the sea, however far away from home he was now. The sea was everywhere, he recalled. In his words, you could fill your eyes with the sea and your lungs with the salty wind, in every corner of the town. When he was a child, he often asked himself, 'how can people live in Milan or Rome without the sea?'

Yet Crotone was his prison, Mirco said, and the large garden of his house was his cell. He wanted to escape. He was thirsty for life. 'My unlucky hometown,' he called Crotone. Rosarno was no different for him; they shared the same Calabrian depression, the same illness. He knew that those middle-aged men who were hanging around the square in the centre of Rosarno town would be unemployed—and had probably been without work for a long, long time. They would be among the majority there, some of whom were on state benefits. The lucky ones who managed to get work were often in construction.

As a whole, almost all the industries in the region were controlled by the local mafia, the 'Ndrangheta, Italy's largest organised crime group, who owned a lot of the land, as well as controlling most of the food supply chains, all the way down to restaurants and bakeries. According to Coldiretti, Italy's largest agriculture industry association, not only the production, but also transport, distribution and sale of food products had become big business for the 'agromafia' groups.[1] Rosarno had always been notorious for being a hotbed of 'Ndrangheta activity and was the birthplace of criminal clans such as Pesce, Bellocco and Ascone 'Ndrine. For years these criminal networks had penetrated all walks of life in town as well as the local government. Back in October 2008, the mayor of Rosarno, Carlo Martelli from Go Italy (Forza Italia), Berlusconi's party, was arrested for having links to the mafia and having favoured businesses connected with the Piromalli family, one of the local 'Ndrangheta clans. That December, the town council was dissolved on orders from Rome as result of its infiltration by the 'Ndrangheta.

In January 2018, it was found that the Farao-Marincola clan had expanded beyond its stronghold of Ciro in Calabria and developed a supply business for wine, cheese and olive oil to restaurants in Germany, where the gang threatened owners of restaurants and pizzerias, forcing them to buy products from the companies controlled by the group. The clan had controlled bakeries, vineyards and olive groves, as well as having hands in asylum reception centres.

The mafia networks had, for years, controlled the recruitment of agricultural workers here. Through the *caporali* who were controlled by the mafia, the 'Ndrangheta was able to determine who were chosen to work and who were not. The *caporali* would pick up their selected migrants and bring them to the farmers, for which they received a percentage of migrants' wages. They controlled and disciplined the workers, who often wouldn't dare to complain, for fear of reprisal.

In San Ferdinando (the council of which had already been dissolved several times as result of mafia infiltration), as well as Rosarno and the Gioia Tauro plain, 88% of workers employed in agriculture were migrants. The farmers, as the norm, would offer meagre wages, no rights and no contracts, and local men would not usually want to work for them—and when a few did, they would normally negotiate their wages to be up to €50 a day. African workers, in comparison, would earn €2.50–€3 an hour, about €20–€25 per day. Even those with documents had not been protected from extreme exploitation. They might be working every day during the harvest, but as their farmer employers would not declare their real working hours to the INPS (social security), workers would not be able to build up the 102 days of declared working time required for them to claim unemployment benefits out of season.

Mirco had grown up seeing migrant workers around his town. He had seen them working in the fields as labourers or shepherds. He saw how they were segregated by the local population who considered them 'dangerous beasts.' When he was a child, his grandmother used to try to scare him, 'if you don't stop crying, I will call the Moroccan man!'

When he reached adulthood, Mirco decided to leave Calabria as he started to feel as if he was 'sinking' to the bottom of a deep well. 'They knew nothing of the world; they had only ignorance, racism, mental scarcity, viciousness and filth,' he would say to the outside world about his hometown. It was eating away his soul with all its humiliation and injustice. He felt he had no choice but to go. He knew that the young had to leave if they wanted to survive. In his words, the only option was crime, or take the first train out. He escaped as soon as he was able to, at the age of nineteen. And most of his schoolmates left, just like him. They all searched their fortunes far away from home. The statistics are as sad as the region itself appears: youth unemployment (fifteen to twenty-four-year-olds) in Calabria is 65%.[2]

Mirco left on a warm day in August. He brought with him many books, his concert guitar, a photo of his dog. It was a long car journey with his father who drove him to Bologna far to the north, where Mirco was to study archaeology and music in the university there. It was a moment that he had dreamt about for years, and Bologna was, for him, paradise. There he saw so many libraries, cinemas, theatres, and people strolling. There he received an emotional education and discovered all that he was missing back home. At nineteen, he finally learned to be a social person. He remembered his first year in Bologna as a beautiful year, when he became fully immersed in his studies, the passion of his life.

Memories of Calabria came back to him a little later, in solitary Sunday walks through the snow. The smell of the sea came back to him, and the long sunsets in May, when the sea and the sky became one. Mirco realised later that he felt guilty—guilty for running away. He felt guilty because somehow he was different from most of 'his people,' which gave him the ability to leave. Years after his departure and when he had built his new life in Bologna, he would still constantly refer to Calabria as being 'like a beautiful woman whose body is corrupted by a spreading cancer.' He had abandoned that woman for his freedom.

Everything that Mirco had done since leaving Calabria was a statement defying his hometown—and its harshness and prejudices. He had a job that most people back home would consider middle-class, even though it didn't bring him a comfortable standard of living: performing and teaching music. He also taught music and languages to non-Italians and asylum seekers. He continued to see the new arrivals to Calabria as those who were bearing the brunt of the rotten society from which the local younger generation had escaped and left behind. He wanted to do all he could to compensate for what his hometown was doing to these new arrivals.

Mirco had never been tricked into feeling nostalgic for his hometown. Some of his schoolmates returned to the region, but others went even further away, to live abroad. For him, the longer he was away building his life, the more unbridgeable the distance between him and his past became. He grew to feel disgust for the idea of returning to Calabria—a feeling of which he was not proud.

Mirco's last visit to Calabria was to his grandfather's funeral. He met relatives that he had not seen since his teenage years. They hugged him strongly. But his hometown felt like a desert to him. He still had the memories of those sunsets of his childhood, but he never found them the same again. The home visit left him sad and tired. He realised that, even if you escaped from your hometown, it would always follow and burden you, hanging behind your shoulder. You would never entirely escape it, even if you ran half the world away.

* * *

Now in Rosarno, Benjamin and the team followed his friend, carrying their plastic bags of shopping, along a dusty, nearly empty road. A couple more African boys rode past on their bikes again, westbound. 'They're going back to the camp,' his friend said, referring to the *tendopoli*, the shanty town built from wood, corrugated iron and tarpaulin, a couple of kilometres away. It was located in an industrial park on the outskirts of San Ferdinando, a tiny seaside resort that had only around 4,500 residents. 'It's not far from the seashore,' he added. They walked in the same direction as the cyclists, along the back road connecting Rosarno with San Ferdinando.

This makeshift camp was the latest product of the authorities' management of the housing issue for migrant workers, which had been completely based on an emergency approach. The handling of the 'Rosarno emergency' was delegated to the Department of Civil Protection, a body set up in the aftermath of the earthquake in Irpinia to coordinate assistance during natural disasters. Rosarno's emergency approach towards migrants had been the same for years. Treating the migrants' presence as a temporary arrangement, dealt with outside of town, made it less intolerable for local residents. More than 2,000 seasonal migrant workers arrived each year in the Gioia Tauro plain from November to March for the citrus harvest, and before 2010, many were living in an encampment and derelict farmhouses not far from the latest *tendopoli* in San Ferdinando.

Back then, besides the tough conditions inside the camp, there was also a huge amount of hostility and resentment from local residents towards African workers. Unreported stories about racist incidents and attacks were shared and passed on by migrant workers. In December 2008, a gunman went into a derelict factory building where over a hundred African workers were sleeping, and shot two of them, seriously injuring a twenty-one-year-old from the Ivory Coast. African workers took to the streets in Rosarno in protest.

Two years later, on 7 January 2010, a group of local youths used air rifles to shoot several Africans on their way back from working in the fields. This sparked a protest in the streets and more than 2,000 people demonstrated in front of the town hall. They shouted 'We are not animals!' and carried placards saying 'Italians here are racist.' They had put up with racism and racist abuse from the local community for a long time. But they would not tolerate physical violence, which had continued for two days. During this time, some local racists had even set up a roadblock and hunted down Africans in the streets of Rosarno, many of whom were beaten with metal bars or wooden clubs. One of the locals arrested for the attacks was Antonio Bellocco, related to members of the Bellocco clan, which had control over many of the local fruit farms.

All this happened while Silvio Berlusconi was still prime minister of Italy and Roberto Maroni from the League (La Lega) was the interior minister. Instead of condemning the violence against African workers, Maroni claimed that 'tensions were a result of too much tolerance towards clandestine immigration.' He said this after twenty-one Africans had been injured during the attacks. The violence was such that the police had to bus all African migrant workers out of town, to other parts of Calabria, Naples, and Bari. Their departure was cheered and applauded by local residents. Meanwhile, Rosarno was nicknamed 'the world's only all-white town.'

Later, on 20 February 2011, the local authorities set up a temporary container camp for seasonal workers, however it only provided 200 beds and documents were required for entry. Therefore the majority of African workers were kept out and continued to find shelter in the countryside. A tented camp for the seasonal workers was then set up by the Civil Protection authorities and the Ministry of the Interior. With funds of just €40,000 allocated for the season by the Ministry of the Interior, there was no proper plan from the local and national authorities on how to manage the place. It was practically abandoned from the start. With discontinuous funding and the absence of management during the winters of 2012 and 2013, it fell into disrepair. The tents housed up to 450 people, and as time went on, the encampment pulled in more and more people. By 2014, the number of occupants had doubled. Apart from the numerous tents, people built wooden and corrugated iron shacks, too. However, basic facilities were still absent. There was no electricity, no hot water, let alone heating during the winter.

The appalling living conditions in the encampment were revealed by the mobile clinic of Italian NGO, Doctors for Human Rights (MEDU), who were providing assistance to around 150 African workers each month in the encampment as well as in abandoned farmhouses in Rosarno, San Ferdinando, Rizziconi and Taurianova. The African workers who were treated by MEDU had not only endured terrible living conditions that harmed their health, they were also subjected to appalling working conditions as well. Around half of them had already been granted humanitarian protection status, yet nearly 90% of them were not given a work contract and 64% were paid an average of €25 or less per day. As pointed out in the report 'Governing Agricultural Migrant Workers as an "Emergency": Converging Approaches in Northern and Southern Italian Rural Towns,'[3] far from being a solution for the migrants' housing situation, these 'emergency' structures contributed to reproducing labour exploitation.

MEDU launched an appeal to the PD government to get their act together to combat exploitation in agriculture. The authorities did nothing until October 2016, when the first step in cracking down on labour exploitation and *caporali* was taken when a new law was passed, introducing sanctions on employers and mandating organised labour inspections. However, the law did not address the problem sufficiently, as the huge inspection efforts required to verify exploitation simply didn't happen. Also, the law failed to promote a supply chain approach that aimed to increase transparency of the whole chain to combat *caporali* and exploitation.

The conditions continued to deteriorate at the *tendopoli*. It was laid out in large fields miles away from San Ferdinando town which itself had plenty of empty apartments. The distance from and relationship with the local towns was itself the story of the *tendopoli* and why it existed in the first place: the towns didn't want Africans in their midst. The structural racism that informed the attitude of the town and the emergency approach of the authorities was the context in which racial violence was able to thrive. The racism that motivated the violence of January 2010 had never gone away; it carried on in the daily segregation of African workers.

In October 2017, a gang of four local men were arrested for a series of racially motivated attacks on African workers. The men drove around the area at night in a Fiat Punto looking for Africans on their bikes—and when they saw one, they would lower their car windows to attack them with clubs and knives. Dozens of Africans were assaulted, suffering broken noses, shattered bones and serious concussions. One man was run over by the gang and seriously injured. Attacks continued even after the arrests: at least thirty more attacks by hit-and-run drivers were reported by emergency services. The threat was constant and frightening. The danger was always around and often behind you.

No one could be adequately prepared for the sight of the ten acre *tendopoli*. It was much larger than the makeshift camp in White Grass in Campobello, more densely occupied and with more and more people moving in by the day. The visibly overcrowded tents and shacks made of wood and plastic were built so tightly next to each other that it not only felt claustrophobic but posed an obvious fire risk. Bed space was very tight and Benjamin and his team had to share one shack, some sleeping on filthy mattresses, others on the floor. People divided themselves into communities of Senegalese, Gambians, Malians and others. Benjamin's group, as newcomers, tried to stay close to his friend and keep themselves to themselves. As more people arrived, Benjamin felt more vulnerable. Living day-to-day without basic facilities was exhausting—let alone doing it with a much bigger crowd. He felt so stressed that he couldn't sleep much at night.

The biggest problem for Benjamin were the *caporali*. They had penetrated the *tendopoli* for years—well after the anti-exploitation law was passed in 2016. As soon as Benjamin and his team arrived, in winter 2017, their work fell under the control of a *capo*. Only €15 per day was left after all the deductions. There were no exceptions for new workers. You had to stick around for three or four years to learn the ropes and eventually you might get to work directly for local farmers.

Benjamin and his team regretted the decision to come to Rosarno. 'I wondered if we had left Libya,' he said bitterly. The stress gave him headaches. He often stayed awake into the early hours wondering how he had jumped at the idea of coming to this hell-hole and where his life was going from here. The team toughed it out for two weeks. But after that Benjamin felt he had to leave and move on again. He could stand it no more. He went all the way back to Campobello. Alieu, however, wanted to stay on. After all, he had invested in the travel fare to come all the way to Calabria. His family was waiting for support. Turning back after two weeks was not his style. He continued there for another month after Benjamin had left with his six other fellow workers.

* * *

'If I had a place to go to, I wouldn't have come back,' Benjamin thought to himself when he arrived back at the same bus stop in Campobello. It was freezing cold. Benjamin pulled up the zip of his only black jacket and wrapped the scarf tightly round his neck. He then dug his hands in the jacket pockets, shivering as he walked on. He felt as miserable as the weather.

When Benjamin came back to the makeshift camp in White Grass, instead of asking everyone for an update, 'Che,' a fellow resident in his thirties, beat him to it. He also came from Gambia and always wore a Che Guevara beret. 'It's been so tough here in the winter, I'm telling you, brother,' he said. There was not enough work around for everyone. Che and others sometimes found casual work trimming olive trees. The local farmers needed them to tidy up the fields. But during the off-season, these farmers paid €20 per day, on average, without a contract. However, those who remained here preferred to stay and earn €20 than going to Rome or elsewhere and risk failure. To move out of Campobello, train or bus fares would be the first thing in which to invest. Was it worth the while to move away, to look for work outside the region? The answer would be 'no' for those with little cash, like Che. These Campobello farmers were the devils they knew. Some of the Africans had been here for six or seven years and the farmers would come to them when they needed workers. Even lowly paid, they would still be able to earn when there was work. Most felt that this was a safer bet than going blindly into the unknown.

Benjamin was massively dispirited by the conditions at White Grass. Having returned from Rosarno, he knew that he now had even fewer choices. The lack of basic facilities and the poor hygiene were depressing enough, but everything was made worse by the cold of winter. Often he stayed inside his shack, covering himself in layers of plastic sheeting which protected him from the dropping temperatures and the wind. It was so cold that he never took off his only jumper and jacket when going to bed.

Daytime was no less easy to get through. Benjamin often sat with others around a fire they had made, talking about any options for finding work. Che was in charge of the fire and of boiling hot water in a large metal container, to be provided to people for a wash or a shower. Young and fit, he sighed at the absence of work. 'How we are going to get through the winter, I just don't know,' he said to Benjamin. The world outside seemed as quiet as ever, except for the old tractors that rattled around the area every day. Benjamin had not told his family back home about his situation. Che hadn't, either. 'It will break their hearts,' he said. And for everyone here, it was heart-breaking to know how they were perceived in locals' eyes. Locals thought they were accustomed and suited to these appalling conditions because they were from Africa. Che had always tried to explain to the farmers, 'We don't live like this in Africa,' and pleaded for help with housing. But the walls of their hearts were far too tall and thick, said Che, and his pleading always fell on deaf ears.

Che had been here for over two years and things had not improved for him. You started to realise that you could end up living here for years because your choices were extremely limited and you had no means of turning the corner.

In truth, the Africans knew well that their labour was seen as a desirable commodity, while as humans they were seen as undesirable by the local community. In this off-season when most farm labourers had departed, local people continued to refuse to rent out rooms to them. It was not about money, because even when you could afford it, the locals would still not rent a room to an African. It was not about migratory status, either. Those who had residence permits were no exception to this treatment. As a habit, locals simply did not want to let places to Africans, who continued to be denied space and were kept out of sight.

In the middle of the winter, as the disused building where Sanji had been squatting now had more than a dozen occupants, he decided to move back into White Grass. In late December, the encampment had around a hundred occupants, down from 1,000 during the harvest. By January 2018, the number of people had dropped to sixty. All of them had been in the asylum reception system. Some were waiting for documents and to be regularised, like Benjamin, people whose situation of limbo had prevented them from demanding a contract and having a place to stay. Around a third of them didn't have the possibility of ever becoming 'visible' or 'documented' again.

Sanji's mother and sister, who were looking after his now five-year-old daughter, called him regularly and were waiting for him to send money. Each time his mobile phone rang and the picture of his mum appeared on WhatsApp, he felt an immense sense of guilt. Guilt for not being able to give them the regular support they needed.

Sanji was gradually building up contacts in the Campobello farming community. When there was work, he would bring friends whom he trusted to join him and work in the fields alongside him. He wanted to help his friends as much as he could. Farmers were pleased that he was able to bring a team of trusted people. They came to pick them up and drive them to work. However, Sanji was not content with the irregular amount of farm work from the limited contacts that he had. He started looking around for any sign of a job in town. He had been told that the 'normal jobs' in town were closed to Africans. Having lived in Campobello for several years, he knew that Africans did not do town jobs. But being as stubborn and strong-willed as he was, Sanji wanted to experience it for himself. He looked in each and every café, shop and restaurant in town, to ask about any possibility of a job—only to receive a frown and a disapproving shake of the head. Before long, Sanji got his answer: Africans were practically barred from the service industries here. As the saying went, 'Even if the employer doesn't mind black people, customers would.'

* * *

Mohammad was one of the few African workers who had left not only the region but the country as soon as the olive harvest ended. There was no hanging around for him. He'd managed to save up for a flight from Palermo to Barcelona in Spain. He heard from a Gambian friend that there would be plenty of farm work to do in areas surrounding Barcelona. There, you could earn €50 per day, fixed rate, for the same hours as in Campobello. Mohammad did not want to sit around waiting for work during the winter. As autumn ended and most workers were getting ready to leave, he had already boarded the plane to Barcelona, where he had no social networks except that one friend. His courage was immense, driven by his determination to earn for his family, which had always sustained him through adversity. He knew he would be able to get through.

Mohammad's friend was waiting for him when he arrived in Barcelona. Together, they then travelled four hours by bus, to Lleida

(Lleida is in Catalan; Lérida in Spanish), in the west of Catalonia. Lleida, the capital city of the province of the same name, was the largest city he had been in since he set foot in Europe. It was also one of the oldest towns in Catalonia, with ancient settlements dating back to the Bronze Age. Instantly, he liked the vibrant feel of the place and the people. They seemed friendly and approachable. He followed his friend to a village outside of Lleida where they were to live for four months.

The region around Lleida was the leading producer of apples, pears and peaches in Europe. Every year during the harvest season, an additional 5,000 to 6,000 workers would be needed. Around half the extra demand had been met by local workers and by Spaniards from other provinces. At least another 2,000 vacancies were filled by African migrant workers.

On the first day, the farmer to whom Mohammad was introduced requested a 'probation' period of a few days, during which the farmer would watch him work. He was told that this was a process that he had to go through. He couldn't say no. Mohammad passed the test after several days, and since then was given more work.

Spain's agricultural production supplies much of Europe. It has depended on African labour for decades. Farming is generally shunned by local workers; only 9% sell their labour on farms.[4] African migrants came to fill this labour shortage. Most of them were undocumented or had insecure migratory status—less than a third of Africans had documents, like Mohammad. They were without rights or protection. Like African workers in Italy, they were seen as a security problem for local communities and were dealt with as such by the police.

Back in Campobello, inside the community of the White Grass encampment, people looked out for each other. Collective communal living was the only way to survive the hardships of winter. All put their earnings into a shared pot, which fed everyone. When one person was out of work, he could fall back on the community fund. Sanji saw residents of this place as his family, be they from Gambia, Senegal, Sudan or anywhere else. You had to stick together in adversity.

In the winter, people burned more coal and kept the fire going for longer at night, to keep warm. There was always the risk of fires in makeshift camps like this, due to the flammable building materials—mainly wood and plastic sheets. Some people used old gas canisters collected from nearby factories, others made stoves over piles of wood picked up from the fields. There was obviously no fire fighting equipment on site. On Christmas Eve, before most people returned to sleep in their shacks, a fire quietly broke out in one of them. The occupant of the shack was not there, so the fire was not spotted early.

Sanji was working in the fields that day and stayed out visiting his young friend Omar at the minors' shelter in the evening. A Gambian fellow resident of the camp called him.

'Call the firemen!' Sanji cried out. His belongings—some clothing and, importantly, his documents—were stored by his sleeping space inside the shack. The man, his voice shaking, told Sanji that he had already done so. But twenty minutes had gone by and there was no sign of the firemen. 'What should we do?'

Sanji decided to call the fire brigade himself. The phone rang once, twice, and they picked up.

'*Pronto.*'

'Our camp in White Grass is on fire. Please come help us! Please!' Sanji tried to explain in Italian. There was no sound or response at the other end of the line. Then they put the phone down.

Sanji was not surprised by this treatment. Emergency services were often the frontline on which Africans experienced racism. Even during the harvest, the ambulance service never responded quickly to calls from African workers seeking medical help. The ambulance would normally arrive an hour after the calls and its staff would complain that 'the blacks use us as taxis.'

Panicked, Sanji called the police. By this point, he was running back to White Grass. A fellow Gambian man in his thirties had jumped out of his shack, with his belongings and a plastic bag filled with oranges that he had picked and brought back during the day. Sanji saw smoke in the distance and quickened his pace. Then, as he reached the gate, he saw many others standing there, Benjamin among them. They had all run out with their belongings. They were shocked and confused. In front of them were so many shacks that had already burned down. The Gambian man who had first rushed out stood there, still holding his plastic bag of oranges. The sight of the fire brought him to tears. He did not move, looking lost. Sanji sprinted past him, and without a moment of hesitation, ran to his own shack, now most of it already a charred mess. The burnt-out part of the shack was his bed space and everything he owned—a jacket, a thick winter jumper, and all his documents. The loss of these things probably wouldn't have been the end of the world for anyone living a normal life in the outside world. But for Sanji, this was devastating. It had taken him two years to receive his papers; he had no idea how long it would take to be issued with another copy, knowing how very lengthy it could be to apply for any documentation in this country.

That night, half of the makeshift camp had been destroyed. It was only luck that no one was hurt.

7

BECKY AND THE 'INTEGRATION' VILLAGES

Not long after Benjamin's departure from Rosarno, news of a tragedy came through on the night of 26 January 2018. Becky Moses, a twenty-six-year-old Nigerian woman, had been burnt to death during a fierce fire that swept through the *tendopoli* of San Ferdinando, where more than 1,000 people lost their shacks and tents and their belongings.

Becky Moses had arrived two years before from Nigeria. She was placed in a CAS in Riace, a village on the other side of Calabria from Rosarno. At that time, Riace was gaining a worldwide reputation as the 'model of integration.' This reputation could be traced back to the summer of 1998, when a boat left Greece in poor weather conditions and ended up beached at Soverato, 40 kilometres north of Riace. Two hundred and eighteen people were on board, men, women and children; they were all Kurdish, most of them from northern Iraq. Domenico Lucano, locally known as 'Mimmo,' who later became the mayor of Riace, proposed that the Kurdish people should stay in the village and be housed in the properties that had been left vacant by the villagers who had migrated to northern Italian cities like Milan and Turin or abroad. Lucano came up with the idea of regeneration, in which the incoming migrant population would help revive the village. Subsequently, he and his colleagues set up several projects, the most prominent of which was known as City of the Future (*Città Futura*), with a focus on 'integration.'

This all happened in the context of the continuous depopulation of Italian villages. Following the post-war decline of Italy's rural communities due to decades of inadequate investment, around 6,000 villages had become 'extinct' while another 15,000 had lost 90% of their residents and faced extinction. During the six years from 2012 to 2018, almost 80,000 citizens had abandoned villages with fewer than 5,000 inhabitants. Emigration was ongoing and permanent. According to ISTAT, nearly 157,000 people left the country in 2018, most of them going to Western European countries.[1] These 'ghost towns' and 'ghost-towns-to-be' were mainly concentrated in the poorer central and southern parts of the country, where living standards had always been the lowest.

In recent times, various ideas about how to revive these places have been developed. Some turned to renovating empty buildings into hotels and holiday homes, pulling in tourists in order to save the dying villages. Then, in the past few years, well-meaning people have started talking of migrants settling in these villages and reviving them as models of 'integration.' This has been celebrated as a positive example of migrant contribution and highlighted as a 'win-win situation' where Italy received migrants and they 'paid back' the country's hospitality by re-populating its villages. 'Integration,' in other words, referred to a process of assimilation: 'We receive you, you fit in, adopt our ways and values, and make the necessary economic contribution.' The 'contribution' would be the migrants' agrarianisation in exchange for village regeneration—the result of which would not be equally beneficial to migrants and local communities.

* * *

Contrary to the optimistic portrait in the media, migrants who were sent to Riace were surprised by its isolated location and dismayed at its socio-economic prospects. Given the choice, they would ideally have wanted to live in industrial centres and cities where the employment opportunities and existing migrant communities were. But if they resettled in the cities, would the new arrivals be given the same welcome? Would they not then be called 'foreigners coming here to take our jobs' (instead of 'migrants rejuvenating our economy')?

Joseph was a friend of Becky's. He had been a soldier back in his home country Togo, in West Africa, and had to flee from factional fighting and persecution. He left his five-year-old son behind. Since then, he had promised himself that he would do everything to give his son a good life. He travelled from country to country looking for work. He never thought of coming to Europe before he reached Libya. For him, Libya was where the work was and he still believed that it would have been an ideal place to work and make money had it not been for the lawless anarchy that had engulfed the country.

Following a horrific sea crossing and rescue, Joseph was sent to Italy and placed in a camp in Taranto. He was the only resident there who was transferred to Riace on a SPRAR project in 2016, which he very much resented when he arrived at the village. 'I'm not coming to Europe to retire,' he said to his family and friends in frustration.

The City of the Future scheme, set up by Lucano, was run by an association whose declared aim was to 'help refugees without treating them as a burden on public welfare,' which meant that it expected refugees to contribute in order to 'deserve' protection. The funds that came with the projects started changing the face of the village. Abandoned apartments were renovated; jobs were created for villagers and there was turnover in the shops. Within two decades, Riace's population grew from 900 to more than 2,300 in 2016. The village's economy was, indeed, improved by the migrants' arrival.

Joseph was placed under Project Welcome, a project being run alongside City of the Future and Project Migrants. He never knew what these projects were really about but saw the manager of Project Welcome as a 'crook' who had made a large profit out of migrants and owned a big mansion next to the main square where Joseph waited for work every day. The 'crook' was running a CAS, under which Becky Moses was placed in one of its houses to the left of the square.

Becky had revealed to Joseph that she left Riace because the 'crook' was about to send her and three other women to the most terrible place, the Sant'Anna CARA camp in Crotone. Sant'Anna had grown to be one of the largest camps in Europe, and was notorious for a series of corruption scandals exposed in May 2017. Back then, the police sequestered goods and property worth €84 million in a raid and arrested sixty-eight people, including thirty-five-year-old Father

Leonardo Sacco, the head of the Catholic Misericordia association that managed the Sant'Anna camp. As the police revealed, of the €103 million state funds allocated to the camp between 2006 and 2015, at least €36 million ended up in the hands of the mafia. Many of those arrested belonged to the Arena clan of the 'Ndrangheta mafia active in the local area, who had managed to infiltrate the camp a decade earlier, taking charge of key services. Thanks to Father Sacco, the clan won contracts for supplying catering and other services to the camp, allowing it to grab millions in EU funds. It was also discovered that the management of the camp had inflated the number of migrants living there. While the criminal networks profited, migrants were given poor-quality food, and never received their daily allowances of €2.50 'pocket money' but instead were given a card that could be used only at vending machines inside the camp. The reputation of the criminal networks and appalling conditions in which asylum seekers were living had for a long time made the camp notorious among the African migrant communities throughout Italy.

Becky refused to go to Sant'Anna for good reasons, but as a result, she was given three days to pack her bags and leave the CAS accommodation. The three other women felt they had to follow orders and go to Sant'Anna and they did so grudgingly, but the 'crook' who managed the CAS in Riace did not even inform the Sant'Anna camp about their arrival.

At the time, the situation for Becky became desperate as she was soon to become homeless. She couldn't be transferred to a SPRAR because her asylum claim had been refused. The refusal made it impossible for her to carry on living in Riace. Therefore, she went to Lucano and begged him to allow her to stay a few more months in Riace. He said he couldn't do anything. She was left on her own and had to ask for help from some of her friends who were living in the *tendopoli* of San Ferdinando. Becky set out to join them, 60 kilometres away, on the western coast of Calabria. Joseph said good-bye to her at the square. He watched her waiting for the bus on the other side of the road. That was the last time he saw her.

Becky had just turned twenty-six on 11 January. She arrived in the makeshift camp of San Ferdinando only two weeks before her death. At around 2:00 am that Saturday, a fire broke out inside the *tendopoli* that many suspected was caused by a brazier left unattended overnight. An inferno consumed more than half the encampment, built as it was of plastic and wood. Becky was burnt to death and two other women were badly injured. Apart from a hundred people who went on a protest organised by the workers' union USB (*Unione Sindacale di Base*) in the town of San Ferdinando the following Monday, Becky's death hardly caused a ripple in the local community.

In the aftermath of her death, Lucano claimed that it was 'the institutions and the mercenaries of hospitality' that should be held accountable for her death. However, he never mentioned that some of 'the mercenaries of hospitality' were working right under his nose. Lucano said that the provincial authorities of Reggio Calabria, where Riace was located, had decided not to pay the funding due to the CAS (where Becky lived) from June 2016. He had reportedly asked the prefecture to send the funds in December 2017, to no avail, which he believed was 'a sort of embargo on Riace.' With payments being withheld for the reception system in Riace and a huge debt of €2 million having accumulated, wages were not paid, and asylum seekers feared being made homeless. Meanwhile, there was another aspect of Lucano's story: among many Africans who were living in Riace, the belief was that the shelters were often poorly managed and consequently came under more scrutiny. A local source, close to Lucano, also said that the poor management of the reception centres and improper book-keeping had long raised suspicions.

Those who knew Becky knew that the appalling management of the CAS where she was placed in Riace was one of the reasons why she ended up in San Ferdinando. 'Integration is a lie', Joseph said. He saw it in Becky's death. He saw through it in his three years in Riace, where he had become thoroughly disillusioned with the entire project, calling it 'all about politics and money.'

Lucano was said to have created jobs for the new arrivals. However, what was actually created were four artisan laboratories for woodwork, glass, ceramics and embroidery; none of the skills were useful to migrants' future employment prospects. Since Joseph had been in Riace, he had never been given employment advice, vocational training, work placements, or any paid work under the project. There was no real work for migrants, according to Joseph and his friends.

The world media reports had portrayed and photographed African women working in traditional handicraft shops in the 'Global Village,' an area in which stalls and shops were set up where they sold the products they were taught to make. In reality, there was no daily wage for the migrants. The profits from the sales of products did not go to them, either. Learning the skills to make handicrafts and manning shopfronts could not bring in an income for them. For the Africans in Riace, those were 'shop windows' for the press. Joseph believed that the media reported what suited them. 'They're not interested in our real situation.'

Even though work placements in the Global Village shops were not proper paid work, not everyone could get on them. As Joseph and many other Africans observed, those placements were mainly reserved for 'a specific category of people,' i.e., those who were seen as 'genuine refugees.' There was clearly preferential treatment in terms of work placement opportunities; those seen as 'economic migrants' were put at the end of the queue. For three years, Joseph and many fellow Africans felt cut out of the project. They had to look for work on their own and had been doing casual farm work, for a maximum of €30 a day.

For those who managed to find casual work in the village, non-payment was common. On the rare occasion when Joseph got work as a security guard in a minors' centre run by Lucano's brother, he didn't get paid for five long months. Lucano's brother used to run four minors' shelters and had a big part in the reception system. Joseph practically worked for free. The employer's justification for not paying was always, 'We haven't received cash from the local government.' Joseph did not dare to challenge him, since he was 'Mimmo's brother.' That was how power worked in the village. So much for the aims of the SPRAR project for people to become independent and part of society. Most migrants in Riace actually ended up impoverished and desperate. Despite Joseph wanting to be independent, he could only live on the state allowance of €75 per month during his time on the project. Later, after much pleading, Lucano's brother tried to pay back the owed wages to Joseph by letting him stay in his friend's apartment, rent-free.

Daraja, a Nigerian woman in her twenties, was transferred to Riace in 2016. She eventually found work in a nursery doing cooking and childcare, but had not been paid since 2017. It was the same for her four colleagues at the nursery. Daraja desperately wanted to leave Riace but was trapped there because she was still waiting for her humanitarian protection documents—she had waited for three years already.

The desperate situation had compelled several African women to look for alternative employment and eventually accept requests for sex work by certain farmers in the area. A particular farmer for whom Joseph had worked, had asked him to 'introduce him to African women,' a request which Joseph refused with contempt. The farmer had a habit of picking up female migrant workers in Riace for the orange harvest in his fields. Young African as well as Romanian women were chosen by him—the farmer was interested in 'trying it on with everyone,' as he put it. He would employ them to work on the farms and paid €30 to have them around for the day. During work time, he would then make his advances. Some women accepted it as an exchange, for €30 each time, because they desperately needed the money. However, if the women workers refused his requests repeatedly, he would never employ them again on his farms.

* * *

Camini, a tiny village situated a couple of kilometres north of Riace, had followed a similar path of regeneration. It sat in the ancient Locride area, amid the heights of Punta Stilo, facing the Ionian Sea. It survived on agriculture based on many small land holdings which produced citruses, oil and wines. Like Riace, the young of the village had deserted Camini two decades before, seeking employment outside the region or even outside Italy.

The village mayor in 2020, Giuseppe Alfarano, nicknamed Pino, was once part of that exodus. His father was a flour miller in Camini and his mother came from Riace. Alfarano told me he had left the village in 1998 when he was eighteen and had gone to study architecture at the University of Florence. Florence! How attractive it would be, with all its culture and affluence, for a young man who had grown up in a tiny village. At that time, almost every young person had left or was leaving the village. Ultimately it was the lack of employment and opportunities that pushed them to leave. They would go to the north of Italy to study and find work, or go further to Germany to seek a livelihood. Wherever they went, they would eventually settle there. Almost no one would return to Camini to live.

As a result, as years went by, the village suffered the fate of steady depopulation, with only 250 people remaining in the 1990s. Alfarano recalled Camini as a 'dying place' in those days. The population was ageing. You would mourn deaths much more often than you would celebrate new lives. As young people moved away, there were fewer births: between 1998 and 2001, the total number of children in Camini was eight or nine. The school closed.

After his studies in Florence, Alfarano stayed there to work. His wife, also from Camini, worked as a school teacher there. However, during all those eighteen years in Florence, Alfarano never stopped missing his home village. He used to return to visit three or four times a year, and without fail during Christmas and Easter. It was always emotional to be back. Somehow Alfarano felt that his destiny was to return to Camini some day. Years later, when someone told him about a job back in Camini, Alfarano decided to take it up and return to his home village to live.

Back in Camini, Alfarano became involved in working with the social cooperative Eurocoop. Along with Rosario Zurzolo, its president, they saw what happened with the Riace project and how it had transformed the place. They went to consult with Lucano regularly. They were inspired and their work has been informed by the Riace project ever since.

In 2010, Alfarano and Zurzolo went to visit the Ministry of Interior in Rome, to seek state funding for the setting up of a SPRAR project under Eurocoop and to be managed by the Jungi Mundu (World Together) Association in Camini. They had the advantage of just the right timing: the ministry was looking for locations to take on projects for refugees at the time. The Jungi Mundu project has been entirely state-funded since then. In 2011, when the project started, it had only thirteen placements. The number later increased to thirty, and then to 113.

With the funds that came with the migrant placements, the project aimed to revive the village. Abandoned houses were refurbished and redeveloped in the historic centre, the school was re-opened, and jobs were created for the villagers. The project manager's office in the well-decorated Jungi Mundu building was staffed by numerous people—all of them Italian. Overall, around thirty Italians were employed on the SPRAR project, including administrators, kitchen staff and a cultural mediator from northern Italy whose job involved showing guests around the various workshops where 'migrants are taught by locals to make wood and ceramics artworks and pottery.' Local residents were also employed in construction and other work created since the project started.

The project had brought in a lot of interest from the outside world, and with it reporters, researchers and the like, which boosted business in the village. With a lot of optimism, Alfarano said to me: 'With the project, events and the media interest had transformed Camini into a place like Taormina.'

Then, the mayor at the time advocated getting rid of the project. That was when Giuseppe Alfarano thought he had to stand in the mayoral election, which he did in May 2016, when he argued for continuing the project. In his proposal for the five-year tenure as mayor, the project was hailed as being a positive thing for the regeneration of Camini. The villagers did not need much convincing.

Under the SPRAR project, more people from Syria, Eritrea, Nigeria, Gambia, Pakistan, and elsewhere have been transferred to Camini since April 2016. The village population increased to an estimated 820 people in 2017. Between 2017 and 2018, twenty children were born in Camini, both of local and migrant families. Before the project, the village had about one child born a year. As the number of children grew, the school was re-evaluated. Previously, when there had been a school, the classroom had been in the building which was now the village library. It was now relocated to a newly refurbished building.

Most people transferred to Camini were families; there were also eight single men. They had occupied over twenty of Rosario Zurzolo's properties in the village. Some farmers also rented out their empty houses to the project in return for a good, stable income. Gino, born and raised in Camini but now living in Monasteraci not far away, was one of the farmers. He rented out his three houses in Camini to Syrian families under the project, one of them for €500 and the other two for €300 per month. He said he paid special attention to one of the Syrian families who had been traumatised by the wars and were in need of counselling. He would bring oranges and shoes for the children, who called him 'Uncle Gino.' He could talk with them in English because he used to work for Alitalia and lived in Germany when he was a young man.

Being part of Camini's project, Gino seemed to have full confidence in it. He also employed Syrian and Iraqi men to work on his olive groves in the autumn and orange farms in winter. He knew that local Italians did not want to work on farms. 'The money is too small and so they prefer to stay home, and ask mama for support,' he said. Family networks were the safety valve for the unemployed younger generation. Gino gave a job to one of his daughters, too: she managed the family shop in Monasteraci. While appreciating the project and what it had done for him, Gino thought that Matteo Salvini of the League was 'all right' and that 'he just wants people to have work.'

The Syrian family to which Gino brought oranges and shoes were living in one of his houses on the edge of town overlooking the terraced fields flowing down the hillside. The family had been there for two years. The mother had been hospitalised after a breakdown. She had suffered tremendous emotional turmoil on the journey, and then discovered her disabled baby son's paralysis could have been made worse by the hardship and poor diet during their escape to Lebanon and resettlement to Camini. Now the family was barely coping with her absence. Her husband was looking after their six children on his own, with help from a carer, who came in several days a week. For the time being, he could not consider finding a job, with all the childcare responsibilities. The exhaustion was written on his face.

His disabled baby son was three, and despite being paralysed, was an active child and enjoyed talking with all the adults around him, in Italian. For a few days a week, John Hampson, from London, who had been volunteering in Camini for a year, would come to their house and pick him up to go to 'baby parking' (the Italian phrase for a crèche). The father would have his schoolbag prepared and hang it on the back of the adapted pushchair, and then gently and carefully lift the child up and into his seat. John would then push him up the road from the house, talking to him along the way.

They would then turn into a narrow lane into the centre of the village. The 'baby parking' consisted of two well-maintained playrooms in a building renovated by the project. It was a well-staffed place, open to villagers and migrants alike. John carried the child up the stairs and sat him down in the middle of one of the playrooms. The three-year-old was always excited to be there, surrounded by toys and other children. Without being able to move, he would sit on the padded mat in the playroom, playing with toys around him and interacting with other children. 'Baby parking' did not exist before the project—not only because the funds weren't there, but also because there were few young children in the village.

If anyone asked this Syrian family about their home country, the father would show a video on his phone of the bombing and destruction on the streets of Damascus. Right now, all they could do was try to recover, although it looked like they had a long way to go. They were trapped by illness and the youngest child's disability on top of the difficulties of trying to rebuild their lives in the middle of an isolated village. They had no means to think of the future.

The project had provided basic facilities for the nine Syrian families to find a safe and tranquil home for a while. In this sense, Camini provided a sanctuary for them. Meanwhile, there was not much interaction between the Syrian families and the villagers, who mostly kept themselves to themselves. Such isolation was clearly not a long-term option. The families were only hoping that time would give them some answers. Eventually, whether these families could move on or not would depend on their own networks and resources outside of Camini. Those with little would be more likely to stay longer, whether they liked it or not.

* * *

Charlotte was a close friend of Becky's. She and her family were one of the African families under the SPRAR project in Camini. She came from Nigeria with her two girls and two boys, and they had been placed in a shelter in Milan when they first arrived. Then they were told that they were to be transferred to a place called Camini in southern Italy. She had no idea what she was to find there. After a long bus journey, they were driven further and further into the mountains and wondered where on earth they were being taken. Then, an unassuming grey stone hillside village came into view and Charlotte was shocked by how small and isolated it was. She instantly felt angry with the authorities' decision to transfer her and her family here.

'Why were we sent to a place in the middle of nowhere?' she asked. It was so remote that even her mobile phone didn't always get a signal. Charlotte looked around and saw no business or trade in the village and that many locals were unemployed or had moved to Germany for work. There was certainly no space in the virtually non-existent local job market for a newcomer like herself. From the start, she feared that she would not be able to find a way to support her children. She wanted to move to Agrigento in Sicily where she had friends, but the project team persuaded her to stay and try it out.

Having had no choice and no possibility of moving away, Charlotte accepted her situation and tried to come to terms with it. She tried to get used to living in a village. She gradually got used to climbing the steep winding lanes and relying on a couple of tiny convenience stores for food to feed the family. She made friends. She tried to feel settled. She got to know several Nigerians living in nearby Riace and sometimes went to visit them. She came across a new face, Becky Moses, and they became close. Charlotte loved Becky's warm nature, her humour and her kindness. 'She was just beautiful. When you were around her, you couldn't help feeling cheered up. She made you laugh,' Charlotte always told everyone. Becky came to Camini to visit her and her family sometimes, and she went to see Becky, too.

As someone with a family, Charlotte was offered a basic apartment for the duration of her time on the project. But she had to try to find work to support her children. It was clear that the many workshops set up under the project could not really bring employment to the new arrivals. Charlotte was frustrated. Rosario Zurzolo tried to help and offered her a first-floor room space for her to use as a fashion and design workshop, so she could practice her handicraft and dress-making skills which she had brought from home. Charlotte had studied fashion for two years in Nigeria and having a space like this to use as a workshop was a thrill to her. She started to work and display her products for sale. Stunning colourful women's dresses, handbags, purses and jewellery were all laid out and hung on walls inside the workshop. Over two years, Charlotte invested a lot of hope in her work and tried to reach out to villagers so she could earn from her products.

Eventually, though, she saw that she wasn't going to make a living out of this—villagers could hardly afford these handicrafts. A while later, she began to see group after group of Italian tourists coming into the village. With the model of 'integration' widely advertised, people on the SPRAR project found themselves becoming a tourist attraction. 'Refugee tourism' was flourishing. Charlotte's workshop had become part of the attraction to bring in revenue for the village. When some Italian tourists travelled to Camini to 'take a look at the brown and black people' while relaxing in these hills, Charlotte took the opportunity and tried to sell her handicrafts to them. Often, they treated her like an exotic object and her work as a souvenir of their 'refugee tour'. Some were rude. Once, an Italian tourist questioned Charlotte about the time she came to work and shouted at her for not opening her shop on time for them.

The living expense allowances Charlotte and other migrants received at the time were given in vouchers, which could be used in the only three shops in the village. The voucher system, as always, was stigmatising. It highlighted the 'outsider' status of the migrants and limited their ability to purchase things they needed. It surely was the opposite of inclusion.

Then, she met a Nigerian man during her time in Camini, and they decided to get married. She was feeling hopeful about life again. She made her own Nigerian wedding dress and all the dresses for the bridesmaids. Rosario Zurzolo gave her away at the wedding ceremony, a glamorous event in the village when at least half of the population took part. She cherished the memories and the professional photographs taken of her wedding that were compiled as part of '*Un Mondo Nuovo*' (A New World), the photo album of the project. In this well-produced colour volume, pictures of children of all origins sitting together in classrooms spread across the pages, depicting a society *paradiso*.

The reality—and particularly the reality of employment and opportunities—for migrants who were transferred here, had been much less pleasing to the eye than the bright 'diversity' signposts and flagship workshops. The majority of Africans felt no chance of finding work in the village and looked for farm work nearby.

In 2017, Charlotte's time on the SPRAR project ended, thus ending the allowances and the accommodation. She then had to get her own apartment and live without any support. It was like being thrown into the rough sea before learning to swim. Over the next year, Charlotte increasingly felt that her life was going nowhere and that Camini was not the place to settle. She tried to bring in an income by taking up hairdressing and making braids for people—but customers were limited to Africans. Her husband, despite having formal refugee status, was only able to get casual jobs. He DJ-ed once a month, in a makeshift Nigerian disco in the middle of an olive grove in Riace Marina a few miles away. Throughout 2017, many of the original arrivals in Camini gradually moved away, one by one, because there was little prospect of employment.

Then, in early January 2018, Charlotte had to say good-bye to her friend Becky, who was having to leave because she was being evicted from the CAS and couldn't stay in Riace anymore. Charlotte was saddened by Becky's departure, but wished her all the best in her destination: San Ferdinando. However, a couple of weeks after Becky left, Charlotte heard the worst news. She had died. Charlotte could not believe what she was told. She died? No one wanted to believe it was true. Every African, not only the Nigerians, in Riace and Camini, was shaken and upset. How could such an innocent young woman die such a painful death? Charlotte could not get over it.

She went to Riace to attend Becky's funeral. People of all origins were there to pay their respects. The mayor Lucano brought her body back to Riace for the funeral, a gesture that probably revealed his sense of guilt over what happened in Riace, which had led to her departure for San Ferdinando. But it was far too late, especially, for Becky's family and all those who knew her and loved and cherished her friendship.

8

'IF YOU CAN DREAM IT, YOU CAN DO IT'

In the following months, Benjamin came to learn just how unwelcoming Campobello was. Living inside the White Grass community with fellow Africans, you could switch off from the sights and sounds of the prejudice in the outside world. But when in town, you were faced with reality. It was then that he truly felt like an alien.

Benjamin felt deflated when walking past a group of school children led by teachers who stared at him suspiciously. 'Don't bother with them,' Alieu said. Alieu always tried to avoid a walk to town if he could help it. But Benjamin was not the type to stay indoors to stay out of trouble. Besides, he needed to recharge his mobile phone. He walked around town several times trying to find a café or a bar that might do him a favour. But so far, he had no luck.

By complete chance, one day, whilst he was walking around town aimlessly, he stumbled across a small bar tucked away on the side road opposite a church. It was three o'clock in the afternoon, during the usual siesta time, but it looked open, so Benjamin poked his head in through the doorway. A woman in her thirties, with short, dark brown hair, was serving behind the bar. 'Ciao!' she said.

'Ciao!' he gladly responded. It was the first time anyone greeted him in this town.

'Come in,' she said, with a warm smile. She had a tattoo on her left arm and was dressed casually for her job: a white T-shirt and blue jeans. The most out of the ordinary thing was that she looked friendly. As Benjamin walked inside, the first thing he saw on the wall facing the front door was a sign with a Walt Disney quotation, written in English: 'If you can dream it, you can do it.' The place had a non-Italian, non-Sicilian feel to it; in fact, it was anything but local. There were packets of crisps, of all flavours, on the shelves, just like in an English pub. The band AC/DC was playing on the stereo in the background.

'Where you from?' she asked in English.

'Gambia, I'm from Gambia,' Benjamin replied shyly. This was definitely the first time an Italian person had ever asked him about his country of origin—except the police, of course. He decided to tell her that he was living in the open fields of White Grass and was looking for a place to charge his mobile phone.

'Ah, I understand, I understand!' the woman said sympathetically. 'Of course!'

Then she added: 'It's terrible that you live in that place. It's a very bad place.'

Benjamin nodded deeply. God, someone was listening to him, he thought. 'It's true, it's terrible place. We have no other place to go, you see.'

'I know, people in Campobello are very, very bad,' she said, shaking her head.

Her words stunned him. Benjamin couldn't believe that an Italian person was telling him this, critical of her own people. This was a first.

'My name is Camilla,' she said. 'Give me your phone, please.'

Benjamin took the mobile phone out of his pocket and handed it to her. Surreal as it was, he had the feeling that things were going to improve from now on. His phone would be charged—and he could come back here to charge his phone every time.

'You can always come to my bar to recharge your phone,' she said, as if reading his mind.

'*Grazie*, Camilla, *grazie mille*,' he didn't know how else to express his gratitude. He felt so fortunate at this moment.

'Would you like a cup of coffee?' she asked, again with a smile.

'Sure, sure.'

That would be his first free cup of coffee in Italy. She didn't want to take the money. He used to think nothing was free in this country.

'This place is so relaxed, so peaceful,' he mumbled, looking out into the rear seating area, with the winter sun shining in. Just then, several young men and women walked in. They had just come from the college nearby.

'My friend studies in the college just over there,' Camilla said to Benjamin.

He nodded, and observed the students who were now drinking and chatting at the bar yards away from him. He had never been this close to local people. This had got to be the strangest experience he had had since he arrived. He chuckled to himself at this thought.

Pure chance had brought Benjamin to this bar where Camilla was working. She seemed kind and compassionate. She was the closest thing to his 'saviour' in this town. Not only had he found a perfect place to recharge his phone regularly, he had also found a safe space to recharge himself—and take a break from the misery of White Grass.

At the same time, it was also pure chance that Camilla happened to have voted for Tommaso di Maria, the local Five Star councillor who had requested the demolition of the makeshift camp at White Grass. Benjamin had no way of knowing this, of course. He had never heard of Five Star and had no idea about the people who voted for them. All he knew was that the people in this town seemed pretty miserable and were unkind to outsiders. Camilla appeared to be the only exception. She had been a Five Star supporter as long as they had been around. She often walked past the Five Star office on the main street Via Garibaldi. She never went in as she had never been the type to take part in political public meetings, but she read the notices on their wall and followed their news online. She believed that Five Star was for the 'common folk,' like her family and everyone else she knew in town. She didn't know who Tommaso di Maria really was, except that he was the Five Star candidate for whom she was voting in the local election. And she was sure to vote for Five Star nationally too, when the general election came in 2018.

For a long time, Camilla had been feeling miserable about the way things were in Campobello, her hometown, which she referred to as 'mother' because she loved it dearly. She hated to see the town suffering for so long. She hated to see its health deteriorating and it being unable to recover. It hurt her deeply. Campobello had been going from bad to worse—'It was poor, but now it was finished,' she said to Benjamin. She could see no future for the town where there was little employment apart from agriculture and most young people had left to find work in the north. It looked as though most of the young people that still remained in Campobello gathered in her bar. What chance was there for the young here anymore? She herself had only got this bar job to do, often overworked and feeling exhausted. There was no other work around.

* * *

Sanji fell into a depression after the fire that destroyed his documents and belongings. He moved into another shack left empty after the harvest. He sat there in the pitch-dark, thinking about what he was supposed to do from this point onwards. Was he going to rot his life away in this place? He had nowhere else to go. Now, he had no papers, either.

A young friend òf his, named Adama, who was living in an asylum camp in Marsala, invited him for a visit, to take a break from the encampment in Campobello. He didn't wait a minute to jump on the train to Marsala, only half an hour away. Bumping along the track and looking out of the windows over the green fields already felt like taking a break. Acres and acres of vineyards came into sight as he neared Marsala. He was curious about the town, where many fellow Gambians lived. His friend Adama had just been transferred from a minors' camp in Salemi, a medieval, landlocked town on the hill in the Valle del Belice, 35 kilometres east of Marsala.

Sanji was interested in the names of the Sicilian towns and found out that the name of Marsala derived from an Arabic name, 'God's harbour.' He liked the sound of it. The town was also the most populated area in the province and eight times bigger than Campobello. It sounded like a proper city.

However, Marsala was nowhere near as glamorous as its name suggested. Coming out of its unassuming-looking station, you encountered a quiet provincial town. But as you walked further into the town itself, you would find that its charm lay in its calm, modest outlook. Visitors associated the town with Giuseppe Garibaldi and

Marsala wine. Garibaldi's 'thousand-man' landing in Marsala— eventually conquering the Kingdom of the Two Sicilies in 1860 and unifying Italy, meant nothing to Sanji. He had certainly heard little about the English merchant John Woodhouse who accidentally ended up in Marsala in 1770, where he drank and fell in love with the 'tanned wine,' *Perpetuum* (meaning 'perpetual' in Latin), produced by the local farmers. Woodhouse started to import the wine to England to compete with port and sherry and added brandy to it during shipping in order to preserve it, thus creating the wine known as Marsala.

After exchanging a warm hug, Adama led Sanji over the level crossing by the station, then along a long, commercial street. Abandoned winery buildings were all that stood out. Further down the road was a café serving freshly made pasta of all shapes and the only *Bolognese* in town. Workmen from nearby building sites came here for their quick lunch. They were always given a generous portion of pasta to keep them going for the rest of the day.

Sanji and Adama reached another old winery built in the 1930s on Via Mazara. Adama pointed ahead, just 100 metres away, 'There, Acos.' It was a former hotel where he now lived—a two-storey yellow angular building with the sign 'Acos' in white paint above the first floor. A young African man was standing behind the sign, looking out into his 'front yard,' which was a large petrol station.

The Acos Hotel was not making money and had been converted to an asylum reception camp for adults, housing around 180 people in 2018. The majority of residents here were sub-Saharan Africans. There were also Moroccans and Tunisians. Over the years, residents had protested against its conditions, which caught the attention of UNHCR, the IOM, and Borderline Sicilia in August 2014. Among the complaints were those of corrupt conduct by the staff, i.e., the living allowance money due to the residents was delayed for a month or more. When a Nigerian resident protested, he was threatened by the staff, who told him that they would destroy his documents for international protection and deport him back to Nigeria. Despite the protests, things continued as they were and the camp carried on receiving a steady allocation of asylum seekers.

Some of the African boys at the Acos Hotel camp had been relocated from Casa di Riposo Giovanni XXIII a couple of kilometres away, a care home where up to a hundred asylum seekers were housed alongside mental health patients. The building looked like an abandoned hospice. Standing in the front yard, you could sometimes hear elderly patients crying and groaning from inside. You would seriously wonder why those in charge placed these patients in the same place as asylum seekers who had entirely different needs.

The young African boys at the Acos Hotel camp all tried to look for work. Clearly, the monthly allowance of €75 was insufficient. Each time Sanji's friend Adama received this money, he would send most of it to his family and kept only €20 for himself for the entire month. Living on €20 a month meant that he could not do anything much except stay inside the shelter. He had to look for work. But sadly, it wasn't easy in town, as most service and hospitality jobs would not hire Africans. The only avenue open to them was, once again, in agriculture. The boys would come to wait for recruiters outside the petrol station in front of the Acos Hotel building, where they would be selected for the day's work in the fields. The recruitment point was nicknamed 'kalifoo grounds' by the boys, a term often used by sub-Saharan Africans in Libya to mean 'slave market'. (*Kalifoo* is the Libyan word for day workers; 'kalifoo ground' is where people are selected for work, like slaves).

The boys, Sanji's friend Adama included, would always be taken to work in vineyards and other farms in the region. The middle of winter was a tough time for them as there was not enough work around and they couldn't travel outside of the region to work on different crops because the camp wouldn't allow them to be away overnight.

* * *

Fifteen minutes away by car from the Marsala town centre was the well-known Stagnone Lagoon, a marine area with salt ponds and windmills. The country lane followed the coast, with salt production on one side, and vineyards on the other. Here, farm work in the winter was as quiet as the tourist season, except for the greenhouse crops. In the early spring the planting and tending of vines started; the first shoots looked tiny and bright green in the gentle sunlight, waiting to burst into rapid growth.

Further down the lane, a two-storey house stood on the right-hand side of the road behind several palm trees. It was a former hotel called Borgo della Pace, the Village of Peace. Converted into an asylum shelter, it had been a CAS since 2014 and was now home to thirty-two people from Gambia, Senegal and other African countries, three or four to a room. Most of them had been there for one or two years. Winter for them was mainly spent waiting for work.

Saikou was among them. He had once sold food on a stall in Gambia and was now a farm worker in Marsala. As he often said to his friends, occupations had changed, but the money had not. He looked painfully thin, but he would tell you that it was not only because of the poor-quality pasta meals delivered from outside the shelter. He had also lost weight as a result of the anxiety and stress during five long years of being transferred from camp to camp and waiting for papers in the chain of bureaucracy ever since he had arrived on the island. He devoted most of his waiting time to work. He looked to the left of the lane, at the mass of newly planted vines. 'This is the work for Africans,' he said to his friends still living in the shelter in Marsala town from which he had been transferred. 'No locals are doing it.' As for the salt flats across the lane, that was work for local men only.

Everyone, as a habit, came to sit on the short fence in front of the shelter every day. In the winter and early spring, local farmers would come here to select their workers for the day's work in the greenhouses. In the early summer, Saikou would get quite a lot of work tidying the fields. When the grape harvest started between August and September, he worked every single day. One year, he went to Campobello for the olive harvest. It was there that he heard about Ousmane's death, which saddened him. He was only there for nine days, as the living conditions in White Grass were very poor and it was too far for him to cycle there and back every day.

One early morning on a winter day in early 2018, as Saikou waited in front of the shelter, a farmer approached him for work in his tomato and strawberry greenhouses on the outskirts of Marsala. Greenhouse tomatoes that were planted in September or October started to be harvested from December and throughout the winter, so there was always some work to do at this time of year if you had the contacts. (Tomatoes grown in the fields were normally planted in March and harvested from June to August).

Farmers would agree a pay rate before work started, and the day rate was set at €20 on that occasion, with which Saikou didn't try to argue. But when the day ended, the farmer refused to pay the agreed amount and offered him €15 instead. Fifteen euros for a day's work. Saikou could hardly believe that the farmer was so shamelessly cutting down what was already a substandard wage. He argued and argued for the originally agreed fee, but the farmer would not back down. In order to get paid at all, Saikou eventually had to accept the €15. This was the first time this had happened to him, although he had heard a lot about this practice.

On another occasion, Saikou was promised €25 for a day's work in another tomato greenhouse. But after an eight-hour day, the farmer refused to pay him at all. Saikou tried to dispute this and demanded his wages to no avail. Eventually he felt he had no other choice than to walk away with nothing. He felt so frustrated and found it difficult to contain his anger. At the same time, he felt completely powerless. What could he possibly do about it? The absence of a work contract meant that he did not have a leg to stand on. It was his word against the farmer's.

Every African he knew at Borgo della Pace was in the same boat—non-payment was something they would experience every now and then, as if a part of their normal life as agricultural workers. But no one wanted to kick up a fuss, fearing the consequences. There were no unions working in this area, to their knowledge, and in any case, few workers could be convinced that collective bargaining or protesting would do any good. They all knew that farmers could simply walk away and find other migrant workers who would be willing to do the work cheaper without a contract. Many could remember back in 2013 in this area, when some local farmers were paying Romanian workers better wages—around €5 per hour. When the sub-Saharan Africans arrived in larger numbers, the farmers saw that they could get away with paying less and sacked all the Romanians and replaced them with sub-Saharan Africans. As a result, some of the Romanian workers left the area because they could no longer make a living here. This now often happened to sub-Saharan African workers here: either you accepted your status as practically slaves or you got out of the area. 'More slaves are waiting outside the door,' was the farmers' attitude.

Many times Saikou wanted to talk to his fellow workers about the need for them to resist their enslavement together, but he stopped himself. He felt it would be difficult to unite people and fight against the farmers because there were differences among the different nationalities here. He didn't think he was capable of resolving these differences in order to fight the common enemy. This feeling of powerlessness turned everyone inwards. Saikou now felt that all he could do was carry on working as much as possible, to achieve his immediate aim of supporting his family back home.

By late spring, Saikou was given more work on the vineyards, clearing weeds. The minimal wages drove him to think of alternatives. Could he simply go to find work in other countries, such as those in Scandinavia? Were the conditions for African workers better there? He had no information and no contacts there. At times, he discussed his ideas with fellow residents at Borgo della Pace. No one really knew what to do. However, Saikou saw life as a test. He had age on his side.

* * *

Benjamin, Alieu and a team of people from their encampment went out early in the morning to look for work every day. They were able to find two to three days' work harvesting oranges in a week. The rate of pay always varied between €20–€25 for an eight-hour day during the off-season. Benjamin worked his hardest, hoping to be given more work, and he always came back to White Grass with scratches on his forehead and hands after a full day's work picking oranges. Che teased him for not being an experienced picker, and gave him some hot water that he had boiled for a shower.

Benjamin still refrained from telling his family about his farm work. He made them believe that he was doing casual work in restaurants and cafés. He couldn't bear the thought that his family would see him as a 'failure' who couldn't find suitable work in Europe. Every time his brother, who was an office clerk, called him on Whatsapp and asked how he was, Benjamin would tell him that he was 'managing' and that he continued to do casual catering work.

In the late winter, small groups of Romanian women could be seen picking oranges in the fields not far from White Grass. Some women were working in the fields near the olive oil factory minutes from the town hall. The factory had an antique olive press outside the gate which attracted the attention of Italian visitors and buyers in the summer. They would come in and purchase bottles of freshly made olive oil. But in the winter and early spring, the factory shop was securely locked up. The main factory door was open though, and modern oil extraction machinery, different from the traditional olive presses, could be seen on the factory floor, with no workers around. Notice boards on the walls displayed information about olives—green olives are those picked before ripening, and black ones are harvested when fully ripe.

Tommaso di Maria, the Five Star councillor who had pushed for the closure of Benjamin's makeshift camp in White Grass, finally had his wish granted. On 12 February, when it was still freezing cold, an official notice was served on the encampment. It was delivered by police officers. This piece of A4 paper brought a great deal of panic straight away. Everyone crowded around it to read and see what it all meant. Sanji read it out loud for everyone to hear and take in. It had come from the mayor of Campobello, Giuseppe Castiglion, and, as few African residents here could read Italian, the notice had been translated into English—rigid, formal English with long sentences that only happened in poor Italian-to-English translations. The tone was authoritarian—and although Benjamin and others didn't understand every word it said, they got the gist. The notice served its purpose of intimidating the residents and eventually clearing the site. 'Evacuation is due in twenty days from the time this notice was issued.' Failing to leave would mean prosecution and paying fines of up to €500, for which the notice cited several articles of legislation that no one had a clue about.

Everyone felt more frightened than ever. Benjamin was literally shocked into silence. He sat with everyone quietly, nervously chewing on a tiny twig like a toothpick. Alieu had immediately got on the phone to every Gambian he knew in Sicily to try find a solution. Perhaps a spare bed somewhere, or a short stay at someone's shelter? So far Alieu had no offer of help from anyone. Benjamin watched him pacing up and down and felt so helpless—Alieu was supposed to be the better connected and more 'clued-up' person among them. When Alieu panicked like this, it felt like their world was collapsing in on itself. Besides, with the level of stress it was causing, Benjamin had the feeling that Alieu would soon be suffering from his stomach ulcer. This chronic illness always returned to torture Alieu during particularly bad times, preventing him from eating properly or even working.

Che was quiet too, sitting at his corner by the fire he made. He felt his eyesight weakening—it had been worsening since he started working in the fields and he had no idea why. For the moment, everything was hazy in front of him. Everyone's misery hung like the smoke from the fire. His own destiny now felt like a hazy mess, too. He was still waiting for his asylum commission interview and there was a long way to go in the asylum application process. He was still limping from the leg injury that he had suffered in Libya when he was beaten and locked in a cell by his employer who never paid him a penny. But he had learned not to cry long ago. The biggest question he had in his mind at this moment was how far he would have to walk, with his bad leg, to look for an alternative sleeping place.

Benjamin pinned the mayor's notice up on the wall of an empty shack near his, so that everyone could come for a second look. He had read through it several times. 'The failure to comply with what was ordered, within the prescribed period, will entail, according to the law, forced eviction with the use of public force.' 'Public force,' he repeated to himself. They would be evicted by 'public force'—enabled by the institutions and politicians who wanted to push the issue of housing for seasonal workers under the carpet by making the encampment illegal. 'Public force' endorsed by associations and those who said and did nothing to oppose it. Twenty days to go. Where could they go? Would the officers actually be on time? Was there a way out of this?

Benjamin, his friends and co-workers, now in the middle of a miserable situation in Campobello, had not yet realised that the country in which they were living was steadily moving towards even greater hostility towards Africans and anyone considered an outsider. The seeds had been planted long time ago. For years, political parties in Italy had been able to successfully scapegoat migrants when the country had been faced with stagnation for years, with one of the highest debts in the EU and an 11% unemployment rate nationally. Despite the fact that migrant labour had filled the severe shortages in agriculture and had been sustaining it, the Right had been able to manipulate public opinion and channel public anger onto migrants, and Africans in particular.

The League was, at this time, campaigning for the 2018 Italian general election as part of an alliance with Berlusconi's Go Italia (Forza Italia) and Brothers of Italy (FDL). 'Berlusconi is the one who thinks for the south,' was the thinking of many Sicilian voters, particularly in working-class communities. The League was campaigning under the slogans 'Italians First' and 'Stop the invasion,' with its leader Matteo Salvini pledging to deport over 500,000 'illegal immigrants.' Salvini had preached hatred against migrants for years, and had claimed that 'Islam is incompatible with Italian values,' in the same vein as the 'clash of civilisations' propagated by Geert Wilder and Marine Le Pen. During the election campaign, the League's candidate in Lombardy, Attilio Fontana, had called on people to 'defend our white race.' 'We have to decide if our ethnicity, if our white race, if our society continues to exist or if it will be wiped out,' he said.

As Benjamin and his fellow residents were being given twenty days to leave White Grass and were frantically searching for a place to move to, Italy's general election had 'migrants' squarely at the centre of the campaign. The 'migrants' in question were not seen as human beings who were living outside of their place of origin. The 'migrants' in the public mind were 'brown and black people' and the 'illegals,' i.e., those unwanted in Europe. The 'migrants' were a cut of meat being displayed on a butcher's slab, its price being noisily haggled over, its value scrutinised by everyone. At the same time, this meat was being blamed for a disease that had been spreading among the populace.

As the election drew to a close, on 5 March 2018, Idy Diene, a fifty-three-year-old man from Senegal, was shot dead by a local man in Florence. Diene had lived in Italy for over twenty years. He was making a quiet living as a street vendor, selling tissues and lighters to passers-by. He was about to go to Florence's central mosque for noon prayers when he was gunned down in broad daylight, on the bridge Ponte Amerigo Vespucci. This was one of the busy bridges where many different lives crossed paths: the townsfolk, tourists, middle-class shoppers, students, and migrants who were rarely seen in the city centre except when selling handbags and handicrafts made in nearby Chinese factories to tourists.

No one would forget that Diene's cousin Samb Modou, who also worked as a street vendor in Florence, was killed in December 2011, by a fascist named Gianluca Casseri. Idy Diene was targeted for the same reason. Also, his murder happened only weeks after another racist shooting of six African-born migrants in Macerata, a central Italian town, at the beginning of the election campaign in February. The shooter was Luca Traini, a fascist and former candidate for the League in a local election. In the aftermath of the shooting, Berlusconi blamed migrants, saying that they were 'a social time bomb ready to explode.' The neo-fascist party New Power (Forza Nuova) ran a demonstration in Macerata, where its leader Roberto Fiore called the fascist shooter a 'victim.' It was clear that the environment in which racial violence had been bred was part of the broader toxic politics of race that was 'common sense' at the top of society.

But the wind was blowing in their direction. As it turned out, the League won 123 seats in the general election, nearly 18% of the vote. The Five Star Movement, to which councillor Tommaso di Maria belonged, was the largest single party nationally with 231 seats, that is, just over 32% of the vote. Five Star's founder Beppe Grillo had said in 2016 that 'all undocumented migrants should be expelled from Italy.' Its 2018–19 leader Luigi di Maio had also said that he wanted an end to the 'sea taxi service' that rescued migrants; he was not dissimilar to Salvini in policy rhetoric on migration. During the election campaign, Five Star gained a large amount of support from working-class voters by committing more talk time to issues such as a minimum monthly income and labour laws, and as a result saw a surge of support in the south—in Sicily, it gained all twenty-eight seats.

Idy Diene's death on the day of the final vote count seemed symbolic—symbolic of the ushering in of an era to be marked by a further normalisation of racism by the state, and with it a much higher level of racial violence in society. With the far-right government coming into power, it felt as if Ousmane, whose death was a consequence of racial segregation, had been killed a second time around.

9

EVICTION

The police finally came. Mid-March. Every day before this day, Benjamin had hoped for a delay from the authorities. And every day he had dreaded the sound of police vans driving down the lane. This day, he knew they had arrived, as the loud barking of the German Shepherd guard dog chained up outside the farm cottages alerted the residents of White Grass. Everyone came out of their shacks and walked towards the gate. Benjamin quickly got up from his mattress, got dressed and joined the others.

Then officers came out of their vehicles and approached the gate of the encampment. 'You must leave this site by Monday,' one officer announced. That would be in three days' time. The demolition was to start right away, he said. Benjamin and everyone stood listening. Where would they go? Benjamin still had not worked it out. He was as clueless as he had been twenty days earlier when the notice was officially pinned up. He had been asking for help, mostly from Camilla and her circle of friends, as she was the only person he knew in town. She was the only hope that he had to find a bed somewhere.

As the police officers surrounded the camp and got ready to start demolition work, shack by shack, everyone stood around, discussing what to do. They were all here because they had no alternative in the first place. Where could they turn now? Benjamin felt the panic rise in him. In a cold sweat and virtually speechless, he went back to his shack, sat down and tried to get his breath back. Soon enough, he could hear officers storming around the shacks. He took a peek outside and could see that they were taking down strips of wood from the shacks and piling them next to a bonfire in the middle of the camp. A short while later, the fire became fiercer as the wood was thrown on. He could hear it crackling. The sound was a reminder to everyone that time had truly run out. It made Benjamin's heart beat faster.

People started to organise their exit from the camp. Several Gambians were saying that they might be leaving town, to go to their friends in other parts of the province. Benjamin walked over to Alieu. 'Where are we going?' he asked. None of the Gambian men in the group had a clue where they were heading. They had three more days until the final day, when the entire encampment would be flattened. Benjamin looked up at the rain clouds, the late winter rain that never went away. His heart sank thinking about sleeping on the side of a muddy country path. 'God help us,' he said under his breath. At that moment, an officer walked past. Benjamin acted on his impulse of asking anyone for help. 'Could you help me, officer?' he said. The officer looked puzzled, paused and responded, 'What do you want?'

'Could you please help me find a place in town?' pleaded Benjamin. 'I don't have a place to move to.'

The officer looked him up and down, then replied, 'You have money to pay for a room?'

'Yes, yes, I do,' Benjamin said, thinking that he would try his very best to put any money together, to be able to rent a room, even a tiny one.

The officer looked amused. It was the first time anyone from the camp had made such a request. No Africans were able to rent a room in this town. Perhaps it was the thought that Benjamin actually believed he would be an exception that amused the officer. 'OK,' he said, 'Let me ask around and get back to you.' And, of course, the officer never did get back to him.

Police officers patrolled the site throughout the demolition. No visitors were allowed. The tight security was to limit negative publicity. What went on at White Grass had to be kept under wraps. However, something had to be said about the demolition, and the authorities relied on their friends in the media to give the official line. A news report on the planned day of demolition said: 'There will be no eviction this morning in the district of White Grass in Campobello di Mazara, because the migrants will have left the camp before the intervention of the police scheduled for today.'

* * *

On Sunday, one day before the encampment was to formally close, a third of the shacks had been taken down and burned. People were taking with them whatever things they could carry, such as mattresses and blankets, along with their few personal belongings. They started to look for deserted farmhouses and barns, all in complete disrepair, dotted around the olive fields across Campobello and beyond.

Alieu came up with an idea. He was one of the few who had got onto the good side of some farmers around here, and had been working for one particular farmer for over a year. He decided to ask him for help with getting a place to move to. The farmer said yes and offered him a temporary space to stay at a derelict farmhouse just outside Campobello. Alieu wanted to help his friends at such a difficult time, and invited six of them, Benjamin included, to come along with him to the place. Benjamin felt so grateful to his friend for his kindness, as he knew that Alieu would be in trouble if the farmer found out that he was bringing a group of people along.

Alieu, Benjamin and five others started the four-kilometre trek to the farmhouse, which they nicknamed the new jungle. Everyone was carrying their bedding, walking in a line, to avoid the passing tractors. Alieu led the way, across the border from Campobello to Castelvetrano, where they were hemmed by olive fields on both sides of the country road. The young olives shone in the sun, thriving. These were the black gold of the region; they were the crop that kept it going. Along the road were olive and wine producing factories and businesses that came into view one after another, as if boasting of the abundance. The large signs with the words 'Seidita Olive Oil & Olives' impressed Benjamin. Opposite it was an equally huge factory with prominent glistening metal pipework. Hundreds of barrels outside the building told you that it was a wine-producing plant, a big business in the region, too. Benjamin walked on, behind Alieu, eagerly wanting to reach their promised, new lodgings.

Half an hour later, an earthy yellow-coloured, two-storey concrete building and compound appeared in the distance. It stood out in the midday heat haze, their oasis in a desert. It was like civilisation had emerged in the distance, just as during Benjamin's four-day journey across the desert to Libya—but for him, somehow, it still felt like the misery wasn't going to end so soon. As they arrived at the deserted farmhouse, Alieu pushed open the front gate and everyone gasped at the state of the place. The front yard was filled with wild grass and piled high with all kinds of litter. The farmhouse itself was filthy and there were no windows and no doors to the building. It appeared to have been uninhabited for decades.

Alieu walked around the place, and as he expected, found no water supply or electricity. He then went to take a look at the back and saw a six-square-metre room—if you could call it a room, partitioned by a wall. It was pitch-dark, even at midday, as it had no windows. Alieu took out the torch in his bag, turned it on, and shone it around this room. Nothing. Just the four walls made of concrete. 'At least there are no dead animals,' Alieu said to Benjamin, who was standing behind him, in a confused state. They smiled a helpless smile. Alieu then dragged his bedding over to this 'room,' put it down, and gave a long sigh. 'Why don't you share this space with me?' he said to Benjamin.

Benjamin nodded, but he felt like crying. He felt the panic again; he knew that he might have to stay in this place for a while. It was bad enough at White Grass, but they had managed to overcome some of the major difficulties, such as the lack of gas, electricity and hot water in the winter. Here at the new place just outside Campobello, there was nothing. No basic facilities, not even water to wash your hands, let alone to take a shower. Water, as they found out a while later, had to be brought from a standpipe at a junction fifteen minutes down the road.

Several more people had joined Alieu's group and followed them to this place. Alieu found himself unable to turn them away as they were so desperate. There were now sixteen of them in total. No one could use the space upstairs as it was too visible from the road and they didn't want to draw attention to themselves. Alieu led ten of them, all Gambian men, to the other sections of the compound adjacent to his room. Three or four of them had to share a sleeping space, as there were not enough partitioned rooms. Being given a bed space here was seen as a gesture of friendship; it was clear to everyone that Alieu had gone out of his way to offer help to as many people as possible.

The bonfire was still burning in White Grass which could be seen from a distance. Police officers were still on site, supervising the demolition, well past 9:00 pm. Police vans continued to patrol the streets of Campobello, in the light overnight drizzle.

Well past midnight, Benjamin couldn't get to sleep. The thin blanket he had brought from the old camp was not enough to keep him warm. He sat up, his feet on the cold, concrete floor, and thought of his mother and his now nine-year-old son. His mother wasn't well, and he could not tell her about his current situation. By the light of his mobile phone, he looked at his son's photograph, taken a couple of years ago, wrinkled inside his old wallet. What worried him the most was the reality that he had not be able to send cash back to support them for quite a while. He did not even know how long he would be able to stay in the farmhouse to even have this roof over his head.

Since the demolition had started, it was said that several charity workers had been handing out food parcels at White Grass. Unfortunately, no one in Benjamin's group actually saw them. Benjamin believed that the group had probably left the old camp earlier than the charity's arrival and missed the opportunity to get some basic provisions. With less than €20 left to his name, Benjamin was feeling desperate. He had no idea how to get in touch with any NGOs or charities and did not know where they were based, to ask for help and collect food donations.

As Benjamin and the group worked as a collective, they shared out what they had. At this moment, as Benjamin wasn't earning, he had to rely on the support of others, for which he felt both grateful and guilty. He tried to do the daily chores for the group to compensate his lack of cash. He did food shopping, with money from the collective pot, and walked a couple of miles to Eurospin, a supermarket near White Grass, to bring back the provisions needed by the group. There, he picked up large bags of rice, chicken drumsticks, onions and tubes of tomato paste. This would make several days' dinner for everyone. Following the shopping, he pushed the trolley, with bags of food, along the country lane on the edge of town, all the way back to their compound.

Back in the farmhouse, people were eagerly waiting for the food to arrive. Some of the Gambian boys, aged no more than twenty, had not eaten for a day or two. They came up to see what Benjamin had in the trolley. Then Alieu set and lit a fire, with everyone standing around him. Chicken in a tomato and onion stew, with a large pot of rice, was what they were going to have. When ready, the boys stood queuing to dish out the fluffy white rice from the large old pot that Alieu had brought with him from White Grass. Benjamin shovelled down the white rice faster than anyone. He had been hungry for days. The smell of the cooked stew was comforting for everyone. They were able to temporarily put aside their misery and focus on getting their energy back. When their hunger was gone, they put away the remains of the stew, saving it for the next two days.

Benjamin's former fellow residents at White Grass had all been split into small groups and found their sleeping places in different disused farmhouses and barns across the Campobello and Castelvetrano border. A dozen people found sleeping space in an area just 200 metres away from Benjamin's farmhouse: a large gated site of a disused factory that belonged to the cement company Calcestruzzi S.P.A. It used to be a large mafia-run business that had infiltrated the construction industry for years. The managing director, Mario Colombini, was arrested for fraud, breach of public supply contracts and facilitating the activity of Cosa Nostra in 2008. The factory had subsequently been confiscated and closed down by the authorities. The place had been left empty; the windows were all broken. A group of Gambian and Senegalese boys from White Grass had moved in. You could now hear people's voices echoing on the factory floor from a distance away. Attached to the factory were deserted plant rooms, also occupied by Gambian and Senegalese boys. This was the landscape of the destitute.

As people were scattered around the area, it wasn't always easy for them to bump into one another except when they returned to White Grass to pick up any useful material that remained. Benjamin would go back to White Grass every day, to see people and to check up on what was happening generally. After all, he had spent more than three months here, and the encampment had become a community where he could feel connected with those in the same boat as him. That sense of solidarity and the feeling of a collective in the most desperate circumstances had drawn many to return for a visit, even when the site was almost all flattened.

As Benjamin walked down to White Grass, he saw Sanji on his second-hand scooter rattling past with its loud, tired engine. They both stopped at the same time to greet each other. Sanji told Benjamin that he had gone to search for a place to stay with a small group of six, including his nephew who had joined him in Campobello a short while ago. They had come to a junction in the west end of town, and instead of turning left to take them to the train station, they decided to try their luck and turned right. They then walked along a main road past olive groves to the horizon, and a six-metre-high modern statue of Jesus, arm outstretched, as if to indicate the direction for travellers at yet another junction: turn right here and you would reach Castelvetrano, but if you kept to the road on the left you would get to Mazara. Sanji and the group decided to go left, as they saw buildings dotted around in the distance.

The road wasn't easy to walk on. As it was the main road going to Mazara, a constant stream of Land Rovers and tractors roared by. The buildings in the distance turned out to be some large disused barns that they couldn't get into. However, opposite them stood a deserted petrol station facing the main road. The state of the building resembled a scene from a low-budget post-apocalypse film. It told Sanji that it had been abandoned for possibly more than a decade—and peculiarly left empty on the main road all this time. Its blue paint has almost peeled off. There was no door, and all its windows were broken. The group walked up and took a look at the inside. Piles of broken tiles and rubbish. Unsurprisingly, it was filthy with no basic facilities.

Sanji and his group had no alternative options. There were other disused buildings like this in the area, and conditions would be identical. It seemed pointless to carry on searching. They decided to stay and make the petrol station their temporary shelter. They spent the day cleaning up the place, put their old mattresses on the concrete floor, and put a white sheet over the broken windows, to fend off wind and dust.

'Life is wrong put,' as Sanji would say. But no one had time to lament their miserable existence. Living rough for a long period of time had equipped them with skills to survive in difficult conditions.

Sanji and his group dealt with the lack of electricity by getting torches to light the space in the evening and using a second-hand generator which they bought from a shop and on which they could recharge their mobile phones. Sanji also relied on his young friend Omar, who was still living in the minors' shelter in town. Omar and the other teenage boys looked up to Sanji as someone older and streetwise. They came to him even more often since he and his group had moved into the petrol station as it was closer to them than White Grass. They used the one bike they shared, going to and fro between their shelter and the petrol station. They liked spending time with Sanji.

For water, Sanji had to fetch it from the same water tap on a farm not far from White Grass a couple of miles away. Each time he carried two gallons of water in a container for daily use, on the back of his scooter, and rode all the way back to the petrol station where he stayed. Sanji and others in his group also went to the water tap every few days to take cold showers.

As they soon came to realise, the forecourt of the petrol station was where local drug dealers frequently did their exchanges of cash and cocaine. Sometimes, during the night, cars pulled in and shadowy figures conducted business right outside where they were staying. The boys always kept silent to steer clear of any trouble.

During the first month of their stay in the petrol station, the group had some luck with a surprise visit—from two nuns who drove by with lots of food supplies. Sanji didn't usually have good impressions of the volunteers from various organisations that had visited White Grass because many of them had given out incorrect information to the media about the encampment. This time, it was different. The visitors were giving the much-needed help to Sanji and his group. One of the sisters came from Castelvetrano, the other based in Mazara. Sanji didn't catch the name of their charity, but the food they brought, pasta and many canned products, was a blessing; it fed the seven of them for two weeks. The two sisters never came back, though.

Sanji's nephew, thin and rather frail, was quietly chopping wood to make a fire. This wood had been brought to them by a kind-hearted local woman, a rare demonstration of compassion in Campobello. They had no idea where she lived, but judging from the size of the tree branches she brought, she must have been living on the outskirts rather than in Campobello itself. Sanji's nephew seemed to be using all his strength chopping the wood. He was also in charge of making 'China green' (tea) for everyone. He looked nothing like Sanji, no dreadlocks, no bracelets on his wrists, but a simple red T-shirt that he wore on most days. He was shy and never talked much, but always smiled and helped Sanji whenever he could. He added lots of sugar into the China green, to boost everyone's energy levels. Sugar; at least they had plenty of that.

Sanji was the only one in this group able to make contact with several local farmers, as he had been here for years now. One of the farmers, who came from Mazara and owned land in Campobello, would call Sanji and get him to work on his orange fields, and often asked him to bring several workers with him. The farmer was a member of the local mafia. He used to work in a shoe factory in Milan, owned by Silvio Berlusconi. He liked Sanji's hard work during the orange harvest: he was able to pick sixty crates of oranges in a day, faster than anyone else. Each crate paid €1.50, so he was making €90 a day when there was work. The boss liked him, and sometimes paid him some of his wages in advance when other workers had to wait until the end of the month. The boss trusted him so much that he made Sanji supervise the work, trimming and sorting the picked oranges. Sanji was paid €75 for it. Although he brought friends and relatives to work on the farms, he never charged them a fee. They were all his brothers, as far as he was concerned—they shared out the work as long as it was available.

Although everyone talked of Sanji's boss as being part of the local mafia, Sanji ignored it as much as he could. At work, in the fields, his boss rarely looked him in the eye when they talked, often looking away and around him, as if constantly checking his surroundings for danger. Sanji heard him saying to someone, 'I could die anytime.' No one knew what sort of trouble he was in. Once, as a joke, he pointed a gun at Sanji, saying, 'I can do what I want with you,' laughing. Sanji didn't take it well. He said to his boss, with a firm voice, 'Don't do this to me again.' And the joke was never repeated.

Then, one day, several Italian men came asking for Sanji's boss in the fields. Sanji did not know why, but the following day, he heard that his boss had been murdered. He never found out how and why, but people thought it was the result of a mafia territorial war. Unfortunately, it was also the end of Sanji's most secure source of employment.

Sanji carried on working for other farmers, but the work was not always regular. He and his group never had a regular supply of food. It was five months before the olive harvest. Still, people in the group followed the principle of sharing food provisions—Whenever anyone earned something, the cash would go into their shared pot, to purchase food for the group. One man's good workday would be everyone else's good luck. But when no one was earning in the group, then they starved together. For a couple of days, all they had was water. The only regular supply that they had was music, which they played loud on their mobile phones even during the most difficult days. Sanji liked Jamaican dance hall and played artists like Beenie Man, popular in Gambia. It kept their spirits up. You could hear music coming out of their old petrol station from some distance away.

'I would leave this town if there were a job somewhere else,' Sanji always said to his nephew. But deep down he knew it was not that easy. His insecurity about what might be out there outweighed his desire to escape destitution in Campobello and kept him here. This collective of people he lived with had been all that he had known. Outside Campobello, there was no one else with whom he had spent a night in a deserted camp, no one with whom he had shared all the misery. Beyond Campobello, he had no one else to trust.

Like everyone else here, Sanji wanted to live in a room, a 'room' in the real sense of the word, like a human being. 'The living at the moment is the opposite to everything about being a man,' he said quietly to his nephew.

Since the demolition of White Grass, the authorities had continued to lie about the situation of the Africans, to offer up some justification as to why they had been living in such a way. Their line was that 'migrants refused to accept accommodation offered to them by the authorities.' Sanji would never have found this out had he not been asked by the aunt of the owner of Futuro, the minors' shelter, 'Why did you refuse the accommodation given to you?'

Hearing this question, Sanji was stunned. He refuted the claim immediately. Lies were also spread by journalists, who quoted the authorities' line: 'Out of a total of fifty people, a group of four or five would have found a home between Campobello and Tre Fontane. More than half would have just left town... Others would eventually settle down in the country cottages provided by some employers.' The journalists did not talk to anyone who was evicted, and certainly never saw their 'home' or the 'country cottages.'

* * *

It had been an exhausting day. Not only walking to and from the farmhouse and Campobello town, but also the mental strain of finding ways to improve conditions. Benjamin had not had a shower since they had moved into the farmhouse. Then he heard that some people were returning to White Grass to take showers. He wanted to give it a try. That evening, Benjamin walked all the way back to White Grass. The sight of a fire from a distance away was reassuring; he could see several people gathering around it. The camp had been completely flattened by now and there was no trace of resurrected shacks. No cops. But the fire was as it had been before.

Approaching it, Benjamin saw that it was still Che, the man with the Che Guevara beret, minding the fire. He was quietly boiling up water in the large metal container, just like he always had. He looked more worn-out than ever, his eyes half-closed. 'You want a shower?' Che looked up and asked Benjamin, as if he were running a shop. Che had walked back here from his new 'jungle', just to look after this.

'Yeah, I'd like a shower,' Benjamin said, kneeling down by the side of the fire.

'It's 20 cents, please,' said Che.

It hadn't been easy for him in his new place, not having basic facilities. There was little work and therefore no cash to buy food. He came up with the idea that he would return to White Grass to sell hot water for a shower. He'd been doing it all day, and many people had come to him for a good shower. He had made enough cash to pay for a few days' food. Benjamin didn't mind paying 20 cents for a shower. He absolutely needed one.

Walking past several Gambian boys on the way back, Benjamin had to tell them, 'I just had a shower!' He felt energised. He walked back slowly alongside the olive fields by the light of his torch. At this moment he felt so clean and light.

The next day, Benjamin had an important task to do for the group. He was asked to get a fresh gas bottle from a nearby factory. Alieu had brought in the last one and it was now Benjamin's turn. He had to transport it in a supermarket trolley, all the way to the farmhouse. He then connected the gas pipe to a portable stove and prepared the tomato and onion stew for everyone.

The following afternoon, Benjamin walked into town to visit Camilla. There were few people in her bar at this time of day, and this was when Benjamin was able to have a chat with her. 'When I spend time in your bar, I feel human again,' he said to Camilla, who always welcomed him when he visited. Here, he felt he could put aside the world of harshness for a short while.

As Camilla placed the cup of coffee in front of him, Benjamin told her that he was in need of help once again. 'I've got to get out of that place,' he said. 'Please, please, could you help me look around for a cheap room, somewhere? Somewhere with water and electricity, somewhere warm?'

Camilla looked at him with sadness. Since she had known Benjamin, he had never been okay. He had never had the dignity and respect that he deserved—from farm employers, from the people in town, the town that she loved. And she knew about the people from Gambia and Senegal who had led a subhuman existence in White Grass all these years. Things had not changed for them. If anything, they had got worse. Camilla wanted to sound optimistic, but she found it hard.

'I will ask around in Campobello and Castelvetrano, about a room for you,' she said to Benjamin. She started calling friends and acquaintances, to ask about accommodation in town. But the answer from landlords in Campobello was always the same: a work contract was required to rent an apartment or a room. Knowing that the majority of African workers were not given work contracts, the landlords had the best excuse not to let places to them. Camilla shook her head at this standard excuse. She knew that the colour of his skin was the real reason why Benjamin and every other African would never be able to rent a room here. This was when there were so many unoccupied apartments and houses in the town, large numbers of them low-priced and affordable to rent for most people.

When the bar got busy in the early evening, with students coming in from the nearby college, Camilla couldn't talk so much and Benjamin went to sit in the corner, sipping his coffee. He did not speak enough Italian to talk with the students that came in. He simply sat there, tapping his foot to music from the 1940s swing era. Perhaps the Americans who came to Sicily in 1943 used to listen to this music. He tried to hum along with 'Chattanooga Choo Choo', and for a short time, the stress and worries left him.

Benjamin came to Camilla's bar almost every day, to ask about a room in Campobello and nearby towns. As the days went by and there was no good news, his small glimmer of hope dwindled and he felt more and more depressed. Late at night, he would sit in the pitch-dark farmhouse with Alieu, with a torch, and often there were no words exchanged at all. They were both exhausted, in every sense of the word. Benjamin's feeling of gloom took over when it rained heavily. The thumping of the raindrops felt like a portent of misfortunes yet to come. He listened to it, finding it hard to breathe.

Benjamin always went to bed early and got up at 6:00 am, almost every day, to walk up to the crossroads fifteen minutes from the farmhouse, to wait for work, any work. Local farmers came there to pick up workers whom they would organise to work on the day. Benjamin had not had any luck so far, and he guessed that it was because farmers did not know him and so would not pick him first. He had relied on Alieu to bring him along to the fields when they worked. But Alieu had not been well enough recently, due to his stomach ulcer, and wasn't able to work.

One day, when Benjamin was in Camilla's bar, she told him that a friend of hers was checking out a spare room in an apartment shared with their friends. Benjamin's eyes lit up. Maybe his luck had finally come. This friend of Camilla's later showed up at the bar, telling Benjamin that she was waiting for an answer from these friends. Could they actually be letting this spare room to him? Camilla's friend promised that she would let him know the following day. He hoped and prayed.

But the woman did not show up at the bar the next day. Or the day after. She vanished. Benjamin asked Camilla where her friend was. She had no idea. Days went past and still no sign of her. Perhaps the answer from her friends was so negative that she couldn't bear to tell him and explain why they turned him down. Benjamin couldn't get to sleep as it was especially cold that night. Alieu was kept awake, too. They gave up trying to sleep and got up to set up a fire. Then they sat around it for a couple of hours, just to stay warm. The fire, helped by the wind, was burning bright. Benjamin took out a photograph of his mother and son to show Alieu. He was missing them terribly, and worried about them and their future. His voice grew weaker as he had no energy inside him. Alieu simply looked at the photo and nodded.

Then Benjamin took out another photo from his wallet. It was himself, hair combed and dressed in a black suit. Alieu burst out laughing, at the contrast of the photo and what Benjamin looked like now. Benjamin laughed, too, shaking his head. 'You see, my life wasn't always this bad.'

10

FIVE STAR AND THE ILLS OF THE TOWN

One evening, on Via Garibaldi, the main street running through the town centre of Campobello, the local Five Star Movement was having its branch meeting in their ground-floor office. It was not long after the general election where the party had won over 32% of votes in Italy and became the largest single party nationally. Five Star saw a big surge of support in Sicily and the south generally. On the window outside their office, a large handwritten poster celebrated the election news: 'Five Star Movement is the number one political force in Campobello di Mazara, with 2,760 votes (nearly 50%) in the Lower House and 2,512 votes (49%) in the Senate. We thank our electorate for their support.'

Everyone that came through the door to the meeting was smiling and in good spirits. They greeted each other warmly and exchanged excited comments about the election results. The sense of optimism and triumph was clear. Some of them were between twenty and thirty years old. Five Star had attracted many young voters, especially among the working-class, as youth unemployment was well above 50% in Sicily. In Campobello, there was a strong sense that the decline was permanent. This was a town built upon agriculture, and apart from agriculture and its related industries, there really was not much else to it. What jobs were to be had apart from working in agriculture, which most of the young people here didn't want to do? Working in a shop on a low wage clearly was not a prospect to keep them here. What alternatives did they have, if they did not want to be stuck in dead-end jobs for the rest of their lives? The only option would be to get out of town—to leave Campobello, and Sicily. Many young people had already left.

The son and daughter of Giuseppe and Francesca were among the leavers. The couple had lived in Campobello for four decades. Giuseppe, now in his sixties, owned a small piece of land growing olives and lemons in the nearby seaside town of Tre Fontane. He sold his olives directly to merchants from outside of Sicily who came to the town in the autumn. Giuseppe usually hired a man from Senegal to harvest the olives for him—this was not the work that his children wanted to do. Giuseppe's wife Francesca thought that Campobello was not for those who wanted to do something with their lives. Not only had nothing much changed here, but it had got poorer in the past forty years, she believed. The couple thought their son was wise when he decided to leave home and go to Rome to make a living. He did well and eventually became a restaurateur. Their daughter found a career as a pharmacist in Pisa.

Those who remained in Campobello were often embittered by the limited opportunities they had in order to improve their lot. Years and years of misrepresentation and manipulation by politicians and the media had given the locals the opportunity to blame someone else for the failure of their own town. The young people sitting in Five Star's meeting room in town were not like the hard-right racists who formed part of the support base for the League. They did not sit and argue for the deportation of migrants. Many of them hadn't even properly made up their minds, and if asked, they were likely to stutter and hesitate, but most of them would tell you that 'the current migration policy doesn't seem to work for anyone.'

Several of them who were active in the organisation sounded more definite in their opinions. Marco, in his thirties, was such a person. He stood by the door, ushering people in, and acted as the chair of the meeting. He believed that Italy should not have to take in 'all the migrants.' He would use the case of exploitation of migrants as evidence that 'it cannot be good for migrants, either.' He said that

'Europe should aid African countries, so that Africans won't have to come here'—the standard line from Five Star politicians.

Soon, several middle-aged men arrived. In their winter jackets, they appeared to have just been on their evening walk and popped in for a chat with friends. Marco started to pull the chairs around and get everyone to sit in a semi-circle facing the table. He then brought in some sweets to share. People bantered with each other. There was a feeling of community. This appeared to be the 'direct democracy', Five Star-style, that had reached out to thousands in this town and all over Italy. Then Tommaso di Maria, Five Star's local councillor and spokesman in Campobello, walked in. He was casually dressed and looked amicable, with studious glasses and a fashionable young man's haircut, his hair parted in the middle. At first sight, Di Maria wouldn't have struck you as a politician. He greeted Marco and everyone else warmly, as if they were friends. Perhaps it was his non-elitist approach that helped win hearts over to Five Star in this town.

At the same time, Tommaso di Maria was good at adopting the political language of obscurity. He knew how to dodge questions if they did not suit him and give answers in the most elaborate language that circled around the edges of an issue but never touched the core. He had mastered the art of 'giving solidity to pure wind.' While this branch meeting was happening just after the demolition of the encampment in White Grass, it did not appear to be on anyone's mind. No one was talking about it—and certainly not Di Maria, who had had his own part in it.

***

Apart from Sicily, Five Star also did well electorally in the region of Calabria, similarly characterised by chronic unemployment. So did the League, despite its northern, secessionist past. Back in 2013, when Salvini had taken charge of the League, his party got only four votes in Rosarno. Yet, on 4 March 2018, he was elected senator for Calabria, having received nearly 49,800 votes.

It was widely known that Salvini won the seat with the backing of a former mayor of Reggio Calabria, Giuseppe Scopelliti, who was previously elected with the support of the 'Ndrangheta, the mafia that controlled many of the businesses in the region and beyond. A short while after Scopelliti's declaration at a political rally that he would lend support to Salvini and form a close alliance with him, Salvini decided to run as a senate candidate, as he was keen to make electoral gains in the south. He agreed an official alliance with Scopelliti's party, the National Sovereignty Movement (*Movimento Nazionale per la Sovranità*). This political alliance with the local power guaranteed he would win the seat.

On 17 March, Salvini held a rally in Rosarno to celebrate his electoral victory, and, no surprise, among those sitting in the first few rows of his audience were men from the Belloco gang and the Pesce family who were affiliated with the 'Ndrangheta. At the rally, Salvini gave a speech in which he blamed migrants and their *tendopoli* for the town's decline. Not a word was uttered about the mafia and their dominance in the industries there. A month after this rally, however, his ally Scopelliti was arrested and convicted for forging official documents while he was mayor. He was subsequently sentenced to five years in prison.

Back in Campobello, Benjamin and his group were trying to find ways to improve their living conditions. They found a water tap at the junction a little further up the road. Everyone in the disused farmhouses next to them also used to fetch water from this tap. People carried back two containers of water at a time, either on their bikes or on shopping trolleys that they had borrowed from the supermarkets. They now had water to share out in the group, but not enough for everyone to take showers each day. When someone needed a shower and there was enough water, they would boil it in a metal container over a fire. They also built a shower unit using plastic sheets they collected from the old camp.

It was getting warmer in late March and the lack of washing facilities was becoming unbearable. Transporting water was not only inconvenient, but the quantity was far from sufficient for the whole group. 'I need to get out of here,' Benjamin kept telling Alieu. 'I don't know how many more days I can last in this hole.'

Camilla's bar was the one place Benjamin could drop in to use the toilet, something they didn't have in the farmhouse. He could then wash his face properly and not worry about the amount of water that he was using. Camilla had just gone to Palermo for a week to have a break and spend Easter with her friends. She told Benjamin that she would look out for a low-priced room for him there. As it turned out, in Palermo as everywhere else in Italy, private landlords did not tend to want to rent rooms to Africans. Even getting a short-term lodging was not easy. There would first be the suspicion of potential criminality if you were 'black.' Then would come the request to check your immigration documents, which would be the excuse to turn you down. Even on the rare occasion a landlord did not turn an African away, it would still be difficult to find a shared apartment where white Italians would want to have an African for their flatmate.

In Palermo, if an African happened to find a place, it would most likely be overcrowded and shared with other Africans. The conditions would be poor. Plus, you would have to pay around €100 per month for the 'privilege.' This was not something that Benjamin could afford.

Camilla's absence that week was tough for Benjamin. The bar without her just wasn't the same. As Benjamin found out, Camilla was the only reason his presence was tolerated at all. When she was not around, his request to charge his mobile phone was met with a straight 'no' from her colleagues. Benjamin paid for a cup of coffee as it was not free without Camilla being there. He knew he should not be spending what little money he had on a coffee, but he had to stay in the bar to wait for an opportunity to recharge his phone. He was hoping that a staff member on a later shift would say yes.

For now, he walked away from the bar counter, took the chair in the corner and sat down. He kept quiet and tried to avoid meeting anyone's gaze. Several local customers were sipping coffee and gave him a suspicious look. It worried him. But he kept his head down and tried to ignore the stares. That wasn't good enough. One of them, a man in his forties, suddenly approached him, and said to him with a raised voice, 'You should leave. We don't want to see you here.' The man's friends simply looked at Benjamin, expressionless. There were several other customers standing around who saw what happened. No one intervened. They sipped their coffee as if nothing had happened. Not a movement on their faces. Not a flicker in their eyes. Benjamin did not know what to expect next from the man and did not want this situation to escalate. He walked out of the door, without a word.

Sanji, unlike Benjamin, rarely tried to go somewhere that he knew 'belonged' exclusively to the local people. He believed that it would take a long, long time, for the white folk to change. He felt he wouldn't see it in his lifetime. The reality of racism as Sanji saw it, was day-to-day and had a long history. A coloured bar, the practice of segregation, existed here in daily life. In this town, you would never see a 'black' person (sub-Saharan or East African) sitting at the same table as a white Italian. It just did not happen. Not because there were written notices on the walls preventing Africans from entering these places, but because the hostility was often so obvious that Africans would stop going there. If you were 'black,' you would be lucky to go into a bakery to buy pastries without getting a frown from the shop assistant and glances from the customers.

During Easter, when local residents came out in the streets to watch the religious processions, Sanji didn't want to be in town. For him, local residents had always treated Africans as beneath them. Deep in their hearts, even on a day when they remembered Christ and his sacrifice, they would not extend compassion and humanity to Africans. Sanji spent Easter Sunday afternoon napping in his temporary home in the abandoned petrol station.

However, keeping yourself to yourself did not mean that you would be left untouched by racism. Daily chores would bring you face to face with unwelcoming townsfolk. One day, Sanji went to do food shopping in town and walked past a shoe shop. A pair of trainers caught his eye and he walked in, wanting to try them on. Just as he put them on, a middle-aged local woman inside the shop walked up to him and asked, 'Did you steal these shoes?' Sanji was surprised by such an overtly offensive remark. He stood there, looking at her, wondering how to respond. Then he had an idea.

'Do you realise what you're saying?' he questioned the woman in Italian. 'I am human just like you. Don't judge me before you know me.'

The woman was taken aback by his response, not expecting an African to talk back. She wanted to turn and leave. 'Stand there, don't go,' Sanji said to her. 'Maybe you're not an evil racist, but just very ignorant. I want you to spell this word after me: IGNORANT.'

The woman was shocked. So were the customers at the till, watching the confrontation. The shopkeeper happened to be the grandson of a farmer for whom Sanji had worked. He saw what was happening and didn't want it to escalate. 'Look,' he said to the woman, 'I know this boy. He works for my granddad. He's alright.'

'Say it: ignorant.' Sanji wouldn't let it go and repeated the word to the woman. He never shied away from racist incidents and always confronted people who stereotyped or abused him. His shaming of her in public forced her step back. 'I am sorry,' she eventually apologised to him, admitting she was ignorant.

On another occasion, Sanji was walking along and saw a local woman in her mid-twenties turn and walk away quickly when she saw him. She did the same the next time she came across him in the street. Sanji decided to educate her and started running after her. She was shocked, stopped and asked, 'Why are you running?' To which he replied, 'Why are *you* running?' They started to talk, which ended in a conversation about why she had to run away each time she saw him. The woman admitted that it was her father who warned her about Africans. 'Stay away from them,' he had told his daughter.

Sanji asked her to look at him. 'There's nothing to be scared of, is there?' She shrugged her shoulders and walked on. After that, every time she walked past him, she no longer ran but greeted him with a *ciao*.

* * *

Benjamin was chatting with the Senegalese boys in the compound when Mohammad walked into their front yard. He was well-dressed, in a white shirt, and was well-spoken. He stood out, with his warm smile. He said he had come to visit a friend of his from Gambia. Benjamin had never met him before and tried to strike up a conversation. To his surprise, Mohammad had already been living here in Campobello for five years.

Whilst talking to him, Benjamin realised that Mohammad had at one point stayed in the same camp as he did near Trapani. But they hadn't exchanged words until now. One reason for this was that Mohammad tended to keep himself to himself. He stood out as a loner and had always lived by himself. When asked why, he would explain that he was not suitable for communal living because he never wanted to disturb people—and probably never wanted to be disturbed himself. At times, living alone made him seem aloof from other Africans. When the Gambian boys were frantically searching for a roof over their heads in the middle of the demolition in White Grass, Mohammad had moved out from a garage space rented to him by his former farmer employer in Campobello, to a village called Triscina, 9 kilometres away, on the coast.

But Mohammad was always concerned about his fellow Gambians and had tried, on numerous occasions, to talk to his employers and even the *carabinieri*, pleading with them to help find housing for his friends and fellow workers.

In the following months, when Mohammad was living in Triscina, Gambian workers in the disused farmhouses all believed he had moved in to one of his employer's houses in the village. This was something that almost never happened to Africans—and certainly had never happened in Campobello. The Gambians all saw him as someone who had 'made it.' They looked up to him as the model worker who had won the trust of the white man and had 'earned' proper housing in return. In their eyes, Mohammad was the exception to the rule. But at the same time, no one felt jealousy or had any ill feelings towards him, because Mohammad had a big heart and would always give them a helping hand.

One day, one of Mohammad's Gambian friends asked to visit him in Triscina, to have a day away from the stress of coping with conditions in the farmhouse. By bike it was a twenty-minute pedal to Triscina, which appeared to be a quiet little place next to a long beach with holiday apartments and not much else. Mohammad met him, walked him down the lane on a slight slope heading towards the beach, and opened a large metal driveway gate to the farmer's house where he was living. His friend gasped as he saw the large house that stood a few metres away. As Mohammad ushered him in, his friend let out a whistle, seeing the well-maintained garden complete with a stone fountain.

'Wow, this is your place,' his friend said with admiration. He pushed his bike into the garden and followed behind Mohammad towards the house. A small boat on a trailer was parked to one side. The friend shook his head and could not believe Mohammad's luck. It was another world, a world he would probably never have had the opportunity to reach. It almost felt like he should not be inside the gate. 'Come on,' Mohammad urged him, 'Come with me.'

But Mohammad did not walk towards the front door of the house. He walked to the side, towards the rear. 'Where are you going?' his friend asked.

Mohammad walked further until he got to the end of the garden. 'This is my place,' he said, smiling as he opened the door to the garage. Mohammad didn't need a key to get in. It stayed unlocked. It was a garage that the farmer had let him use as a living space. Since the farmer had hired Mohammad to do a great deal of work for him, he had decided that it was worthwhile letting him have that space, to keep it convenient to hire him. The farmer, however, did not forget to charge him a rent of €75 per month, a lot of money for a small space of ten square metres. Meanwhile, the €75 did not pay for the entire garage—the farmer's ladders and garden tools were still in here and he and his family still had access to the garage whenever they wanted.

'This is great, this is beautiful,' said his friend. He understood it now. Mohammad was not living in a room in the farmer's luxurious detached house or any house for that matter. He was living in a garage. Mohammad had won the trust of the white man—but not so much so that he would be treated as an equal.

Like before, Mohammad had done everything he could to make the garage space feel comfortable and look like a home: he had laid a table cloth on the old dining table in front of the stove; he had picked up a second-hand sofa and created a sitting area next to the dining area. His bed was in the corner, with clean bedsheets on it. There was a compartment up a ladder which he had turned into a storage area and spare bedroom for any visitor. This garage had been transformed into a makeshift bedsit. His friend was amazed. Mohammad had done so well with the space he was given. Although it was a garage, this was certainly another world from the squalid conditions in all the derelict farmhouses and barns where the Africans were living in Campobello and the surrounding areas. Mohammad invited his friend to stay over, to get away from the pitch-dark farmhouse for a night.

He and his friend took a stroll down the beach at the bottom of the lane. The sand stretched for miles in either direction. It was clean and quiet before the tourist season began. The two of them stood there, letting the early evening sun shine on their faces. If there was ever a carefree moment in their daily strife, it was this. Mohammad was pleased to see his friend relax.

'Are people OK here in this village?' his friend asked.

'Yes, they seem more open-minded than the people in Campobello,' Mohammad answered, smiling. He knew he had tried his best to 'behave as a good guest' in the village. In a way, living away from other Gambians probably brought him some trust among the suspicious local residents. It was a trade-off that could happen in a racist society.

Mohammad had worked his hardest, as always, and won himself a good reputation among the farmers in the area, who preferred to hire the workers they knew. He had established good working relationships with more than 200 farmers in the region. As a result, he often received calls from the farmers and would be picked up and taken to work on farms miles away from Triscina. Often, it was an eight-hour day, for which he would receive the pitiful wage of €20–€25. He would bring a large can of tuna and a loaf of bread and have it for lunch in the fields. In April, he was often asked to work in Campobello, trimming and tidying up the weeds in the olive groves. He would put on his heavy work boots and go on his bike there. Although he had built up his employment networks over the past five years in the area and was able to get a regular amount of farm work, his wages never rose.

* * *

When Camilla returned from Palermo, she spoke to Benjamin and confirmed what he thought might happen: no landlords had said yes. It dispirited him, and at this point, it did feel like things were never going to get better. It felt like he would have to accept his position as an outcast in society.

As he walked back to the farmhouse feeling utterly depressed, Alieu ran to him, breathless, saying, 'The police have just been!' Apparently, a team of officers had stormed through the front gate of the farmhouse and broken into their compound. Only a few people were there.

'Did they wreck the room?' Benjamin panicked. The 'room' that he had been sharing with Alieu. The 'room' without a door or window, or furniture, or light, or heat.

'No, they didn't,' Alieu reassured him, but added, 'They went into next door as well though, and took some cash from the Senegalese boys.'

Mohammad happened to be visiting his friends in the compound when the police raided. He tried to intervene, in fluent Italian, and talk to the police officers on behalf of his friends. They didn't listen and carried on searching the place. Mohammad kept on, and one officer stopped to listen in the end. Mohammad tried to explain how and why people ended up here in these deserted farmhouses: 'People in Campobello are letting them down. They need Africans for work but refuse to house them.'

Mohammad also went to the police station in town several times that week and tried to speak to the officers there. 'My people need housing,' he kept telling them. 'Please help my people. Please.'

The following day a storm blew across Sicily which lasted the whole afternoon and evening. It came from Africa, a powerful blast from the desert. Plastic bags and pieces of wood in the front yard of Benjamin's farmhouse went flying into the air. People had to take down their clothes from the washing lines. They all had to stay indoors. Alieu wasn't feeling well. The poor diet and the stress of living in these conditions, particularly in the past month, had made his stomach ulcer worse. He was in agony the entire evening, curled up in his bed. 'Tomorrow I will have to go into town to get myself some painkillers,' he said to Benjamin. 'Let's hope that it's not too expensive.'

Later that week, Benjamin was wandering around town looking for room adverts and happened to notice a piece of paper in a shop window in a handwritten scribble, appearing to be an advert for a room. The shop was closed, so he walked up the street looking to ask other shopkeepers for information. Two doors down, it was the Five Star office. Benjamin had no idea that it was the public meeting room for a political party. He pushed the glass door open. 'Excuse me,' he said politely, looking in. There were two men talking in there; one of them happened to be the local councillor, Tommaso di Maria.

Di Maria was taken aback by the African face poking into the office. 'I'm sorry to trouble you, Sir,' Benjamin said in half Italian, half English, 'I'm just wondering if you know if there's a place for rent two doors down. They have an advert on the door, but I'm not sure if the advert is for that building.'

Di Maria was puzzled, not least because the language was confusing. He had never been asked a question by an African before. He got up and came outside the office. 'Sorry? Which advert?'

Then Benjamin came closer, repeating the question. Di Maria frowned, as if he didn't feel comfortable standing so close to Benjamin. He stepped back and maintained his previous distance. Several Five Star supporters happened to walk past on the opposite side of the street; they seemed surprised to see their councillor having a conversation with an African.

Di Maria did what was expected from a politician in a public place. He carried on talking to Benjamin and nodded carefully. He had never interacted with anyone in the asylum reception system before and their interests had not been his concern. He was part of the local establishment which had pushed for the demolition of the camp at White Grass and caused Benjamin's current predicament. But Benjamin did not know that. He was completely unaware that this Italian man had anything to do with his current misery. He did not even know that this man was a politician.

'I don't know anything about the rent advert,' said Di Maria.

Benjamin pushed on, believing that this was a local resident who was prepared to stop and listen to him. 'I don't know if you could help me, Sir. I'm looking for a cheap room in this town. Do you happen to know anyone who might be letting?'

Di Maria shook his head, smiling, 'No, I don't.' But he did not turn around to leave. He kept calm, like a politician. 'But I'll let you know if I see anything. You can leave me your number.'

Benjamin was glad to hear this and gave his mobile number to Di Maria straight away. He thought he had found another person in this town who treated him like a normal human being—and took his number. But of course, Benjamin never heard from Di Maria. Meanwhile, the camp at White Grass that Di Maria helped to remove from public view was now a huge pile of rubble and rubbish waiting to be disposed of.

* * *

That day, Liberation Day, on 25 April, one of the farmers came to Mohammad to pick him up for the day's work. It was a long, difficult day, weeding in the olive fields. It was particularly tough when you had to work around the edges of the fields where there was no shade from the fierce sun. As work finished for the day, Mohammad had no strength left. When the farmer dropped him off at the top of his lane in Triscina, he dragged himself back to his place, had a shower and finally sat down. Then he cooked a Gambian stew for himself as a little reward. After food he would often go online and chat with friends and family back home, or just take a stroll to the beach. But today he was exhausted and just needed some sleep not long after dinner.

As a result of his well-established contacts, Mohammad was doing a great deal better than most of his fellow workers. A farmer even sent him to work on farms he owned on the outskirts of Palermo, sometimes for eight to ten days each time, and during those periods, the farmer would let him stay in the garage in his house in the suburbs of Palermo. Mohammad felt that it was a clear sign that the farmer trusted him—enough to let him stay with him at his residence, even though it was in the garage. Mohammad sometimes talked with the farmer's family and took photographs with them.

For him, these pictures symbolised some level of acceptance from Italian society. Italy was hosting him, he felt, as the farmer and his family were hosting him. His host, Italy, had not always shown a welcome and it was clear from the beginning that the welcome had to be earned. It was hard to earn. These photographs, for him, were the evidence that he had earned his welcome. With the long history of the slavery and colonisation of Africa embedded in his understanding of the world and his place in it, he might easily have thought of himself as a slave on a plantation centuries ago, one who had won the confidence of his owner over the years and felt his status elevated when he was talked to by the owner's family. This elevated status seemed to set him apart from the other African workers.

At the same time, in his heart, Mohammad knew what it was really all about. The favourite slave on a plantation might be treated differently to the other slaves, but he was still a slave. Mohammad was treated as a 'good black worker' who had earned the privilege of staying in a garage within the white farmer's family home, but he was seen as a black worker nevertheless. He was a 'trustworthy black' as opposed to an 'untrustworthy black', but he was still always black. The meaning of his blackness had always been clear to him—not least in the reality that he and all other Africans were barred from most employment except farming. Deep down, he knew that he alone could never beat the system that had always been set against the 'black man.'

Mohammad empathised with fellow Africans and never hesitated to help them; he knew he was forever one of them. When farmers need an extra pair of hands, Mohammad would recommend his Gambian friends and bring them along to work together. Gradually, he became known among Gambians for helping people to find work. He had never taken a fee for introducing people to work. During his time in Trapani, he saw several Gambian and Senegalese men recruiting workers and becoming middlemen in agriculture and making cash from fellow Africans. He hated it. He saw it as a betrayal.

* * *

That evening at Benjamin's farmhouse, the Gambian boys were cooking dinner above the fire in the front yard while others washed clothes in a bucket. One of the residents had just returned from picking oranges, and he was letting off steam after a nine-hour day for a pittance of €15. 'Not only are we Africans so badly exploited, but even our safety is at risk,' he said, seething with anger. 'All the way walking back here, I had to avoid being hit by cars. They wanted to cause me harm.'

He had also heard that a fellow Gambian living in another disused farmhouse was injured in an accident caused by a car driver who wanted to run him over. 'Some cars deliberately drive close to the cyclists when they see we're black... If two of you are riding bikes, one following another, you have to be doubly careful. Some people in this town are very racist and evil. There have been incidents when local people overtook two African cyclists, then braked suddenly, causing the second cyclist to run into the back of the first...It can cause serious injuries. 'Accidents' like this happen a lot around here...' The others nodded in agreement, all of them having heard of similar incidents.

Yet worse things could happen. In the towns of Campobello and Castelvetrano where local youths had few employment opportunities and future prospects, some got into drugs and petty crime. Others resorted to rural hooliganism, robbery, looting and mugging. They targeted the weak and vulnerable. There were no beggars to kick in town, so they attacked and robbed migrants, who in their eyes were just 'unworthy blacks.'

One day, when Sanji was on his way to visit a friend in another disused farmhouse, he was set upon by a gang of local youths. They appeared to have come from Castelvetrano. One of them, who looked like an ordinary young local, suddenly took out a pistol. 'This is a cop's gun,' he boasted. Sanji had never seen anyone actually using a gun in Italy. He froze. The man demanded cash from him, pointing the pistol at his head. Sanji quietly handed over the cash, the €50 that he had saved up from several days of hard work. Then, as the man wasn't expecting him to fight, Sanji grabbed his gun, gripping the breach to prevent it firing. During the push-and-pull, the pistol magazine fell out, Sanji quickly kicked it away into the grass. They broke apart.

'Why did you target me?' Sanji asked him, knowing that the man could no longer threaten him with the weapon. 'We have nothing here. Why do you target us?'

'I didn't want to kill you,' the man lowered his voice, 'I have a four-month-old baby daughter and I need the money.'

Sanji was about to let the young man go when he grabbed a glass bottle from the road side, smashed it and slashed Sanji's left arm. The gang ran, taking the money with them. Sanji was left bleeding heavily. Luckily, his friend arrived, and quickly got him to a hospital. That wasn't the end of it, however. The police arrived. The man who robbed and attacked Sanji had gone to the local police and reported that Sanji had attacked him first and threatened him with a gun when Sanji saw him having sex with an African woman. Clearly, the man had feared that Sanji would report him, so got his accusation in first. Sanji was taken to the police station and questioned for hours. Fortunately, the man and his gang were offenders already known to the police. Sanji's testimony was believed and he was let go.

The entire attack shook Sanji to the core. He did not expect gang violence in a rural setting like Campobello. Since then, he knew that it was not always safe to go about the place on his own. Those who were living with him in the derelict petrol station were also on their guard; they had to look out for one another and stick together as much as they could.

The wound on Sanji's arm required several stitches and had prevented him from going out to search for work for several weeks, and he still had to return to the hospital to have the dressing changed. It had also made it impossible for him to ride a scooter, and as a result the task of food shopping and the transport of water containers had fallen on those around him.

Meanwhile, the townsfolk of Campobello were more worried about stray dogs. It was reported in the local news that 'a medium-sized mixed breed stray dog was shot in the Campobellese seaside village of Torretta Granitola.' A Campobello resident reported it and the police intervened. The Five Star councillor Tommaso di Maria also raised public alarm about several stray dogs being poisoned between Santa Ninfa, Castelvetrano and Campobello, and another dog which had been hanged from a tree in White Grass. 'Who would do such a thing?' Di Maria asked passionately, via social media. No one had a clue who could be involved, but it sounded like the sort of thing that happened with small-town idle youths trying to gain a reputation. The news reports and the councillor's emotional 'awareness-raising' led to an outcry in town, at least in cyberspace. If only they could have extended a little bit of that empathy to fellow humans.

Sanji was feeling down after the robbery and attack and talked to his nephew a lot about the future. One day, he said, he would like to go to Sweden. A friend there told him that it was safe there and wages were much higher. Equally importantly for him, he wanted the opportunity to try to play football professionally again—and that wasn't going to be possible in Italy. But then who knew if it would be truly better in those Scandinavian countries? He wanted to hold on to the idea that things could be better somewhere else, as that was holding on to hope. 'You can only hope.'

* * *

Meanwhile, inside the town there was plenty happening, to keep the gossip going. In late April, a police operation jailed Mario Tripoli, the brother of the municipal councillor Maria Tripoli. He was part of a mafia family in Campobello. He was directly involved in extortion and threats, linking the local mafia networks with the local government.

As May approached, Tommaso di Maria launched an anti-mafia campaign on behalf of the Five Star Movement in Campobello. He sent a proposal to the mayor of the town, and requested him to organise 'a day of legality' involving a symbolic 'wall of legality,' where every citizen of the town could write or draw what they thought 'illegality' was, as well as 'every type of criminal association.'

However, whether it was the talk of a clampdown on the local mafia or ecological issues, the audience for Five Star in Campobello seemed to gradually dwindle. Tommaso di Maria and his colleagues ran a public meeting in their branch office in Via Garibaldi every Monday, but after the summer, the turnout never exceeded half a dozen people. Sometimes Di Maria would sit in the middle of the speaker's platform with just a couple of colleagues each side and no one in the audience. Passers-by would look in through the glass door with curiosity, but no one came inside. The excitement of the election victory was over.

Camilla, who worked in the only bar in town that Benjamin visited, felt a little uneasy about the League-Five Star alliance. For her, the League was for the wealthy in the north who seemed very different to Sicilians. Oddly though, the League's hard-line anti-migrant policies didn't seem to have crossed her mind.

11

SALVINI AND A RACIST MURDER

On May Day, Mohammad wanted to take the day off as he would have done in Gambia. Coincidentally, no farmer had called to book him for work. He was able to have a lie-in and prepare a breakfast of tomatoes and bread, and then get on his bicycle to do some food shopping in the centre of Triscina. The number of tourists in the area was rising. They were staying in the holiday homes just down the road. Mohammad had never tried to strike up a conversation with them but thought that they had probably come from northern Italy as well as northwestern Europe.

Following the shopping, Mohammad slowly rode back home, thinking all about what lunch to cook for himself. Chicken drumstick stew with rice would be good. He cycled down the lane overlooking the sandy beach in front of him, taking a deep breath. It was as if he were spending a leisurely day like the tourists he had seen in town. Having always worked six or seven days a week, Mohammad felt a day off on May Day was well deserved. He did not have to rush lunch, instead enjoying his home stew while texting and messaging greetings to his friends all over Sicily.

The day after, Benjamin got up 6:00 am and walked over to the junction a kilometre down the road where Africans waited for work. Luck was with him, and he got an offer from a farmer who owned vineyards 3 kilometres from Campobello. He was sent to tidy up one of the vineyards for the day, until 5:00 pm. He was paid €20 for the nine-hour day.

This year's Ramadan was the warmest Benjamin had ever experienced. On one of those days when he was not doing any odd jobs on the farms and the temperature reached 38°C, he felt like going for a swim in the sea. He had never done that during his time in Italy. He asked for a ride from a fellow Gambian who owned a second-hand scooter. So off to Tre Fontane they both went, to the nearest seaside spot frequented by tourists in the summer. Benjamin loved the scooter ride along the country lanes, feeling the wind blowing on his face so that the humidity did not matter. The beach was still fairly quiet in early summer, with only a few people sitting about. He was pleased that there would not be a crowd staring at them. It felt good to be at the beach. The water was warm; it was refreshing and helped him release the stress during Ramadan.

Before the sun set, they returned to the farmhouse and cooked some rice. Just before the meal, the housemates all prayed together in the front-yard. As he had not earned much in the past few weeks, Benjamin felt embarrassed to eat with his group all the time. Sometimes he went over to another farmhouse where other Gambians were staying and had his iftar meal there. He got up at 3:00 am for breakfast and prayer, then went back to sleep until around midday. The idea was that if you slept more, you had less time struggling with hunger and thirst in the heat. The fasting was particularly hard for Alieu, with his stomach ulcer that still troubled him.

* * *

For several mornings in early June, the abandoned petrol station where Sanji and his group were living, was silent, with no music coming from the building as it had before. The front window was covered by a torn plastic sheet, and the front part of the room where they stayed before was now empty, with broken wall tiles strewn on the floor. It looked as if the group had deserted the place. But if you looked closer, you would see a curtain that had been put up that separated the front part of the room from the rear. Sanji was hidden behind the curtain. Local residents had made several complaints against him and the group, telling the police that their presence was a nuisance. Although Sanji's old petrol station stood far away from any residential area, the sight of the group had apparently upset the locals living in the neighbourhood. The police were called, and they came to ask Sanji to be more discreet and move to the back of the building, in order to be invisible to the locals. Now, looking from the outside, you couldn't tell there was anyone living there.

On June mornings, everyone went out to work before 7:00 am, some harvesting watermelons, others tidying up the olive groves that were now growing thick and fast along the road. Sanji felt bad about being the only person not working, but he simply couldn't do any physical work using his left arm, injured in the attack several weeks earlier. What cheered him up was a surprise visit. It was a friend from Senegal who came to Campobello just to see him. The friend simply asked around the African boys in the streets and was directed to where he lived. This friend had suffered some really bad luck—he was mistaken for a people smuggler, arrested in Trapani where he had landed, and jailed for a year. Then the authorities determined that he had been innocent all along and released him. A year of his life was considered nothing, and he was not compensated. The only good thing was that he had started dating the sister of his lawyer. Through her, a white Italian, he managed to get a job as a waiter in a restaurant in Trapani—the kind of job that few Africans could dream of having. Now being free and starting a job, he remembered to visit Sanji, who was now in a much worse position than himself.

Soon, Sanji would have to have his dressing changed on his arm. He was told by the staff at the hospital in Campobello that they weren't equipped for this task and that he must go to the hospital in Castelvetrano. Sanji did as he was told. In Castelvetrano, he had to pay the check-up fee of €20 to the hospital, borrowed from a friend who was living in an asylum camp there. Inside, he was asked to take a blood test. Then a strange thing happened: the nurse came and took four bags of blood (2 litres) from him. No one in the hospital explained to him why that was necessary. Sanji left the hospital feeling much weaker. He was to learn later that, this kind of 'blood test' happened to Africans frequently: taking large amounts of blood without consent from the most impoverished was apparently a regular occurrence. Before Sanji

151

left the hospital, the only thing he was told by the nurse was that his injury would keep him from working for another two months.

At this time, there were many teenagers out working in the fields. They came from the minors' shelter, Futuro, in Campobello. There, things were slightly quieter and more manageable for Minh during Ramadan. Only two of the teenagers were Christian, and therefore cooking became less of a task for the staff. Some of the boys slept at midday during Ramadan, preserving their energy. Minh felt sorry for those who chose to go out to work. How could they last the day without any water in the fields? She was concerned.

Minh was worried about her own situation, too. The quiet of Ramadan gave her a bit more time to think things over. How long was she going to carry on with this job? Marco was moaning about not making enough profit to make the shelter worth the while, so much so that he started to cut down staff working time. They were asked to take one month off work, in turns, so that the company could save costs. It would be Minh's turn soon. This seemed such a desperate attempt that everyone started thinking about how long their jobs might last. Marco tried to make everyone believe that they were all in this together and they were one big family. But it was clear to the staff that the future was uncertain, as he started talking about ideas for changing the focus of his business to adult asylum camps and centres for ex-prisoners.

When it was quiet, Minh went out to take a break on the balcony. She leaned against the metal-barred windows, overlooking the detached houses and olive groves in the distance. This had been her landscape every day for two years. Where was her life going from here? She was the main breadwinner, as her fiancé still wasn't able to find work, and her income was so small that they couldn't afford their own place—the average monthly rent in Mazara was €300. She had not been able to afford to visit her family in Vietnam. Despite being legally entitled to one month's annual paid leave, she had never been given it during the past two years. As a result, she had not even taken a single day's leave, because she couldn't afford not to work. And of course, there was no sick pay. She tried not to get ill on this job. She was missing her mother terribly. She had dreams about family meals with her parents, like the old days. It had been seven years since she left Vietnam and now she could only be with them in her dreams. She tried to compensate for her absence by sending them some of the little money that she earned, despite their refusal to accept it.

* * *

Every now and then, Mohammad was sent to work on a farm outside of Palermo. This summer, he decided to pay a visit to his old friend Daniel who was living in a reception shelter in Palermo. He had not seen Daniel since he left Gambia. Mohammad had missed his friend and suggested he come to join him in Italy. Daniel followed in Mohammad's footsteps and had arrived in Sicily months ago. But work commitments had prevented Mohammad from coming to see him, until now.

Since Mohammad arrived in Palermo, his first time in the centre of this city, his employer in Triscina hadn't stopped calling him. It was as if having Mohammad out of his sight for a couple of days was too much for him. Not only did he book Mohammad for work in the next week, but he tried to persuade him to not 'hang around in Palermo.' 'What do you do there in Palermo?' the farmer kept asking, as if he was worrying that the city might lure his favourite worker away from him. Mohammad tried to deal with this employer's controlling ways by laughing them off, saying, 'Don't worry, don't worry, I'll be back soon.' Another farmer also called to book a weekend's work back in his olive farm in Tre Fontane.

It was heart-warming to see Daniel again. They had so much to catch up on. Mohammad could only tell him about the work he had done in these years—he had not really had a rest; he could count on his fingers his days off during these five and a half years. Daniel was amazed and listened attentively. Mohammad told him that he had travelled to many places to do seasonal work. One year, he went to harvest grapes in Licata on the south coast of Sicily for a month and a half. During the previous winter, he travelled to Spain and worked on peach and melon farms near Barcelona.

Daniel was working at a different pace. He was still waiting for his documents, and therefore couldn't go anywhere for work outside of Italy. But Mohammad wanted Daniel to join him in the olive harvest in Campobello. It would help Daniel escape his confined life in Palermo where he knew nothing beyond Ballarò. Besides, Mohammad could do with some company. His time outside work had always felt purposeless, because there was no one to come home to and to spend time with.

Mohammad missed home a great deal and planned to visit his family after the harvest in December. His family was a permanent, sweet burden to him. They meant everything in the world to him. At the same time, the responsibility and duty to support them was something from which he'd never be able to take a break.

During his time in Palermo, his mother called him from home. As often happened, she mentioned that the family needed his support. It was not as if he ever stopped sending cash home. This pressure seemed a little unnecessary to him at times, because they knew he was doing his best. He never took a holiday from the pressure of family duty. His mother went on reminding him on the phone and he never said a word back. He did not tell her that he was visiting a friend, even for a short time. What would she think of that? It never seemed to occur to her that he needed a rest too. He didn't want to give her any idea that he might be doing something that he enjoyed doing, instead of working.

* * *

It was Saturday, 2 June, Italian Republic Day, celebrating the abolition of the monarchy in 1946. The streets of Marsala were deserted. Local folk were resting at home on this national holiday. Inside the lanes and alleyways, many windows and doors were left open, with voices of men and women, chatting in their sitting rooms and kitchens. They were all getting ready to have their pasta lunch with their families in the afternoon. At midday, inside the historic centre, several young couples were having their wedding photographs taken in the square outside the cathedral. Coloured balloons were everywhere, released by wedding guests to enormous applause.

Several miles away, another world moved at an entirely different pace. Out there in the vast green fields that surrounded the town, Saikou and his fellow Gambian workers were working under the fierce summer sun in temperatures of over 30°C. He had got up at dawn, brought a small loaf of bread with him and, as usual, cycled to work. He would cycle all the way past the dock opposite the scenic Mozia island frequented by tourists to get to the fields. He and fellow workers were tidying up weeds and looking after the thriving vineyards, growing thicker by the week. In a couple of months, these fields would be ready to be harvested by thousands of African workers.

For now, and all throughout the off-season, African workers were paid €2–€4 per hour and their daily earnings depended on the individual agreements they established with the farmers. 'Individual' is the key point. At times, the farmer decided to renege on the deal and you would not get paid a penny. Non-payment of wages was particularly hurtful during Ramadan, when workers went through the day without food and water. But why would farmers give a damn?

Salvini, the then new deputy prime minister and interior minister in charge of immigration, had announced that 'the good time for illegal immigrants is over.'[1] Saikou didn't think that Salvini had ever set foot on a Sicilian farm, because no one in their right mind would claim that toiling in the fields in Italy constituted a 'good time.' Meanwhile, back inside the shelter of Borgo della Pace, where Saikou and other Gambian men were living, no one was talking or thinking about the political situation in Italy. At the end of the working day, they were utterly exhausted, and waited for the sun to set so that they could drink some water and have something to fill their empty stomachs.

At 8:30 pm, Saikou's phone alarm rang loud with a call to prayer. He had set the time to tell himself exactly when the fast broke each day, which changed by one to two minutes each day of Ramadan. He and fellow residents shovelled down the usual unappetising pasta meal provided by their shelter—pasta with tomato sauce and nothing else. Once hunger was sated, they sat back and started exchanging greetings and news with families and friends on social media.

It was then that they started to hear the horrific news from Calabria. A twenty-nine-year-old Malian man by the name of Soumaila Sacko who lived in the *tendopoli* of San Fernando was shot dead by a white Italian man. It was apparent to Saikou that this must have been a racist murder. Every African thought the same. This murder, symbolically, happened only hours after Salvini was sworn in as the country's deputy prime minister and interior minister, a man who had built a political career on an openly anti-migrant platform. 'The good times for illegals is over; get ready to pack your bag,' Salvini reiterated. But the police, as usual, dismissed the racial motivation of the murder straight away, before any investigation.

Another young life had been lost, yet little about Soumaila Sacko was known outside Calabria. He had arrived in Italy before 2010, although no one seemed to know exactly when. He had received his papers and was working in the fields in San Fernando. He experienced the subhuman living and working conditions and witnessed the suffering of fellow workers so much that he began campaigning for them through the workers' union USB, which had helped represent thousands of migrants working in agriculture in southern Italy. His regular status had made it easier for him to pursue his activism as a trade unionist for the last two years, during which he became a delegate for USB in 2016.

On Republic Day, Soumaila Sacko wanted to help his two friends who were also agricultural workers, and so he walked with them to San Calogero a few kilometres away to collect some scrap metal from a disused factory so that they could build a shack in the *tendopoli* in San Ferdinando. Some Italians had trouble understanding why Sacko and his friends had to take metal sheets from a disused factory, one that had been abandoned a decade ago after it was seized as part of an investigation for storing over 135,000 tonnes of hazardous toxic waste. African migrant workers in Italy had to build their own shacks and tents because farmers did not provide accommodation for them and town residents did not want to let rooms to them. Sacko's death revealed a world of horrendous exploitation and appalling living conditions in the Calabria region and beyond, where African workers had been utterly segregated from society. Living on the very edge meant that life was filled with real, day-to-day risks to personal safety. Around these segregated communities, African workers often encountered direct racism, racial harassment and racial violence. Those living at the *tendopoli* were all too aware of the history of racism in the province.

That night, when Sacko and his two friends had picked up three corrugated metal sheets in San Calogero, an Italian man drove up and fired at them, four times, with a shotgun. Sacko was hit in the head; he could not be saved and died in hospital. The suspect was named Antonio Pontoriero, forty-three, from San Calogero. It emerged that his uncle had had a stake in the disused factory before its seizure by the police, and that he was among the people accused of illegally dumping hazardous waste there. Pontoriero's shooting at the three Africans, including Soumaila Sacko, appeared a snap decision out of racial spite.

There was huge amount of anger among Sacko's co-workers and friends. They set fire to the encampment the next day, protesting at his death. Meanwhile, Salvini visited Catania and Pozzallo in Sicily that day, rallying support for his party in the municipal elections and consolidating his anti-migrant platform. He reiterated that the new government would set out to increase the number of detention centres in order to deport 'illegal immigrants.' In the days following Sacko's death, Salvini gave orders to stop rescue ships, among them the NGO ship Aquarius, carrying 629 people, from landing in Sicily.

Salvini's aggressive policy moves were made on the foundations laid by his predecessors. The number of migrant arrivals in Italy had dropped sharply between July and September 2017 under the previous centrist PD government as a result of the agreements signed between Italy and Libya in February 2017. These agreements resulted in the trapping of tens of thousands of Africans in horrific conditions inside Libyan detention prisons where they were tortured, enslaved or killed. In the months preceding the general elections in 2018, the number of migrant arrivals were constantly falling, according to UNHCR. The NGO Borderline Sicilia therefore described the policy of the Salvini-led hard-right government as lying 'in a perfect line of continuity' with that of the previous centrist administration. Salvini and his Interior Ministry were building anti-migrant policies upon Minniti's legacy. In particular, Salvini's external migration policy had remained in the same line as Minniti's—although Salvini put less focus on relations with countries of origin or transit. Based on Minniti's restrictive Code of Conduct for NGOs, Salvini went further and adopted a policy of total closure of Italian ports to NGO ships.

The USB called a strike on the Monday following Soumaila Sacko's murder, and his outraged co-workers all joined it in protest. Thousands of workers marched with the USB in Reggio Calabria. The parade became a final collective farewell to Sacko, whose body would be sent back to Mali, to his wife and five-year-old daughter.

Aboubakar Soumahoro, a thirty-eight-year-old Italian-Ivorian and a leading activist in the USB, said at the rally: 'Soumaila was a Malian farmer forced to leave home by climate change. He wanted to stop here, to cultivate the land with other workers, be on their side, organising them together with the USB. A labourer, a man, a trade unionist, a father, a companion. His family asked for three things from us: truth and justice for his shooting; the return of his body to the homeland; the continuation of his union commitment.'

The USB called for a demonstration in Rome on 16 June, to demand dignified living and working conditions for migrant workers in Italy. While 20,000 people joined this protest, Salvini reiterated that no rescue ships were to dock in Italy. Aboubakar Soumahoro had a message for Salvini: 'Your good days will come to an end. Because we will fight back.'

Meanwhile, racist attacks and attempted murders did not stop with Soumaila Sacko's death. That June, a twenty-two-year-old Malian chef named Konate Bouyagui was shot 'for fun' in Naples. Bouyagui survived the attack, but Africans, already fearful, saw their fears exacerbated in a country where the shooting of Africans no longer surprised anyone. 'This is not Libya!' many Africans shouted out in protest.

* * *

Saikou, who was living in the shelter near the salt flats in Marsala, was cautious in his local environment. When you got used to being cautious, it became your second nature. You kept your head down and avoided eye contact. Back home, you did not look people in the eye because that was respectful; here, you avoided eye contact to avoid provocation and trouble.

On his day off in the summer, for some fresh air Saikou would walk up the country lane, with vineyards on one side and salt pans dotted with windmills on the other. He would wear his baseball cap with the word 'black' on it, and a jumper even on a warm day. He never walked far, but just strolled in the surrounding area. A couple of times, he walked up to the docks where tourists took the boat to Mozia island across the shallow lagoon bordered by the salt flats. Mozia, primarily an archaeological site, used to be an important colony of Carthage, the Phoenician city in North Africa. It was eventually destroyed by the Greeks of Syracuse in the fourth century BCE, after which the inhabitants developed a new town on the coast nearby, which became the town of Marsala.

This was all interesting to Saikou, as he was preparing for school exams that included the basic history of Sicily. If he passed the exams, he thought he might stand a chance of being considered for a place on a catering training course designed for those working in tourism. This was the kind of seasonal work that many local young people wouldn't want to do. For Saikou, that would be one step up from working in the fields.

Sitting by the dock, he would quietly prepare for the questions that might be asked and rehearse his answers. 'What do you know about Sicily?' was an obvious question. To which he would answer, 'Sicily lives on agriculture and the work of Africans.'

To the northwest of the salt flats were a mass of fields dotted with farmhouses. Rocco, a fifty-two-year-old native Marsalan, was taking his dogs for a walk around one of his father's ten farm plots. There were acres of vineyards, with wooden posts lifting up the vines, allowing easier access to the grapes. To the right were rows of olive groves, producing a small quantity of olive oil, some of which was pressed and processed by Rocco's family in-house. Farmers here shared out their farming equipment, such as oil presses, tractors and tools. Some of their olives were sent to be processed in the nearby factories.

Then there were orange, lemon, and apple trees, and a tomato greenhouse. Rocco was particularly proud of Sicilian tomatoes. 'They taste different from all other tomatoes. They're fragrant,' he said. However, this tomato greenhouse was the only one his father had left. In recent years, there had been increasing competition in the global market; for instance, imported tomatoes from Morocco, following an agreement signed between the EU and Morocco concerning the liberalisation of agricultural products. It meant that Sicilian farmers had had to think of new ways to improve production and re-establish their advantage.

Rocco tried to persuade his father to make changes, for instance, to the way he grew tomatoes. But his father preferred to keep to the old ways. The result was that it was no longer profitable or even worth the trouble to grow tomatoes: he received only 70 cents per kilogram for the tomatoes he grew, and the high transportation fees—10% of the price—made it even worse. The same went for the grapes; he was earning only €40–€50 per 1,000 kilograms of grapes.

To become competitive in order to increase farming income, a small number of farmers were looking for new ways to grow their crops. A good friend of Rocco's, Marco, was doing exactly that: he was growing organic grapes for his own winery, Cantine Ballotta, near Trapani. No chemicals, no pesticides, but as it cost more to do so, farmers saw it as taking a greater risk and few had been willing to invest. Innovation, however, Marco believed, was the way to find a new niche and to make products more profitable in the long term.

Rocco commented on how the Sicilian mafia are fully integrated into the agricultural chain. Many of the olive oil processing factories and the forty-odd wineries in the Marsala area were owned and controlled by members of the mafia. In Marsala where Rocco's father worked and produced grapes for the wineries, the prices that farmers received had been kept low at the same rate across the industry. Rocco knew that prices outside of the area could be up to three times higher and it angered him. This control had depressed farmers' earnings and in turn kept workers' wages low. The meagre farming income also meant that farmers were reluctant or unable to invest in improving means of production, which led to low productivity and therefore low income. A vicious circle.

Despite the lasting hold of the mafia on Sicily, Cosa Nostra seemed the last thing Rocco liked talking about when anyone asked about the island. He didn't like the way criminality had been portrayed in many of the films made about Sicily. He found the TV series *Detective Maltese* too much of a cliché to watch and the film *Gomorra* too dark and unbearable. Deep down though, he wished that the mafia had simply become history and that descendants of its members were branded for life and had to seek alternative livelihoods, like the son of Salvatore 'Totò' Riina, the Corleonesi mafia chief. Riina ordered the murders of prosecutors Giovanni Falcone and Paolo Borsellino in 1992 after his verdicts were delivered. His son now conducted mafia tours for a living.

Rocco was born and raised in Marsala; he had always loved it here and this was where he felt he belonged. He would look into the fields and the mountains behind them, and take a real deep breath. Home. Since he had come back from his years working in northern Italy and abroad, he had known he would never leave home again.

Three decades ago, Rocco went to fight for his own future and went north to Milan. He worked as a driver in a luxury hotel. There, he used to drive the rich and famous around town. He remembered Kirstie Alley from Cheers, and members of Iron Maiden, the British heavy metal group, and said they were so polite. But obviously, the most important person he met in Milan was his wife, who was born and raised in Milan. They had been moving between north and south, between Milan and Marsala, ever since they got married.

Later, Rocco was able to afford to go to England, where he went to seek his fortunes in the early 1990s. There, in Chiswick, west London, he worked as a waiter in a Mexican restaurant. He worked long hours and lived in a bedsit. As his time outside work was minimal, he didn't have the opportunity to learn the language. But he picked up the habit of trying different cuisines. 'I like curry and basmati rice, and lemon chicken,' he boasted of his broad culinary tastes that he brought back from London. Even now when he visited Palermo, he would often pop into one of the Bangladeshi cafés for a curry.

Rocco's years of hard work in northern Italy and in Britain paid off; it enabled him and his wife to have what they had today—the country house with a large garden, a property in town which he rented out, and three family cars. They certainly wouldn't have been able to send their two sons to Edinburgh otherwise—the elder son studying public relations at university and the younger one working there.

Despite loving his hometown and even having obtained a certificate in agriculture, Rocco didn't want to work on his father's vineyards, which supplied the small local winery collective. The collective was a short distance from the farm and almost symbolised the self-sufficient nature of life in the community here. Rocco strolled back home from the farm at midday. His mother was preparing lunch using olives that they grew, with cheese and risotto, and they drank the white wine from the local winery that processed every farmer's grapes in this community.

Rocco's father, eighty-five, was too old to work all the time. During the summer and autumn, he depended on hired hands, some of them African workers, to harvest his crops. No one here saw Africans as taking local jobs, because few local people—both of Rocco's and his sons' generation—wanted to work in the fields. Rocco's generation, whose fathers were farmers, didn't farm full-time these days, but preferred other employment. Rocco himself found his niche and came up with the idea of running a taxi service and had become the first taxi in Marsala five years earlier. His taxi license plate was clearly marked 'license No.1,' the first of the ten licensed taxis in town. Other farmers' sons also found alternative occupations. Several started up small agro-tourist businesses. Rocco's friend Vito had turned his father's orange farm in Villapetrosa on the southern outskirts of Marsala into a bed and breakfast with a beautiful garden filled with seventy-year-old orange trees. Vito said he wouldn't sell the oranges, 'because the price of 40 cents per kilogram just isn't worth the while, especially after paying workers picking them.'

As for the generation of Rocco's sons, certainly few would want to remain in farming. Labour intensive as the local agriculture and its related industries were, the majority of local youth saw these as more or less dead-end employment that brought little future prospects. Rocco believed, indeed knew that after his father retired, farming would end in the family. As usual, young people here would go to look for work and seek their fortunes in northern Italian cities or abroad.

But others, with fewer options in life, like Saikou and his fellow Gambians, would come and make up for the shortage. Rocco watched his father nearing the day when he would finally pack up farming. His father would not be able to sell the land because the prices were so low. He would have to just rent it cheaply to the local winery for them to use for growing grapes. Rocco predicted that 'farming would become only for Africans in the future,' unless, old farmers were able to sell their plots on to bigger companies who came to buy up land, which might lead to an increase in larger landholdings.

***

Along with sub-Saharan Africans, many Tunisian migrant workers as well as workers from the long-established Italian-Tunisian community suffered long-term severe labour exploitation in Italy. Tunisian migration to Sicily started in the 1960s and stabilised in the 1990s, particularly in Palermo, Mazara, Catania and Ragusa.[2] In Marsala and its suburbs, there were over 1,000 Italian-Tunisians (whom local people referred to as Tunisians) and recently arrived workers from Tunisia. Almost all of them had been working in agriculture.

Ahmed was in his early twenties and knew Sicilian agriculture inside out. He came to Italy with his family at the age of five and had been granted indefinite leave to remain, instead of citizenship. Ahmed spoke Italian like any other local, but he was not seen as Italian. His slightly tanned skin colour would mark him out for life, as people could tell he might have North African parentage. Ahmed was accustomed to being treated as second-class in the country in which he grew up. He didn't think about citizenship. He would tell his friends, 'Citizenship doesn't mean you're Italian or would be treated as one. The truth is they'll never accept you, even with citizenship.'

Like many Italian-Tunisians of his age, Ahmed didn't go to college because his family couldn't afford it. The lack of educational qualifications hindered his already limited occupational choices. Therefore, he went into farm work and had remained working in it for four years. During those years, there was never any improvement in wages or conditions. As the norm, migrant workers never received a pay rise, no matter how long they had worked in the industry. Like most other Italian-Tunisians and the newly arrived Tunisian workers, Ahmed had been working via *caporali*, who charged him €50 for each work assignment, no matter how long the job lasted. On top of that, a driver would charge him a transport fee each time. Ahmed earned between €30 and €35 per eight-hour day. There were white Italian workers working alongside him, doing the same work, the same hours, but they were earning €50 per day—even when they had far less experience. The blatant wage disparity was heart-breaking for Ahmed, because it confirmed once again that he would never be able to become part of society. He would explain this to the newly arrived Tunisians: 'This is because we are strangers to them.'

Moreover, despite Ahmed having been granted leave to remain and obviously having all the documents required, he was still not given a work contract by most farmers. On the rare occasions when he did have a contract, the terms of the contract were entirely fictitious.

Without a contract, Ahmed worked through the three months of summer harvest in the vineyards around Marsala in 2018. Not only did he resent the low wages, he was also frustrated that he wasn't allowed any break. The supervision at work was harsh; he got shouted at for not being fast enough. Ahmed often wondered why he bothered to carry on working on the farms. At the end of a working day, he always felt that, after all the fees he had to pay, he was hardly earning enough to make the job worth going to. It was as if he went out for a day trip in the fields and came back empty-handed.

12

'TELL ME, MINISTER, WOULD YOU YOURSELF LIVE IN A PLACE LIKE THIS?'

Salvini launched his mission to stop NGO rescue boats from docking in Sicily, one after another, with endorsement from Five Star. He stated that he aimed to 'protect the external border' and to 'solve the problem at the source,' which meant strengthening Italy's joint operations with Libya to keep migrants out of Europe. His 'strong man' image had won him a lead in the polls, which emboldened him further. It looked as if he was acting on the 'people's will.'

That summer, Salvini set out to end 'humanitarian protection status,' which he believed should no longer be given to people on the basis of maternity, illness, or experience of torture in Libya. Humanitarian protection is a form of protection for those not eligible for refugee status but who, for various reasons, cannot be sent home. Humanitarian protection status entitles people to a two-year, renewable residence permit and enables them to work. Of the 81,500 decisions handed down by Italian authorities in 2017, only 8% of asylum seekers were granted refugee status and 25% were granted humanitarian protection status. Therefore, to remove humanitarian protection would effectively remove the main mechanism for granting any status to asylum seekers.

Salvini's plans were realised in late September 2018, when a series of hard-line, anti-migrant measures were approved by the cabinet that saw the government abolish key forms of protection for migrants. Among these was the security decree law (*decreto sicurezza*) which would abolish humanitarian protection and replace it with a special permits system. The decree, based on the logic of security and control instead of offering protection, aimed to reform the reception system by transforming SPRAR into SIPROIMI (*Sistema di Protezione per Titolari di Protezione Internazionale e Minori Stranieri non Accompagnati*, Protection System for International Protection Holders and Unaccompanied Foreign Minors). The reform made a clear separation between asylum seekers (those applying for protection) and refugees (those granted protection); the former would be accommodated in first-level reception camps (such as a CARA) and CAS,[1] while the latter would have access to the second-level reception system which was now called SIPROIMI. The two categories of people were to be placed in two parallel systems under the decree.

SIPROIMI would consist of small reception structures where 'integration' services would be provided and where people could stay for six months. By January 2019, there were over 875 small SIPROIMI projects in the country which had a total of 35,650 places of accommodation.[2] Out of these, 155 projects were for unaccompanied minors. As a result of the limited number of SIPROIMI places, there was a 'protection gap' for those who were granted refugee status. Since the decree, it had become even more difficult for refugees to obtain authorisation to stay in first-level reception centres after their protection status had been granted, as the protection status didn't allow them to remain in these facilities. Therefore, many people ended up destitute and homeless before being placed in SIPROIMI accommodation.[3]

Those who had been granted humanitarian protection before the decree and were staying at CAS or CARA centres would be evicted as soon as the centre's funding ended (and their stay would not be extended even if the centre did receive new funds). Meanwhile, asylum seekers, as a section of the 'undeserving' migrants, were to be kept inside the first-level reception camps and CAS shelters where funds had been cut under the decree, and those running the facilities would only receive €19–€26 per person per day for the provision of the services required, which was much less than the amount available for those running SIPROIMI facilities, for whom the quota per person per day was €35. This significant cut in funds meant that those running the first-level reception facilities would maximise their profits by further limiting their provisions. Services inside these places were becoming even more inadequate than before. Asylum seekers who were already in SPRAR facilities before 4 October 2018 were entitled to stay for a limited time (until the funding ended). Under the decree, asylum seekers could only be transferred back to CAS and first reception camps.

In this climate, there was growing anxiety among those still waiting for their asylum decisions. In the Acos Hotel camp in Marsala, the number of residents was decreasing. Some had run away due to the long wait and anticipated rejection under the new decree. Insufficient numbers of residents meant that the camp was facing the prospect of closing down in the near future.

Salvini's ultimate aim had always been clear: to reduce migration by creating maximum deterrents—not only closing seaports, banning rescues and criminalising NGO workers, but also targeting those who were already in the country and denying protection to the majority of them. These measures would make illegal even larger numbers of people already living on the edge of society. These people would be faced with only two options: either go to live in rural ghettos and join the army of labour already keeping the country's agriculture running, or go to other countries and seek asylum all over again, living a life in limbo until the Dublin rules returned them to Italy, their first country of arrival in Europe.

***

A mile outside Rosarno, Salvini's stronghold in Calabria, the *tendopoli* of San Ferdinando was still standing. The living conditions had deteriorated—as if they couldn't get any worse. There was no electricity supply and residents had to rely on portable generators that stall holders had bought from shops in town. There was no proper water supply, but a water pipe connected to a factory nearby. Meanwhile, rows of blue tents, well fenced and guarded, could be seen in the distance on the other side of the road, away from the wooden shacks in the *tendopoli* where the majority of African workers were living. The blue tent area, with six beds in each tent, around 500 beds in all, had the 'luxury' of seven bathrooms, running water and electric floodlights. The tents were erected by the authorities in summer 2017; people called them the 'official tents'. This area was run on a first come, first served basis and entry required official documents. Those who arrived after the bed spaces were taken had to go to the makeshift encampment across the road.

At the same time, these blue tents, opposite an orange processing factory, were clear signs that the labour of the African residents was much needed, although the authorities were not prepared to provide suitable housing and give the workers the opportunity to become part of the local community. As a ridiculously token gesture, a wooden 'hospitality school' the size of a garden shed stood opposite the entrance to these tents.

Soumaila Sacko lived in the *tendopoli* where the majority of workers were living, when he was murdered on 2 June. His shack, still covered in white plastic sheets, which he shared with his brother, was located near the entrance to the encampment, now guarded and patrolled by the police day and night. Sacko's body had been transported back for burial in Mali. The memory of what happened still weighed heavily here and the mention of his name always brought out sadness in people's faces. With the heavy police presence, however, people were talking less about it and had returned to their usual routine of trying to eke out a living.

Summer was a quiet time for work here. The citrus harvest season between December and March in the plains of Gioia Tauro was long over. More than 1,000 people were still here in June and July. A group of young Senegalese men sat leaning against Soumaila Sacko's old shack, warming themselves under the mid-day sun. Lamine, in his thirties, was chatting with several friends after having returned from the morning's search for work. He had found nothing this day. He had been in the *tendopoli* for over a year now, having arrived initially to wait for his documents. His friends came for the same reason: for a place to sleep as well as for some work during the wait.

For similar reasons, many others were still arriving, despite there being insufficient work in the summer to keep them going. Around the site, there were signs of new arrivals: numerous wooden frames a couple of square metres in size waited like skeletons for their flesh of metal sheets and wooden boards to be attached. Dotted around the site, there were also the remains of shacks that had been destroyed by fires. Towards the rear of the camp was a pile of burnt wood and melted plastic. It used to be a shack that accommodated two people. When a fire broke out, one of them called the fire services. But, as usual, firemen arrived only when the shack was nearly burned to the ground. The wreckage was not cleared away and no new shack had been built on the same spot, as if it had become a monument and a reminder to those living there.

Further along was an empty space the size of two shacks, with wooden posts all around it. It was used as a social area. Lamine came here sometimes after work in the evening, and stood around chatting with people. This was the equivalent of the town square in Rosarno where the locals sat around having their social time. Only in this makeshift space, there were no benches or chairs or shade under trees.

Residents here also tried to meet their spiritual needs. Lamine and other Muslims were able to pray in the only makeshift mosque on site. There was also a 'Church of the African Union' located in a large tent. Lamine always prayed that he would one day make a good living and properly support his family in Senegal. He had never stopped looking for work, every single day. He would get paid €25 for a ten-hour day in the fields, from 8:00 am to 6:00 pm. When there was regular work, up to seven days a week, during a harvest, he could potentially earn up to €600 per month.

During the summer, as farm work was scarce, Lamine had to find other ways to survive. He saw that many people were setting up stalls and services to cater for the needs of people in the *tendopoli*. There were butchers, food stores, phone charging tents (€1 each time), a hot water service (50 cents for a hot shower), and even barbers. He once spent €2 on a fairly decent haircut and, when it got colder, he bought a pair of old boots for €5 from one of the stalls. There was also a skilful builder here, assembling many of the shacks for new arrivals. Africans of all nationalities worked as a community. No one could make a big profit here running a shop, but it ensured interdependence among the residents in difficult circumstances, making the *tendopoli* a self-maintaining village.

Lamine decided to run a food shop that opened daily to camp residents. He would still spend his mornings and early afternoons searching for agricultural work, and when he was lucky to have found some, he would work until mid-afternoon. After that, he would ride his bike to the Mama Africa store in Rosarno town to buy €5 worth of chicken, onions and a large amount of rice. At 4:00 pm each day, Lamine would take out his stew pot and frying pan and start preparing his shop's unchanging signature dish, chicken and onion stew with rice, in his tiny kitchen behind the counter of his food shop, opposite Soumaila Sacko's shack. It normally took an hour to get the food ready. From 5:00 pm, he would then start serving the stew and rice on plastic plates for €1 a serving. He was able to feed twenty to thirty people with the amount of food he cooked in that hour. He felt quite proud of it. Not only Senegalese enjoyed his cooking, but Gambian and Malian boys too. With his food shop doing well, Lamine also got to know everyone around and became friends with many of them.

As the summer was a quiet season for work, not everyone had the cash to pay for the food from Lamine's shop. He developed a credit system where he kept a book of names of people who had bought food without paying and they would return the money to him when they earned something. The system worked on trust, and he trusted his fellow residents. Lamine also served simple snacks in the daytime to make extra cash: he would use the onions left over from the previous day to make tinned corned beef and onion sandwiches for anyone who needed a bite to eat before going out to work in the fields.

* * *

In mid-July, Salvini paid a visit to the *tendopoli* in San Ferdinando as part of the PR drive to market his anti-migrant policies. He was, as expected, escorted by police officers when he toured the camp. Many residents came out of their tents and shacks to see the deputy prime minister in real life. They lined Salvini's route through the camp, with police officers surrounding them. They wanted to see the man who was bringing more misery to their lives. Lamine decided to stay inside his shack; he was reluctant to show his face to the politician who wanted the worst for people in his circumstances. A tall Nigerian man in his thirties named Michael went up to within a few steps of Salvini, and

said, 'Tell me, Minister, would you yourself live in a place like this?'
The reporters turned off their cameras as Salvini refused to answer
the question.

After having seen the camp, Salvini predictably told the press,
'housing and work, Italians first.' As to the appalling conditions that
he must have witnessed, Salvini called for an end to migrant landings.
'This tent city is a heavy inheritance and shows that out-of-control
immigration leads only to chaos,' he said, in a similar way to how
Marine Le Pen had talked about La Lanière camp in Dunkirk in 2017.
He challenged those who wanted to open ports to migrants to visit the
tendopoli of San Ferdinando, blaming the conditions in the camp on the
residents themselves.

Two weeks after Salvini's visit, its residents marched and protested
in San Ferdinando, requesting a meeting with the heads of the local
authorities to demand suitable accommodation and a real solution to
their predicament. A delegation met with Andrea Tripodi, the mayor
of San Ferdinando. 'Documents, housing and contracts for everyone!'
they shouted out, loud and clear.

The climate created by the League–Five Star coalition government
had already led to increasing police activity against Africans across the
country. Back in Campobello, the *carabinieri* raided the farmhouse
where Benjamin and his friends were living, after months of quiet. It
became clear that this was part of a 'clean-up' initiative. The authorities
were raiding numerous disused farmhouses occupied by Africans,
evicting them and forcing them out of the area. Three officers came
that day, lining everyone up, searching the farmhouse, piling their
belongings on the front yard and telling them to leave.

Alieu was in the house at the time of the raid while Benjamin was
out at Camilla's bar charging his mobile phone. He panicked and
immediately called Benjamin, as he didn't know what to do. Benjamin
walked back as fast as he could, and on entering the yard saw everyone
standing around, dishevelled and distressed, with their belongings
piled around them, and officers questioning them and taking names.
He burst into tears. Over the past five months he had built this place
up, little by little, and made it habitable. This place, with so little in it,
was all they had. Without cash or resources, there was no alternative
for them but to try to stay.

'Please officers, please!' Benjamin pleaded, his voice shaking, tears running down his face. 'We don't have anywhere to go to!'

He could not stop himself sobbing. Alieu tried to calm him down as it looked as if he was going to collapse. He had never seen Benjamin in this state before.

'You've all got to leave,' one of the officers carried on firmly, 'We will be back in two days' time to see if you've vacated this place.'

'We can't leave! We have no place to go!' Benjamin shouted. 'No place to go!' Everyone else nodded in agreement that they could not just leave.

'I'm afraid you've got to leave the area,' the officer reiterated. Then the three of them got into their patrol car and sped off back into Campobello. Benjamin flopped onto the floor and sobbed uncontrollably. 'All is lost,' he said to himself. 'All is lost.'

In fact, prior to the general election of 2018, the authorities' 'clean-up' initiative had already been set in train. After the demolition of the encampment in White Grass, the various institutions preparing for the next olive season held roundtable meetings in which a variety of conflicting interests emerged.[4] 'The Campobello administration demanded that the task of managing workers be distributed among more municipalities; the Prefecture asked the associations to address the situation in some way; the associations themselves requested responsibility, through a public tendering process, for managing the encampment. Once again, the only voices that were absent were those of the workers.'[5]

As discussions continued, the Campobello council brought local farmers into the equation, and asked some of them to take on the task of providing accommodation to workers. The trade-off was that the local authorities would not intervene or take any interest in the standards of the accommodation provided by the farmers. The authorities convened a public meeting with the farmer on 23 August 2018, at which around thirty were present. The institutions involved made it clear: 'There will be no more bivouacs, but you [farmers] must accommodate the workers. In return, we will ignore the housing conditions that you offer; even a curtain [as a partition] is enough.'[6]

One farmer piped up during the meeting: 'What if they want wifi?' to which Lillo Dilluvio, the then-councillor of Campobello, replied:

'Wifi is not of vital importance.' Most of all, the farmers wanted reassurances that the control of standards of the accommodation they provided as well as intervention in working conditions would be minimal. They were reassured as Dilluvio told them, 'do not worry. Even the CGIL union said that in Campobello there is no phenomenon of illegal hiring.'[7]

From that point on, the stance of the local authorities was clear: show a tough line against the encampment, and at the same time, allow migrant workers to remain, necessary to avoid alienating the farmers who absolutely needed their labour. Instead of seeking long-term solutions and making all farmers comply with their duty to house farm workers and ensure housing standards, the local authorities opted for the most opportunistic and cheapest way out.

As a result, throughout the summer and early autumn, police raids took place all across Campobello. What happened to Benjamin and his group at their farmhouse, happened to Sanji and his group, too. The *carabinieri* visited and asked everyone to leave the disused petrol station in which they were squatting. The group had to disperse. Sanji's nephew had a friend in Marsala who helped him out by offering a bed space in his compound, which was already filling with people in the same situation. But he could not take more than one person, so Sanji had to stay behind in Campobello.

He searched frantically for a place to sleep. He started asking strangers for help, something that he had never done before. He knew that many local residents were small farmers who might have farmhouses or barns that were not in use. One day, he stopped a local woman in the road, asking if she could help him. As it turned out, she said she was a relative of a farmer who owned two disused farmhouses nearby. One of the farmhouses had electricity and water, for which Sanji would have to pay €200 for the monthly rent. He couldn't afford that, of course, and had to go for the second farmhouse, which had no electricity or water, for which he had to pay €50 a month.

Sanji still didn't have the cash to pay that amount up front, as there had not been much work for him lately. He pleaded with her to let him off for a week until he found the cash, to which she reluctantly agreed. Sanji immediately moved in to the farmhouse and stayed there for a week; he relied on a borrowed generator for electricity and looked for a water pipe from which to 'borrow' water. When it came to the end of the week, he still didn't have the €50. The autumn would be coming in another six weeks. He knew he would be getting more work in the fields then. But right now, asking her to wait longer for the rent would be pushing it too far.

Eventually, he managed to pull together €50 borrowed from friends and relatives, paid the woman, and was able to continue staying in the farmhouse. Every week, he would travel to his friend Adama who was living in the camp at the former Acos Hotel site in Marsala and take a hot shower there.

As the amount of work had not yet increased and no friends or relatives were able to help, Sanji was unable to pay the next month's rent. He tried to plead with the woman and buy some time, but she was so frustrated with the delay that she told her two adult sons about it. The two men did not take the news well, and came to pay Sanji a visit. Sanji had no idea what line of work they were in, but they were not the type of people to be sweet-talked. They gave him a beating instead.

Tommaso di Maria, the outspoken Five Star councillor in Campobello, continued to use the rhetoric of archaeological conservation to justify the end of the White Grass encampment and the removal of Africans from the fringes of the town. 'How could the previous government have allowed migrants to 'do their business' on top of our archaeological site!' he shouted out to his followers. His language was becoming more provocative, emboldened by the tougher policy of the new League–Five Star alliance. As the olive harvest approached, he continued to show no interest in solving the African harvest workers' serious housing issues. Instead, on social media he called for a 'change in the tolerance of migrants.' He proudly claimed that 'the Green Yellow government [the League–Five Star coalition] is indeed the government of change.'

***

Lamine was increasingly frustrated with life in the *tendopoli* of San Ferdinando. Not only was it overcrowded and particularly unbearable in the summer, but it was also attracting more and more attention from the media. Then, in early August, tragic news came in from friends living in the province of Foggia.

Sixteen Africans died in two car crashes within forty-eight hours. In both cases, lorries carrying tomatoes collided with vans carrying workers on their way home from work in the tomato fields. Four workers died in the first crash, and two days later, another twelve lost their lives in a head-on crash near Lesina, north of San Severo. It emerged that the *caporali,* who were hired by the local mafia, had driven the workers from farm to farm in overcrowded vans. Despite most of these workers having had documents, their work was still controlled by the *caporali.*

Alsane, the Senegalese man who had worked in Campobello almost every autumn and then went to harvest asparagus and tomatoes in Puglia during the spring and summer, saw the aftermath of the second crash as he and other workers were driven past in another vehicle. He was shaken by it. They were his comrades. Having experienced exploitation in other parts of Italy, they had ended up in Puglia, enduring the worst, until they lost their lives. It was heart-breaking. Two solidarity demonstrations and a strike were organised by USB to protest about the exploitation of farm workers. More than 200 migrant workers, many of them wearing the red caps used by the tomato pickers, marched from Gran Ghetto in Torretta Antonacci all the way to the prefecture office in Foggia city.

Marching along the country lanes, the workers chanted slogans, 'Stop deaths on the job! Slaves no more!' Alsane knew only too well about the extent of labour exploitation in this region. Every summer, thousands of African workers would come to Foggia province to harvest tomatoes for as little as €1 per 100 kilograms. Throughout his time here, Alsane would normally be paid between €3 and €3.50 per hour. He always ended up with a daily wage of €25 after the deductions by the *caporali.* For those without documents, dependence on the *caporali* was a must. You could not get work otherwise. There were around 3,000 *caporali* in the region.

The workers who died in the car crashes were living in appalling conditions in Gran Ghetto. The Gran Ghetto was a *tendopoli* located in between San Severo and Foggia, and often had over 3,000 migrant workers living there at its peak. The ghetto had a long history. The first settlement was located in a disused sugar factory by the motorway between Foggia and San Severo. Every five to six years the encampment was demolished by the local authorities and people would then set it up again later on. On 3 March 2017, thirty-three-year-old Mamadou Konate and thirty-six-year-old Nouhou Doumbia, both Malian, died in a massive blaze inside the ghetto overnight. Following the fire, the ghetto was demolished by a hundred police officers and firefighters on the orders of the local authorities. By the next harvest, however, people had returned to the area and, since there was no alternative housing, they rebuilt the settlement. This had been the historical cycle of the Gran Ghetto—and all the other makeshift settlements in the country. Each time, the Gran Ghetto would be driven further into the countryside, further away and even more isolated.

Since the demolition of Gran Ghetto in March 2017, many had moved to a place called Casa Sankara not far from the ghetto site. Casa Sankara was named after Thomas Sankara, a revolutionary and Pan-Africanist who was president of Burkina Faso between 1983 and 1987, renaming it from its French colonial name of Upper Volta. He was killed during a French-backed coup in 1987. In 2017 and 2018, when Alsane came to the region for the harvest, he joined a friend who was living in Casa Sankara. It was a place closed to the outside world. Flat fields dotted with wind turbines were all that you could see on the way there.

Casa Sankara was an experimental project founded by Tonino d'Angelo, founder of the Art Village based in San Severo. It aimed to accommodate migrant workers and provide an environment free from *caporali* and their exploitation. It was run on a five-year contract won by a network of associations and cooperatives across San Severo, Foggia, Cerignola and Bari, with the lead organisation being 'Ghetto Out-Casa Sankara.' In August 2016, a site of twenty hectares, including arable land and a building, was able to house up to sixty people, from Senegal, Ivory Coast, Morocco, Egypt, and other countries. The number of people grew and the project eventually accommodated up to 200 people at peak times.

Over the years, the ideal of a non-exploitative work model became blurred and eventually buried under a mountain of greed. Local farmers would come in to the Casa Sankara site and recruit workers for around €20 a day. The *caporali* started to organise the workers and control their earnings. As a result, in 2017 and 2018, Alsane and other workers were being paid the rate of €25 per day with a €5 deduction for transport around the area. The rising numbers of *caporali* attracted the attention of the police. But they soon turned a blind eye when *caporali* thrusted bank notes in their pockets. Alsane and the other workers were all aware of the bribery that was commonplace. Sure enough, with the police kept quiet, the exploitation went wild.

For Alsane, the situation in San Severo and its surrounding areas, where Casa Sankara was located, was the worst he had experienced yet. Not only did *caporali* extort fees from migrant workers and control their work, but non-payment of wages was also not unusual. It happened to Alsane and his co-workers once. The *capo* ran away with the wages for a team of twenty-eight workers, €50,000 in total, including Alsane's hard-earned wages of €7,000 for that harvest. Alsane was utterly devastated. That was the money he was supposed to send home. He could not speak for days. Despite the anger, Alsane and his fellow workers had nowhere to turn, no one to report the theft to, certainly not the police when none of them had documents.

Meanwhile, Casa Sankara continued to receive good press. It received much media attention when the mayor visited the site for PR purposes on Republic Day in 2018. Reports hailed the place as a model of 'social integration.' When sixteen workers were killed in the car crashes in August 2018, many of their friends came to their funeral held at Casa Sankara in September. Some of the victims had relatives there. After that autumn, with the anarchy of exploitation, Alsane promised himself never to return to this place.

Lamine in the *tendopoli* of San Ferdinando knew what his fellow Africans had gone through. He had friends who worked for years between Calabria and Puglia; they would leave the *tendopoli* in San Ferdinando and head to the area where the current Gran Ghetto was located for the tomato harvest every year. Each time it took a worker's death for their extreme exploitation to come to the surface—but after a short while in the media spotlight, it was then submerged again. It was as if society was suffering from some kind of collective amnesia, enabling such tragedies to repeat themselves.

One day in August, Lamine received a call from his lawyer in town. It was the good news he had been praying for: his documents had arrived! It had been a painful two years, during which he had felt his hope slipping away month after month. He thanked God for answering his prayers and protecting him. At last, he was able to see a glimmer of light ahead and he had been given the precious opportunity to embrace life. The first thing he had to do was try to move out of the dark hole of San Ferdinando.

And he did. He had saved up and managed to rent a cheap room that he shared with another Senegalese man, in a seaside town called Palmi, three stops on the local train from Rosarno. He worked doubly hard on farms in order to afford the rent. Palmi was an agricultural community of 19,000 people and a tourist resort that enjoyed the title of 'the Terrace on the Strait of Messina.' Lamine felt fortunate and was determined to start his new life here. But he never forgot the friends he left behind in the *tendopoli*, and he would help them out whenever he could.

13

OLIVE SEASON ONCE AGAIN

As the harvest of the vineyards in the Marsala area officially came to an end on 26 September, work in the olive groves had already been well under way for a couple of weeks in the handsome fields of Campobello. The hard, green olives were weighing the trees down, waiting for more workers to pick them. As expected, the most notable sight in Campobello was the growing number of arrivals, often walking in small groups, who got off the regional trains in the station every hour. The sub-Saharan African workers, the majority of the harvest workforce, didn't have hosts to pick them up. They had to find their own way, based on instructions from contacts and friends.

Young and middle-aged Tunisian men were also among the new arrivals, many of whom were recruited by their *caporali* who would pick them up from the station and organise their lodgings. There were also some Tunisian workers who had only just arrived in the country, with few leads, and who seemed disoriented with no idea of where to go.

On this warm early October day, a group of three Tunisian men, in their late thirties and forties, walked from the station, with their heavy suitcases dragging along the pavements now scattered with the first fallen leaves of autumn. They trudged past the construction site of the new, EU-funded cinema, to the square at the town centre. Their luggage was weighing them down. They had to take a little break and sit down on the bench to get their breath back. They knew no one in this place and all they had heard about was White Grass. They were so behind with the news that they were not even aware that the makeshift camp there had been demolished seven months earlier.

They dragged their cases along for another kilometre, zigzagging through the side streets, and finally reached White Grass, only to find that it had been flattened. Huge amounts of rough concrete rubble had been tipped over what used to be the encampment, to prevent people from coming back to rebuild it. The three of them put down their bags and suitcases, looking at the concrete dump and then at each other, not knowing what to say. They had come for the harvest and planned to settle here for a while. But where were the tents and shacks? What were they to do?

* * *

If they had walked across the fields behind White Grass, they would have stumbled across the site of the former oil processing factory, Golden Fountain (Fontane d'Oro), behind tall palm trees. Newly arrived workers would be oblivious to the site's history over the past decade. The site had been used as a camp for seasonal workers, known as Ciao Ousmane, for three harvest seasons between 2014 and 2016. On the left stood a two-storey building, with the words 'Ciao Ousmane' on the light green painted wall. The building had been turned into a SPRAR[1] for adult asylum seekers in September 2017, accommodating up to fifteen asylum seekers mostly from French-speaking African countries such as Senegal, Mali and Guinea.

Many of them had been transferred to Campobello recently, and their stay would officially be six months. When the olive harvest began in 2018, there were ten boys in the SPRAR. They had all been working in the olive fields during the harvest, and despite the official insistence that 'the SPRAR residents are different from the harvest workers,' the boys were part of the reliable army of labour for the farmers here. Floriana, a cultural mediator who joined the SPRAR in 2017, believed that the boys' choice of farm work was a result of no alternative employment, 'because in other types of work, Italians are preferred by employers.'

The SPRAR building and the car park in front of it were separated from the other half of the site by a wire fence, with people's washing drying along it. Across the fence were four large white tents set up by the Italian Red Cross, who were there to provide temporary accommodation for the harvest workers. In early October, each of these tents was occupied by twenty people, making eighty beds in total. These Red Cross tents were not an option for the majority of migrant workers, because they required a residence permit to enter and were charging new arrivals a fee of €2 per day. The theory was that, while the Italian Red Cross managed the tents and took care of the registration of arrivals, the Campobello local council would guarantee the maintenance of the toilets, site cleaning and electricity. But the toilets were in a terrible condition and there was only cold water.

The olive harvest season of 2018 'had opened with an official agreement between all the institutional actors, legitimised by the silent consent of many associations.'[2] According to an insider familiar with how the agreement was reached, the silence of the associations was the result of conflicting interests amongst them and their inability to stand together in order to insist on adequate living conditions for seasonal workers. 'The breakdown of the networks and the failure of these associations symbolises failure in civil society,' the source said. As a result of the new 'consensus' of the institutions, while the White Grass encampment had been demolished and any further informal settlements across Campobello criminalised, there were to be three living spaces allowed for the seasonal workers in the harvest: the Red Cross tents; the site of the former cement company Calcestruzzi S.P.A.; and a large settlement of eighty to a hundred tents built on land owned by an olive farmer. The conditions in these living spaces were never the concern of the authorities. 'The result of about five years of emergency interventions is, therefore, a multiplication of the settlements, each of whose inhabitants is differentiated on the basis of regularity/irregularity (of the residence permit) and the employment contract,' Martina Lo Cascio and Valeria Piro pointed out.[3]

* * *

Outside the fence behind the compound used by the Red Cross, four middle-aged Tunisian men were standing around, grilling fish over a tiny fire. They looked worn out and dispirited. They had flown to Palermo from Tunisia, on a €100 one-way ticket, to work on farms in Italy. They got themselves to Campobello for the harvest, although they had no contacts here. Only two weeks into their stay, the four were talking about returning home.

Upon their arrival, they stumbled across the Red Cross tents; they found the fee frustrating but decided to pay and stay because there was no alternative. They found some work with a farmer who paid them by piecework, an average of €20 for each ten-hour workday. Bechir, the most outspoken of the four, was almost brought to tears when thinking about their subjugation. 'Twenty euros? Was that my worth?' The plane ticket to come to Sicily was equivalent to five days of his wages here in Campobello. With all this happening, what frustrated and angered Bechir the most was racism, as he told friends and family. 'They are very racist,' he said, every time he explained the wage levels and the way farmers operated.

Young Hassan from Chad was another temporary lodger at the Red Cross site. On most days, he wore a dilapidated black anorak with a split seam down one arm. He was one of the few who did not own a mobile phone here but carried a SIM card in his wallet; whenever he needed to call his family, he borrowed a phone from someone else. Hassan had travelled all the way here from Lecce in Puglia where he had been working on farms. He was unhappy paying for the overcrowded accommodation provided by the Red Cross—the number of beds in his tent had risen to twenty-eight in the past few days.

As Hassan was new here, he knew no farmers and therefore had to go to wait for work at 5:00 am every morning, on the street corner off Via Roma, just outside Bar Centrale. It was the usual hangout place for many unemployed local men and pensioners. Now with the harvest season, dozens of Tunisian men could also be seen standing around here every day, waiting for work. Farmers would come and select their workers for the day. Hassan would wait until 9:00 am, and if no farmer wanted him, he would have to walk back to the Red Cross camp site or just stroll around the country lanes purposelessly for the rest of the day. He watched people walk by—like the African men who were walking back to their camp site with plastic Lidl shopping bags.

As most people couldn't afford the Red Cross fees and had no documents, they had to look for temporary accommodation on their own. A large group of 200 Senegalese men were employed en masse by a farmer who owned many plots of land in the area. He housed them in a disused automobile show room, with no facilities, 400 metres away from the Golden Fountain site. It was a gated plot with an empty garage at the back. These 200 people were able to avoid public attention here, shielded from the outside world. Those who knew this place called it 'the Senegalese camp.'

There were also Nigerian workers who had arrived in Campobello for the first time and had to search for their temporary housing alone. Frank, a Nigerian man in his late thirties, had travelled with a friend from Trapani where they were sharing a room after his departure from an asylum shelter known as 'Telefama' in Salemi. They looked around the area and decided to take a detour at the junction near the train station. They followed the road and saw the deserted petrol station with faded blue paint where Sanji used to live and had been thrown out by the police a couple of months earlier. Frank peered in and saw that it was a filthy space piled with rubbish. But just like Sanji before them, they learned how to overcome these difficulties—they found a factory water pipe nearby, from where they could fetch water, and relied on a friend in the Ciao Ousmane shelter to recharge their mobile phones for them. It was not a safe place for the two of them to be on their own, with the possibility of random violent attacks. But Frank was more worried about the police officers on patrol. He had to keep his torch switched off in this place during the night.

Frank had received his humanitarian protection residence permit a long time ago, which now enabled him to obtain what he called 'a sort of a contract,' one that came from a work registration service. Employers were said to be hiring migrant workers 'via a public register without illicit intermediation and following contractual rules,' meaning, indeed, that workers' union FLAI-CGIL could claim that 'public placement in agriculture [as a tool] against illegality in the province of Trapani has worked.' The 'contract' given to Frank, contrary to the union's optimism, was not in fact signed by any party, but this was how he was employed at Bono & Ditta (S.P.A.). Four other African workers were on the same 'contract' as him, employed at the same factory. Their duty was water pressure washing olives for a fixed rate of €30 for a seven-hour day (plus a one-hour unpaid lunch break), from early November to the last day of December.

His contract stipulated the dates of the work, but there was no mention of the pay rate. He was actually paid €3 per hour; €20 for five hours' overtime. Throughout each step of production, Africans were paid the 'Third World rate'. Frank did overtime twice in the entire two months, and couldn't cope with more—seven hours of standing was quite enough. As time went on, he was looking forward to his work ending in Campobello, after which he would travel to Salemi to work on the orange farms. There at least he would no longer need to sleep rough: a woman called Nina who ran the Telefama shelter, with whom he got along well, would let him sleep there until the orange harvest ended. These days, as Sicilian ports had closed to rescue ships, Nina's shelter wasn't receiving sufficient numbers of people. It was a matter of time before it would close down. As long as it lasted, there was plenty of room and Frank's request for a sleeping space was sure to not be turned down.

* * *

Since early September, many workers who arrived in Campobello had had to walk a further two kilometres from White Grass to look for a place to stay. One of the first disused farmhouses that came into view on the border with Castelvetrano was the one where Benjamin and his group were living. With their luggage in hand, new arrivals poked their heads into Benjamin's compound and asked for shelter. Benjamin and his fellow residents had to tell them that the place was full and that the police could be returning to evict them anytime soon. And so, people walked on and found shelter in other deserted farmhouses and barns further along the road.

In a large, empty compound right behind Benjamin's farmhouse, several Tunisian men found shelter and started setting up tents inside. By November, there were eighty to a hundred people from North Africa living there. The walls around the compound were high, providing a natural shield from the outside world.

This 'Tunisian camp' was as well-maintained as could be. Near the entrance, a row of shower cubicles with plastic curtains were built right next to a huge metal container with hot steaming water. Benjamin came here every few days to buy a bucket of hot water for a shower. One euro per bucket; there was nothing more precious when you had been working hard for days. To the right of the shower area was a large charcoal grill where cubes of lamb meat were being cooked and sold. Then, behind the grill was a makeshift café shop with a line of soft drinks on the counter area where you could buy bottles of Fanta from Tunisia. You could also get a sip of espresso at any time of the day. The Tunisians also sold lamb stew with couscous here. Right outside the shop was the area where sheep were butchered.

Most men came here as part of a group, except one man, named Mustafa, who was the only person from Morocco. In his forties, Mustafa had been everywhere—he had worked on farms in Turkey and Greece before coming to Italy. He had originally come to join his father in Bari, in Puglia, but sadly his father had died, and Mustafa had since travelled from place to place in the country, doing farm work to support himself. Twenty years had passed since he arrived in Italy, but his work conditions and wage levels had never changed. He was so disillusioned and had little good to say about Italy. 'They are very racist people; it's a bad country,' would be his introduction to a newcomer. One of the worst things in this line of work, he said, fuming with anger, were the *caporali*.

'The Italians [farmers] sit and watch us being cheated by these *capo*, and they keep on making the profits!' The younger Tunisian men nodded, agreeing with Mustafa. Several had travelled from Rosarno where *caporali* were rampant. As their next destination was the winter orange harvest back in the Rosarno area, there would be no escape from them.

A few steps further from the Tunisian camp, sub-Saharan African workers started to congregate in the gated site of a disused cement factory that had belonged to Calcestruzzi S.P.A. This campsite in the shadow of the huge cement processing pipes and machinery was even larger than the one in White Grass. Once the first group of young Gambian, Senegalese and Malian men started to set up their tents, more people came and joined them. Several of Benjamin's Senegalese friends in their farmhouse had moved here, too, after the police visit and their eviction threat. The new encampment grew, in no time. In early October, well before the official olive harvest commencement date (15 October), the numbers at the cement factory site had swollen to more than 300.

An official notice addressed to residents in all the disused farmhouses had been pinned on a wooden electricity pole a few yards from Benjamin's door. One of the paragraphs said: 'It is mandatory for all non-EU workers who intend to go into our municipality and work here in agriculture to obtain suitable accommodation.' As if there was 'suitable accommodation' around.

As the cement factory camp site happened to fall just in the territory of Castelvetrano, rather than Campobello, any measures concerning the camp would be the responsibility of the police authorities in Castelvetrano. And soon enough, the Castelvetrano police came to visit the site and asked people to leave. This happened while the local council of Campobello was 'allowing' the site to be used during harvest because the town needed the workers. The workers treated the police activity as their habitual cat-and-mouse harassment, and simply ignored it. They walked out of the front gate when asked, in front of the police, and then, when the officers left, went back into the site through the rear.

At the height of the harvest season, the number of workers reached 2,000 in Campobello and surrounding areas, all of them without adequate housing and kept out of sight. Apart from the Red Cross, none of the NGOs and groups previously involved during the harvest at Golden Fountain were around this year. And they weren't talking, either. The silence was peculiar at first, but soon became revealing.

It revealed the complacency upon which the 'consensus' was built. In the name of legality and the law, the prohibition of informal settlements was served as an order from the mayor Giuseppe Castiglion. Making them formally illegal was in line with the new government's management of migration, leading to an even deeper invisibility of migrant workers and to their increasing criminalisation.

* * *

The practice of 'out of sight, out of mind' had been the norm for years—yet now it was being trumpeted as some kind of 'new normal'. The plan was to scatter the migrant worker population as widely as possible and prevent it from congregating in one place. In Campobello workers were ordered to stay with the farmers for whom they were working. 'Stay in their backyards,' mimicked some workers when they heard about the order. In reality, what this meant was that many workers were placed in derelict farmhouses and outbuildings by farmers, without basic facilities like electricity and water. Some of these places did not even have roofs. Yet many farmers were charging their workers a fee for the space.

Under this 'new normal,' the 'problem' of the migrant worker population as perceived by the local community would seem to have gone away. The White Grass encampment on the edge the town was no more. 'They' weren't living near 'us' anymore. They were now more than a kilometre away—and with this distance, not many townsfolk even claimed to know their whereabouts. 'Out of sight, out of mind,' indeed.

Some migrant workers found work with particular farmers who preferred to hire a team and would employ them on a regular basis throughout the harvest, to have a regular supply of labour for the season. Mohammad, one of the most experienced workers around, was in such a position. He had been living in Triscina in the garage of a farmer for over six months, and as early autumn began, he received an offer from his main employer, an eighty-year-old Campobello farmer who knew him well. This elderly farmer owned a large area of olive fields and needed the best, regular workers upon whom he could depend for the entire harvest. He offered Mohammad daily work throughout the season, from mid-September to early December, as well as living space in the garage of his sisters' house in Campobello town. The boss himself lived two streets away. Considering the convenience of living in the town and working in an adjacent area, the offer was too good for Mohammad to turn down. He moved to Campobello straight away.

The sisters of his employer lived a street away from Mohammad's former shelter on Via Roma, the place that had suffered two terrible fires that drove away most of its residents, including Mohammad himself. His return to Campobello brought back memories of his early days in Sicily—the time when he was still struggling with the language and knew no more than a couple of people in town. To return and live there was as if he had achieved a small victory. The shops, the coffee bars, the supermarkets, all within reach. The farmer's sisters, Elena in her late sixties and Josie in her late seventies, welcomed him at the door of their two-floor house. Elena pulled up the shutter and showed him into the garage. It was a large area of about twenty square metres, full of farming tools, long ladders and old household equipment. Sometimes a couple of small tractors were parked in there, too, leaving little space to walk. With a dim white light against the concrete floor, the space was more like a factory floor. Mohammad didn't mind. He was used to moving from garage to garage. He made use of the middle part of the space as a makeshift kitchen. There was no furniture except a plastic garden chair. He made himself a suitably comfortable bed space in a raised loft area up a ladder. The two landladies lived on the other side of the building and rarely needed to come into the garage, thus allowing him enough privacy.

Although only a garage, Mohammad's situation was unique in Campobello: you just did not see an African living in town, let alone living in the same building as white Italians. He knew how rare his landladies' hospitality was, and often expressed his gratitude by talking with them and asking them how they were. He sometimes walked past Elena's window and would always stop to greet her. Elena would hold Mohammad's hand in hers and say to him, 'God created men and we're all equal.' She was a devoted Catholic and didn't like the way the townsfolk in Campobello treated the Africans. She would tell everyone who came by that Mohammad 'is a very good boy.'

In the long term, Mohammad wanted to live in a place like everyone else in town. He had had enough of making do with a garage. He started checking out rented places in town. He discussed it with one of the farmers that he knew, who happened to know about an empty apartment on Via Garibaldi. Mohammad was thrilled and went to view the place immediately. It was a first-floor apartment with a balcony. He would have a street view from here! He stood there, looking down on the street below, taking several deep breaths. Campobello town was alive and there, all within this view. Perhaps this would be the start of a new chapter of his life. He would become the first African to live in an apartment in Campobello. Unbeknown to Mohammad, this apartment was just a hundred metres away from the office of Five Star, whose politicians did not welcome the idea of Africans living in their midst.

Mohammad wanted to move in straight away. The monthly rent would be €300, still a large amount for him to pay. But it was a price worth paying. His solution was to find four friends to share the place with him, to manage the costs. He had been on his own for too long and felt he needed company. He was convinced that flat-sharing would work. He just had to wait a short while for the apartment to be ready.

Mohammad had always been helpful to his fellow Africans even though he had always lived apart from them. During his stay in the garage, four of his Gambian friends living in the tents at the cement factory site would give him their mobile phones for him to recharge. At that time, no one at the site had started a mobile-charging service on their generators. When the phones were charged, Mohammad would cycle a mile to their camp to return them to his friends. He did this every single day after work. He didn't see his daily visit as helping people, but rather spending social time with friends. They chatted about life and work in Sicily, and often asked Mohammad to help them find work as they were new to the farming community here. He would bring his four friends to the fields every time his employer, the farmer, said he needed extra workers.

When the sun had set, the camp was partly lit by lights attached to the small generators some people were using. There was smoke from stoves set up for cooking. You could smell stews from outside the entrance. Sometimes Mohammad's friends invited him to stay for dinner, which was a simple Gambian stew cooked on a basic stove next to their tents.

On the way back from the encampment, the country lanes were dark without any lights. Mohammad would cycle slowly and shine the torch on his mobile phone, so that vehicles along the lanes would see him. After 8:00 pm, the wineries on the route back were still operating, with the plant machinery making loud noises. It never seemed to get truly quiet at night here.

* * *

Many farmers were saying that the 2018 harvest had been worse than the last. The quality of olives seemed inferior, as olive trees had been affected by erratic rainfall, early spring frosts, strong winds, and summer droughts. The impact of climate change[4] resulted in both the

2018 and 2019 harvests being the worst in over two decades. Workers were toiling just as hard as ever. Except for rainy days, Mohammad had been working every day of the week, without any day off, since early October.

His employer sent him along with a team of workers to one of his farms five kilometres outside Campobello. On a normal workday, Mohammad would get up at 6:00 am, with the cocks crowing and dogs barking loudly in the neighbourhood. He got dressed, and tried to make no sound so as not to disturb his landladies when he walked out of the garage. The day had not yet broken, but the main street, Via Garibaldi, was filled with seasonal workers waiting outside shops and cafés for their pick-up transport to the fields. Many were smoking on the pavement. Mohammad walked up to the main café there, to have a quick, stand-up espresso. He was well and truly Italian in this respect. After that, he would pick up a baguette from the bakery, warm and fresh.

Mohammad then walked over to the entrance of his employer's compound, to wait for his pickup. The team of workers were already standing there, looking like they had only just woken up. They handed their documents to the farmer's daughter-in-law. She then put each worker's documents in a separate plastic wallet and kept them until they returned from work at the end of the day. The team for this particular job consisted of two Tunisian men, one Romanian, Mohammad, and two other young Gambian men. Some of the Tunisian men working for this employer had been brought in by a Tunisian *capo* who had lived in Italy for three decades and had been recruiting his countrymen for the farmers here. Mohammad's employer also had his family members help out in the fields when they were able. The farmer's grandson Alessandro was the supervisor and Alessandro's nephew came along to drive workers to the farm.

Half an hour passed until all documents had been checked and the two vans were loaded and ready to go. Then down the country lanes they went, setting out for the day's work. The sun had just risen.

Mohammad sat at the back door of the van, holding onto the door, keeping it ajar to let in the fresh air and light. The sunshine of the dawn shone through, he looked out the van, seeing the bumpy lane and town disappear behind them. He still had not had enough sleep, his eyes were swollen. Five minutes later, the lanes got even bumpier, and people held on tight in the back of the van. It was a twenty-minute ride.

When they arrived at the vast fields, stretching out for miles and miles in all directions, the vans parked on the side of the road and everyone got out. The air was fresh and a little moist at dawn. They hung their lunch bags on a tree, and chose their line of olive trees, put their plastic harvesting boxes around their necks and started working. Mohammad looked ahead at the boundless fields in front of him, knowing that it would take the team several weeks to finish harvesting. And then after that, they would be sent somewhere else by the same employer, to another piece of his land.

Mohammad crossed the webbing straps on the harvesting box and placed them around his neck, so the plastic box was hung high in front of his chest. This was to ensure that the picked olives fell straight into the box. Three fully loaded harvesting boxes amounted to one crate. Soon enough, the plastic box was pushing down on Mohammad's chest, filled with olives. The boxes resembled square washing-up bowls used in households and weren't designed for harvest work, although they were commonly used in the fields. Mohammad had got used to it— and to having red strap marks on his neck by the end of the workday.

The large green olives looked fresh and plump, ready to be picked. Mohammad started with olives at the lowest level—those hanging down from the trees on the outside. It took him no time to pick those. He simply ran through the long, pointed oval leaves on the branches with both hands and the olives fell into the box. The movement was gentle but fast; there were no sharp stems or branches to slow you down. The olives simply tumbled into the box on his chest, with a satisfying thumping sound.

Sometimes you might frustratingly miss catching a few olives and they fell on the ground. Mohammad would always try to pick them all up after he had worked on a tree. Other workers often left the fallen ones behind—the work was strenuous enough without hurting your back by bending down.

In the first hour, the farmer's grandson Alessandro prepared and passed around cups of espresso to everyone who needed them. 'Fuel,' he said, 'fuel.' He was better at supervising and overseeing the team than harvesting olives—when Mohammad had famously picked twenty-six crates of olives the other day, Alessandro only managed ten. Even he would admit and joke about how his work rate was far inferior to Mohammad's. Alessandro's grandfather, the farmer, who was always on site to make sure things ran smoothly, slowly steering a tractor up and down the lane, came by to have a sip of morning espresso.

By this point, after working on layers of olives, Mohammad had reached the top of the tree on a wooden ladder. He had learned how to stand stably at the very top of the ladder—something that was not always easy for a new worker. He looked out over the field from the top and could see other members of the team doing the same, with their heads poking out at the top of the thick olive trees.

The team worked one tree to the next in a straight line, each looking after their line for the day. The quantity and quality of the trees always varied—sometimes you got a good tree weighed heavily with olives and then further down the line you got a much less healthy one with far fewer olives. Many of the trees had been there for four or five decades, mixed in with the more recently planted ones in the same row. Mohammad got frustrated with the less healthy trees, as it obviously meant less olives and less earnings for him. He was, however, always working his hardest and was, without fail, faster than others. He was six trees down the line within a couple of hours. Crates of olives were stacked up by the path in between rows of trees.

The temperature had risen by five degrees to 27°C by ten o'clock. Some workers stopped to have a sip of water from bottles which they brought with them. Mohammad had worked non-stop so far, not even taking a sip of water. He did not even have time for a toilet break—not that there were any toilets around. He looked up the path between the rows of olive trees and quickly counted up the amount of work he had done so far. Eleven crates of olives. Not bad, he thought. Then he went up the ladder and continued.

Alessandro was in charge of quality control. When workers loaded their boxes of olives into the crates laid on the ground, he would come and separate them into two types of crates: the green olives and everything else. Large green olives were for food use (you soaked in water and salt for three months) and small green for the production of oil; black and other non-green olives would be for food use only (pickled in salt for two months). When people brought over a box filled with a big mixture of olives, Alessandro sighed and murmured '*Mamma mia!*' to himself. Sorting them had to be done meticulously and he preferred it when workers sorted the olives themselves while loading them into the crates, to save his time. But of course, as the pay was by piecework, workers were only too keen to get on with picking as many olives as possible so that they could get paid more.

At midday, people were getting hungry and food was talked about even before they stopped to lunch. '*Mangiare'*, *mangiare*': the word was shouted out by the Romanian and Tunisian workers. Then the Romanian and Tunisian men sat down first by the trees to have their lunch. Mohammad came down from the ladder, turned over an empty crate and sat on it, in the shade of a tree. He took out a tin of tuna from his bag, opened it and tipped it out on a plate which he had brought in his work bag, and had it with the baguette he had bought earlier. He was the only one who used a plate here. He always ate alone, to get some peace and quiet and a little break. He didn't spend all his one-hour unpaid lunch break eating and taking a rest. As it was pay by piecework, the longer you rested, the less you earned. Time was precious. After finishing his tuna and bread in ten minutes, he put away the plate, smoked a roll-up, and went back to work.

The afternoon sun did not get less fierce. Mohammad paused to have a sip of water a couple of times, and worked through without a break. Alessandro's father, also in charge of supervision, came and helped with sorting the crops and counting up the crates, which created pressure for people to speed up. Mohammad was still way ahead of everyone else in the team. He looked back and saw the Romanian worker up on the ladder, four or five trees behind in the row next to his. Their earnings would not be more than €40 for the day if they did not speed up right away.

At 4:00 pm, Alessandro came over and counted up the crates and the amount of work Mohammad had done for the day. Twenty-three crates of olives in total, which earned him €69 (€3 per crate). In the presence of his employer and the family, Mohammad was content with the earnings. He said it was the best he could do, given that the trees in his row were not all good today. He knew that, on the days when he was feeling tired, he would earn around €60 a day. On his perfect days when trees were good and he was in the best physical condition, he would be able to earn just under €80 a day.

However, deep down, Mohammad knew he was being badly exploited. Workers did not need to look far to know that. When the harvest came, buyers from Naples and elsewhere came to purchase large quantities of olives directly from farmers in the Campobello area. They came to Mohammad's employer and would pay €1.50 for each kilogram of large green olives. Each crate contained twenty-five kilograms of olives, which made it €37.50 worth. When Mohammad picked twenty-five crates of olives and earned only €75, his employer would make €937.50. That is, his wage only constituted 8% of his employer's earnings from his day's hard labour. He was well aware that farmers were making huge profits across the region. He saw them living a comfortable life during the off-season—their profits in the harvest months were sufficient to keep them and their families going for the whole year. Then he looked at his own family back in Gambia, his mother and siblings who were waiting for his support each month—the support that would keep him working and working, underpaid, even with the knowledge of how he was being exploited.

Having stacked up all the olives harvested by the workers, Alessandro was grinning at the total: 110 crates today. So was his grandfather. This was considered a good day. The farmer drove his tractor around each pathway next to the trees; Mohammad and other workers helped with carrying and loading the crates onto the tractor. When all was done, the farmer happily drove off with a full trailer behind his tractor. Job done for Mohammad and the team. It was now 4:15 pm. The workers had worked for nine hours, and with the time spent travelling and loading, it amounted to ten hours in all. Sixty-nine euros for a ten-hour working day. This clearly wasn't the European rate.

Still, the breeze from the crack of the door at the back of the van felt good on Mohammad's face on the ride back into town. He was exhausted, and was looking forward to cooking his dinner and having a rest when he got in. When the vans arrived back at the farmer's compound and pick-up point, the workers got out and queued to collect their daily pay, in cash. In Campobello, from this hour to dusk, tractors criss-crossed town, loaded with the day's crops.

14

OUT OF SIGHT, OUT OF MIND

Since early October, Benjamin and his group of seven had been working several days a week on the outskirts of Campobello. This soon increased to every day of the week. The team also grew to twenty people. As Benjamin was still relatively new to olive picking, he was much slower than Alieu who had been doing it for two years. As a result, Benjamin earned €20 for an eight-hour day while Alieu made €60.

Members of the team looked after one another. On a particularly difficult day when they were picking black olives, the variation in the condition of the olive groves was huge and some trees had far fewer olives on them. The team decided to share the earnings equally among them at the end of the day, to avoid inequality caused by the arbitrary choice of the row of trees on which they worked. They kept to this principle of sharing and collective earning, which they believed was in everyone's interest.

Back in their compound, friends visited on a daily basis. The police had not returned since the harvest officially began. Benjamin and Alieu tried to make their living space as habitable as possible by further tidying the front yard. Even the shopping trolleys and plastic water containers were now all put away. Alieu brought back a plastic house plant one day and placed it next to the sofa that they had picked up from a dump. It made the concrete space look a little more like a living area and made visitors smile. The general hygiene of the place, however, could not be improved much without basic facilities. There were still rats around—they had chewed holes in a pink T-shirt that Benjamin had found in a nearby dump. He often wore it with a pair of distressed jeans (also found at the dump) with fashionable holes in them, which were not the result of rodent activity.

* * *

The cement factory site continued to draw in African workers throughout mid-October. Masses of small tents had been put up, each one butting up to the next. The number of people rose to above 500. Makeshift stores and services were set up in wooden shacks by workers who'd been in the area for a longer time, ready to cater for the growing community. They sold soft drinks, tomato ketchup and tinned foods, such as soup and stew. A general store named itself 'Palermo Shop' and there were even a couple of taxi services; one of them had the sign 'Palermo Taxi' outside.

At dusk, several people loaded food products from a minibus into the camp shops. It had Romanian number plates. In its previous life it had carried Romanian workers all the way from home to Italy, and then continued to transport them to and from work on various farms. Now it had been sold on to several Africans here. Later on, a people carrier with Bulgarian number plates also appeared outside.

A third of the workers at this site had been living in the area between three and six years. Others came from all over the country, as far away as Foggia. Old timers like Alsane, from Senegal, had come to Campobello almost every year since 2013, and thought that the living and working conditions were inferior in the Puglia region where he worked much of the year. But Alsane was trapped having to return to Foggia because the official processing of his residence permit tied him there.

There were many Senegalese workers staying at the site. Young Bill was one of them. He had travelled all the way from Florence to join the harvest for the first time. He had been a soldier, then a security guard back in Senegal. Following the dangerous sea route, he was rescued and sent to Sardinia. To his dismay, conditions inside the asylum reception camps were appalling and the island presented few positive prospects for him and his family. So he went all the way to Milan, spending months sleeping rough in the central station area. Subsequently he moved on to Florence to join a friend. He felt fortunate enough to be able to start a new life in this beautiful metropolis.

Many Senegalese were still leaving home to seek a better livelihood and Bill believed their number was steadily growing. On average, fifty-five people emigrated from Senegal every day, according to the UN. The Senegalese in Italy, the established community as well as the new arrivals totalled 111,380 in 2019, with three times as many men as women.[1] Making a livelihood in Italy was very hard, as Bill himself found out. Along with five fellow Senegalese, he was able to pay for his rent in an apartment on the outskirts of Florence by setting up a street stall selling shoes that he bought from Chinese merchants. He also purchased fake brand labels from them, be it Saucony or Nike, and stitched the labels onto the shoes and sold them in the streets. Working life on the streets was tough and you met people of all sorts, but it never intimidated him. The only fear he had was of the police.

In the three months Bill had been in Campobello, he got to know people of all origins, be they from Senegal, Mali or Gambia. He would walk around the cement factory camp in his flip-flops and stripy socks, and confidently chat to anyone from anywhere. Social butterfly that he was, he also worked really hard. He waited for work outside the camp gate at 5:00 am, and as a new harvest worker, he earned €25–€45 per day.

Inside the cement factory site, many new people had also come from other parts of Sicily. Fallou, in his twenties, arrived from Marsala with a friend in early October. Like many Gambians here, this was his first time in Campobello. He came from a farming background back home in Gambia where his parents were tenant farmers growing rice and maize. Their earnings were small and Fallou took on the mission of helping to provide for his family.

He had lived in what he called 'the famous hotel' in Marsala, i.e., the Acos camp, for two years. After he received his documents in 2016, he moved out of the shelter and, via someone who knew a landlord, found a cheap room in town which he shared with his friends. To afford the place, he looked hard for any work available in town, and through a Gambian friend was introduced to a local builder. The man needed to hire labourers to help him on site, and offered to pay Fallou a low hourly rate of €2.50–€3 to work as a casual labourer. During the good times, Fallou was given around twenty hours a week painting walls, but most of the time he was only given a few hours' work each time, hardly enough to pay the rent.

Fallou was someone who believed that if you tried hard enough, you would get through difficulties. But as time went on he saw there were truly very limited work options around for people like him. Italian shops and stores were uninterested in hiring him; he began to think about asking for work in the Chinese wholesale shops he walked past every day. In Marsala, he knew that the Chinese businesses sometimes employed African boys to do loading work. But the money was as low as that for a casual construction labourer and the hours were so flexible that you could not depend on them to make a living.

Fallou needed extra income to keep his room in Marsala. So he spent the entire spring picking tomatoes in greenhouses and the entire summer harvesting grapes in the nearby vineyards. When the grape-picking season ended, he got on the train with his friend to travel to Campobello for the olive harvest.

Here, nestled behind a concrete wall in the cement factory site, Fallou and his friend set up their little tent. There was hardly any room to walk between the rows of tents. Fallou found it a difficult place to rest after a strenuous day at work. When the weather was bad and it rained during the night, he and his friend were kept awake as their tent flooded. They had to spend the following day trying to dry their clothes. As a solution, Fallou followed the other residents and collected wooden pallets from a nearby factory and placed them under the tent, which lifted it up a few inches from the ground. Someone had picked up a blue plastic liner from an outdoor pool from a dump and used it as a rain cover for their tent. The manufacturer's label in English, 'garden pool', was visible on the roof.

In mid-October, despite having documents, Fallou had not yet managed to obtain a work contract from the farmer for whom he was working. He was paid the piecework rate of €3–€3.50 per crate of olives, the rate varying between farmers. Fallou worked as fast as he could and was earning €35–€40 for an eight-hour day. For this effort, he also developed back ache, terrible neck pain, and sore arms.

The transport of water was a strenuous daily task for everyone here. Several people who had been in the area longer than others developed a way to supply water for people to take showers: they made an arrangement with a nearby factory to fill several containers of water per day, which they then heated over a fire, and charged €1 per person to anyone for a hot shower. As for the lack of electricity on site, a couple of people spent around €100 on a portable generator, charging 50 cents to recharge mobile phones or other electrical appliances. Since then, Mohammad's friends no longer depended on him to help them charge their phones a mile away.

People were finding ways to sustain their temporary community for the season as institutions and associations looked away and did nothing at all. As time went on, when the police did not return, it was clear to everyone that the local authorities had 'allowed' the existence of the camp—for as long as the harvest lasted. At the same time, the authorities had literally 'allowed' the camp's residents to be abandoned. The residents of the makeshift camp were, once again, left to look after themselves without any basic infrastructure.

In the early evening, Fallou and his friend burned some coals in their little metal stove next to their tent, cooking dinner for themselves. He did not want to spend €25 to buy a gas canister, which wasn't always safe to store. Following some chicken stew with rice, Fallou and his friend tried to get some sleep early, so that they could wake up in time for the farmer's pick-up outside the gate at 6:30 am. It continued to rain overnight. The morning after rain was always difficult, as the ground was muddy. Many still went out to work, despite wearing damp clothes.

Then it rained every single day during the last week of October. Fallou's work was cancelled all week. Due to the weather and lower quantities of olives, the harvest was set to end much earlier than normal, towards the end of November.

Tommaso di Maria, the Five Star councillor, still resented the continued presence of migrant workers in the area and tried to mobilise support for a motion to the mayor, via social media, demanding on social media that the authorities be equipped with drones to 'patrol the territory,' to 'allow the surveillance of sites in which the outsiders are staying.' The hashtags of his motion included #the League. Among those supporting the motion were members and supporters of Five Star and the League.

* * *

Mohammad had been ill. It was the official start date of the olive harvest, 15 October, and for the first time in six years, he had to ask for a day off. He had back pain and a bad headache, due to weeks of strenuous work without a break. He had picked twenty-four to twenty-six crates each day before the official start date of the harvest, until yesterday, when he was so unwell that he only managed sixteen crates. This morning, he had to pick up the phone and tell his employer, the farmer, that he just couldn't make it today. Physically and mentally, he had reached his limit. The gears in the machine were jammed and could no longer move.

Mohammad had been the most loyal worker, whoever he worked for. He had never demanded a day off, never asked for better terms and conditions, because he simply wanted to keep working and earning for his family. However, his loyalty as an employee had never been rewarded. His wage level had never risen in six years. Everyone was made to accept that wages simply did not rise in Europe. Mohammad was also aware that, despite receiving his humanitarian protection documents years ago and always carrying his ID, the contract that the farmer had given him for the current job was a fake one. It said that Mohammad was paid a fixed wage of €60 per day, which was a lie. Instead, piecework pay had always been the norm at least during the harvest. And as everyone's wages were always paid in cash, there was no record of the amount, except in falsified paperwork that the farmer produced for tax purposes. The contract clearly only benefited the employer; workers simply had to consent to it, to keep working.

Most other African workers were in much worse situations. Many, like Benjamin, could not obtain residence permits as they remained in limbo awaiting asylum decisions or renewal of their documents. As the offer of a work contract required a residence permit, many Africans and other migrant workers simply had to work for a farmer without one. Some local residents and farmers then exploited the situation further: they would ask for a payment of between €250 and €300, sometimes more, from a migrant worker, for the use of a residential address, such as a farmhouse, in which the worker did not actually live. The address would enable the worker to qualify for a residence permit, which would lead to a work contract. Almost every African knew of such arrangements offered by farmers or local residents of Campobello. Benjamin, like many of his co-workers, could not take this up because he had no cash. But people talked about it as if this was a normal business practice. The system seemed to maintain itself in an exploitative circle: migrant workers were asked to buy residence permits from farmers, who would then give them work contracts which were fake. It was a racket.

That lunchtime, on his sick day, Mohammad put on his white shirt and his light brown jacket, looking like an office worker, and walked to the pharmacy a few streets away, to get something for his cold and headache. That was the first time he had ever gone into a pharmacy in Italy.

The rain continued. It was the one thing that both farmers and workers were worried about. Mohammad's employer felt he couldn't continue to cancel work because of the rain and lose any more time. On many days in late October when it started raining, he would ask his team whether they would like to return home or carry on working. 'You decide what you want to do,' he said to them. When your boss asked you to choose to work or otherwise, he was most likely telling you that you had better choose to work. And so that was what the team decided. During those late October days, Mohammad and the team stood picking olives in the rain, without a word. Sometimes the rain stopped for half an hour and then started again. Mohammad was soaked. The harvesting box was heavier with water in it. But the workers all carried on, at least till 4:00 pm.

Mohammad had been looking forward to moving into the apartment on Via Garibaldi. But the farmer who introduced him to the landlord suddenly broke the news that the rent had been raised from the amount agreed. This change of heart was almost certainly due to the landlord's concern about neighbours' reactions to Africans living in the apartment next door. This seemed highly unprofessional, but Mohammad knew he would never get a direct answer as to why. He just had to wait patiently for another place—if it was ever going to be possible for a local person to consider renting him an apartment in town. As the weeks went by, he began feeling less hopeful. Was he condemned to living in a garage for as long as he worked here? Even as the 'model worker,' Mohammad knew that most Italians looked at him as a black man who did not deserve equality. 'For them, Italy is for Italians only,' he told his Gambian friends.

* * *

Sanji had stayed out of sight for a while and few knew of his whereabouts in Campobello. The only people who remained in regular contact with him were the seventeen-year-olds in the minors' shelter, Futuro. As it turned out, Sanji had already moved out of the disused farmhouse after further threats of violence when his rent payment was delayed. He certainly did not need any more harm done to him—he had just recovered from the wound on his left forearm from the attack by local youths. The scar had healed after months of wearing a pressure bandage. All that was left was a three inch crescent of scar tissue that looked like a strange birthmark.

Sanji got out and searched for a new place, and one of his Gambian friends, Sam, said he could come and stay with him. Sam had been through thick and thin with Sanji—they had been in the same camp on Via Roma years ago and shared the terror of the fires there. Since then, Sam had left Italy for Mannheim in Germany and got himself work on a construction site, earning €10 an hour. He had only returned to Italy to collect his long-overdue documents. During his waiting time, he came to Campobello to find farm work to support himself. This was how he ended up earning €25–€45 a day with no contract during the harvest. With or without documents, Sam believed that farmers preferred not to give contracts.

Fellow Gambians in Benjamin's farmhouse had given Sam a temporary bed space, but the police raids had concerned him so much that he wanted to leave. By pure chance, a farmer for whom Sam worked said he could use a six-square-metre deserted storage shed, a hundred metres away in the fields opposite Benjamin's compound. Sam moved in and brought with him three other Gambian boys who were looking for accommodation. Bed space was literally all that they had inside. Once Sam saw that Sanji was homeless, he offered him a bed in this place, too.

Sanji's portable gas cooker had been lost several moves ago, so now he had to rely on a wood fire that they set up outside for cooking in the evening. The fire created a lot of smoke, and his eyes were always red and swollen after a night sitting around it.

By late October, Sanji still hadn't had much work. This was because the circumstances of the 'new normal' had made it much tougher for people without proper documentation. As Sanji said, 'it was because of the big man,' meaning Salvini. In Campobello farmers were now much more concerned about the consequences of breaking the law if they employed workers without documents. More farmers were now checking papers when new workers were recruited. However, for the farmers, 'legality' did not also entail upholding acceptable working conditions. Workers with documents were no less exploited than those without them.

Under the 'new normal', the police had become more aggressive in their approach to migrant workers, the overarching attitude being that they were now being given a free hand to do what they wanted. Local *carabinieri* were certainly more keen to warn workers about their immigration status. Sanji was known to some officers because of the incident of the attack that injured him in the summer. He knew that it was not a good thing when officers knew you by name. One officer had pointed his finger at Sanji, saying, 'Don't let me see you working without documents. If we see you working, you'll be in trouble.'

To avoid being caught, Sanji had not been working much since the harvest started. But he felt anxious about the lack of work, as his family, particularly his younger sister, was waiting for his support. She had another two years before her college studies ended. He had not sent a penny home since the harvest started.

Sanji was eager to get his documents sorted out. He had waited for years for his humanitarian protection papers before they were destroyed in the fire at Christmas in 2017. He had since received a new copy. What he lacked now was a *codice fiscale*, the Italian equivalent of a British National Insurance card.[2] His friend recommended a Castelvetrano-based lawyer and Sanji cycled to visit him straight away to try to apply for a *codice fiscale* for himself. He needed this along with his ID and a residence permit to get a work contract from a farmer. Many farmers in the area would accept an ID and a residence permit without *codice fiscale*, but Sanji wanted to be doubly sure to have all the documents, in case he got into trouble with law enforcement.

While waiting for his documents, Sanji often spent time in the cement factory camp and sometimes had a sip of espresso at the makeshift café with a headless sheep carcass hung up at the butchers next door. This was one of the three butchers in the camp. They all had enormous chest freezers, secured with padlocks, and powered by portable generators. When Benjamin and Alieu earned something, they would come and buy a kilogram of lamb, which they would cook together with the others in their farmhouse as a stew with rice. It would last them two or three days—they couldn't keep meat any longer than that.

Sanji's young friend Omar from Futuro came to see him and followed him around even more often now. Minh, the cultural mediator, had given up on battling with the management and left for a better job in a reception centre in Milan. Mouhamadou, the other cultural mediator, under tremendous stress from the job, left and went back to Senegal for a long visit. The shelter looked half-closed. Omar and the other teenagers rarely spent any time inside. Then Omar reached eighteen in late November and could no longer live there. He held a small birthday party with his friends in the shelter the day before he was transferred to the adult camp at the former Acos Hotel site in Marsala.

Almost immediately after Omar's departure, the Futuro shelter closed down, due to insufficient numbers of children being placed there. The teenagers were transferred to different places, with Omar the only one in Marsala. The remaining shelter staff all cried as they lost their jobs. As Omar put it, 'the business collapsed.'

15

FULL MOON

At dusk on an early November evening in Campobello, tractors rumbled past with African workers riding on the trailers, astride crates of olives. The sunset was painted dark purple and bright pink, as if it was celebrating the end of a week of rain and storms. It had been a full workday for Mohammad; he had picked twenty-five crates of olives. What's more, he and four co-workers were asked to work overtime for two hours in the evening, for €5 per hour, sorting olives on the shop-floor of the compound of his employer's son. At 8:00 pm, he finally dragged himself back to his bed in the garage where he lived.

The following day, Mohammad worked another twelve hours including the overtime in the evening. He did this for the entire week as he was told by his eighty-year-old employer that the olive harvest would end that Friday. Extra amounts of work were demanded while his pay remained meagre. But he persisted. That Friday, as the work for the old boss ended, he agreed to a small new job working for a different employer, picking olives for a few days on a farm eleven kilometres away from Campobello.

Before the next job started, Mohammad finally had a rare day free. He invited three of his Gambian friends to come to his garage space and cook something together. It was respite time for them, and

Mohammad's furniture-less space was still heaven compared to their tents in the encampment at the cement factory.

On 16 November, Mohammad started working for his third employer of the season and it lasted only a week. Then his primary employer, the eighty-year-old man, came back to ask him to start to harvest lemons and mandarins for him from late November. Mohammad had plenty of work options to keep him going for ages. He usually planned his work a year ahead. Whilst busying himself with work in Campobello, he was already considering apple harvesting in Lleida in Spain for a few months next year. The harvest for the 'golden apple', the best variety in that province, had already started in the autumn.

In late November when the weather turned cooler, as Mohammad's overtime work sorting olives increased in the evenings after long days of working in the fields, his back ache returned and he felt he was reaching his limit. He had always taken on work when it was there. He had given his maximum, non-stop, for the whole year, especially throughout the harvest season. He felt he had now been squeezed dry and it should be time for him to take a break and recharge. He wanted to visit home. So, when his eighty-year-old employer requested again for him to work in the mandarin and lemon fields, Mohammad had to say no. It was the first time he had turned down this farmer's offer of work.

There was nothing he wanted to do more this winter than return to visit his family in Gambia. He had not been home for years. His mother had kept his room for him all this time, the way it was the day he left. He was still very much the centre of the family; his absence made this even more clear, not least because they needed his support. Few knew how often Mohammad fantasised about the trip back home. He would take a bus from Castelvetrano to Palermo, and from there, get on a bus to Rome, and then a plane from Rome to Casablanca, then another plane to Banjul. He dreamed about the welcome he would have when he arrived. It was around 28°C there in November, in the middle of the tourist season when there were lots of people about. He missed the sunshine, spending time with family and hanging out with friends he hadn't seen for a long time. He remembered the last winter in Triscina where he felt so alone, especially during Christmas when everyone else in town was indoors with their families. This year, he wanted it to be different. He had promised to build a room for his brother. He also planned to work some odd jobs, too, such as part-time work in the rice fields. He was not the type to do without work even for a short while.

* * *

Benjamin, Alieu and their team had worked for two farmers for the entire season. A few weeks into the harvest, a Gambian man called Fara in their team had developed severe back pain. He felt so bad that he had to take a few days off work. He stayed in the farmhouse when everyone else carried on working. But Fara did not recover, his pain only got worse. Eventually, Benjamin and Alieu had to take him to the hospital in Castelvetrano, from where he was transferred to Trapani and then to a hospital in Palermo. There, mysteriously, Fara became unable to speak or move. He was moved into the intensive care ward. It was suspected that his illness was some sort of pesticide poisoning.

At the same time, there were rumours going round about malicious medical staff in Italian hospitals, deliberately causing harm to African patients. 'We could get murdered in there,' was the belief among quite a few Africans, who felt that medical staff didn't want to help but wished ill on them. This kind of fear was why no African really trusted the Italian healthcare system and they tended to rely on pharmacists when they fell ill. Some of the Gambian boys started to think their co-worker Fara might have been harmed inside the hospital. Benjamin did not know what to believe but worried so much for him. He missed Gambia. 'You are at least safe there,' he said to Alieu.

Fara's employer did nothing for him in the hospital; he didn't even ask after him. Fara was just a replaceable piece of farm machinery for the employer. Everyone had to carry on working and put aside their concerns for him. Then, they heard from the hospital that Fara had died. There was no post mortem or inquiry from the hospital or the police into the cause of his death. Fara's former colleagues felt powerless as they didn't know what to do to demand justice. Their thinking was: many Africans had lost their lives working in agriculture here and there never was a fuss made about it, so why would Fara be different? People from the Gambian communities in Palermo organised the transportation of his body back home for burial. Fara's death did not trigger the slightest interest among the local farming community, let alone wider society.

Meanwhile, Benjamin had given up on his Palermo lawyer, as they seemed to be in a permanent state of misunderstanding. He was subsequently introduced to a new lawyer in Mazara to pursue his documents. One day, he went by train to visit his lawyer and chase up progress. What was hinted at but left unsaid in this lawyer's office was that things were getting difficult under the security decree as it came into effect after being approved by parliamentary vote in November. Public opinion polls showed that 57% of Italians approved of the government.

The work looked like it was going to dry up in the coming weeks for Benjamin and his team. But next to their compound there was no sign of people leaving the cement factory campsite, which looked more organised as the days went by. It appeared that people were planning to remain there for a while. Benjamin started thinking of new ideas to make money. Would it be possible for him to follow the example of several other Gambians and set up a shop to cater for the people in the encampment? He watched people driving old vehicles transporting food products backwards and forwards on the country road outside his farmhouse, and wondered how much cash he would need to start up like they did.

However, things moved on. Benjamin's ideas for a new venture soon faded in the days towards the end of olive harvest in late November, when the number of people at the cement factory site more than halved in a week. The same went for the Tunisian camp. By then, only around twenty tents remained. The café shopkeeper would soon be packing up his van and returning to Bari by early December. On that late autumn night, when the moon was full, shining with a halo through high clouds above the dim orange street lamps in Campobello town, the remaining workers in the Tunisian camp had their plates of couscous with grilled lamb, in their café shop, standing around discussing work options for the forthcoming winter. Everyone knew that there would not be another full moon before they had packed up and were travelling again.

***

Those who had been in the Campobello area for five or six years would have remembered Ousmane, the Senegalese man who lost his life back in 2013. The conditions under which he used to live and work still remained today. Five years later, Ousmane still came up in people's conversations from time to time. Sorrow remained. Young Bill, from Senegal, felt the pain of families and friends who lost Ousmane, just as he felt the pain for those close to Idy Diene, the Senegalese street-seller murdered by a white Italian in Florence in the summer of 2018, creating enormous anger and fear among the Senegalese communities there.

No one saw gas explosions and fires in these settlements as just accidents. Workers took huge risks every single day of their working lives in order to survive and support their families. Alsane had just heard about a gas explosion that had happened in the ghetto of Borgo Mezzanone where he had been living just a few months ago. Two Guinean boys were seriously injured.

On 1 December, news of another tragedy came through to the compound where Benjamin and Alieu lived. Surawa Jaithe, an eighteen-year-old Gambian boy, died while sleeping, consumed by a fire in the *tendopoli* of San Ferdinando in Calabria—where Benjamin and Alieu had stayed two years before. The blaze appeared to have started from a small brazier lit in one of the shacks for warmth during the cold night. Surawa Jaithe had arrived in Italy more than a year ago. For some time he lived in a SPRAR in Gioiosa Ionica, about fifty kilometres from the *tendopoli* of San Ferdinando, to which he was drawn to visit his friends and find work. Alieu knew him, although briefly, and was saddened by his death. It reminded him of the extreme harshness of living there. Gambians and other Africans across Italy mourned Surawa Jaithe's death; they were all too aware of the conditions that led to these utterly avoidable losses of life.

* * *

'Papa, when are you coming back?' Mohammad's son, now eight years old, asked. He had been asking the question for two long years. Each time it reminded Mohammad how long he had been away from his beloved family.

When the dream of renting an apartment in town fell apart, Mohammad made up his mind to leave. He went into a travel agent down the road from his garage and bought a plane ticket to Banjul, via Casablanca, for 1 December. It was such a simple act, yet it made so much difference. The thought of returning home in a week's time made his heart burst with joy and excitement. 'I'm coming soon,' he was finally able to reply to his son, this time, with conviction in his voice. 'I'm really coming home soon.'

The little boy was thrilled. Days later when the idea had sunk in, he started to ask on their WhatsApp call, 'Papa, are you bringing me a bicycle, or a football?'

Mohammad's family was getting ready for his homecoming. Their phone calls became even more frequent, especially from his sisters. His now twenty-one-year-old younger sister called him every day, reminding him to bring her a new mobile phone. She wanted a good phone, she said, a Samsung one only. She asked him to video-call her when he was in a phone shop so she could choose the phone she wanted. Mohammad knew he wouldn't be able to afford the phones she would see, so he invented an excuse not to call her from the shop. He was soft with her and always tried to placate her demands, knowing she was still young and did not understand how tough it was for him to earn money abroad.

Nonetheless, he had to buy two mobile phones, to be fair to his other sister, now twenty-four. Mohammad went to Marsala for his final shopping trip for his sisters, where he could find bigger shops with more choice. Eventually, he gave in and two new Samsung phones were now added to the gifts in his two massive suitcases. It was as if his life in the past few years, defined by his hard labour, was packed into these two cases, for him to take back home with him.

Mohammad wanted to say farewell to his friends in Campobello. Those friends in the cement factory site had already left and gone to Calabria. The ones who remained were living in the same farmhouse compound as Benjamin. They were staying put, ready for the forthcoming orange harvest. Mohammad cycled two kilometres to visit them and broke the news he was leaving. They were pleased for him, knowing how fortunate he was to be able to travel freely, visit home and see for himself how his family's lives had been improved. They had not been able to do so for years, given their asylum status.

Benjamin did not know Mohammad well, but he walked past the friends talking and listened. His hometown in Gambia was far away from Mohammad's. But he said to him jokingly, 'Give my regards to my family for me, please.'

'When are you coming back, brother?' a friend asked Mohammad.

'I'm going home, don't ask me when I'm returning!' Mohammad teased. The date of return to Campobello was the last thing on his mind.

That Friday, Mohammad got up early, just like on a workday, and travelled by bus to Palermo. His friend Daniel who was still in the asylum shelter there came to meet him at the bus station, to say goodbye. They took a photo together, with Mohammad's two large suitcases next to them. From there, Mohammad took another bus to Rome, where another of his Gambian friends put him up for a night. From Rome the following day he boarded a plane to Morocco, then another, home. All his family members were waiting excitedly for him at the airport in Banjul. Even though they saw him often on Whatsapp video calls, it wasn't the same as seeing and touching him in real life. They were looking forward to embracing him and feeling his presence after such a long time away.

* * *

Regardless of what his project had or had not achieved, Domenico Lucano, the former mayor of Riace, Calabria, was an irritant to Salvini. He was arrested on 2 October 2018, for 'aiding illegal immigration' and fraud. He was not a difficult target, as Riace had already been attracting suspicious attention from the authorities way before Salvini got into power. That autumn, Lucano was placed under house arrest in Caulonia to the southwest and denied the right to return to Riace. The 'Global Village' created by his project became a ghost village.

Around 1,000 Africans had left Riace by November as the project closed down. By mid-December, only around fifteen Africans remained—and the only reason was because they were still waiting for the renewal of their documents. They were struggling to make ends meet. Joseph and his friends were among them. They stood in the square, warming their hands in their jacket pockets, looking and waiting for farmers to walk past and give them orange-picking work for the day. The square was also the only hangout for them, as it was the only place they felt comfortable to gather.

When it neared Christmas and the air was cold, Joseph still stood there waiting for work. A religious procession with a band playing saxophones and trumpets paraded past. He didn't give it a proper glance. He was full of worries about paying his next bills. He was sharing a small one-bedroom flat with friends and they all found it difficult to afford the rent without regular work. Three winters had passed since Joseph arrived in Riace, and his situation only seemed to get worse. When recalling his years here and how his youth was wasted, he laughed bitterly. 'Prison life,' he called it, and then reiterated, 'Integration is a lie.'

Back in Camini, by December, the majority of African residents who were originally transferred here on the SPRAR project had left the village. However, transfers into the village still continued under the project.

Charlotte remained for the time being, because her humanitarian protection documents needed renewing, and this was where they had been issued. She promised herself that she would wait for no more than six months. After having to leave the original apartment provided under the project, she had to move to a smaller place at the top of a steep lane. The place was too small for her four children. Arriving upstairs on the second floor of the block, she would walk straight into the kitchen, behind which was the small sitting room where her children sat waiting for dinner. Their food provisions were always barely sufficient, especially for her nine-year-old boy and ten-year-old girl, who were growing fast.

That Christmas, like the last, Charlotte did not have anything special to give as presents to her children. Nor was there anything special on the dinner table. She would cook a large pot of rice, fry some plantain and boil some eggs. The family had had the same Christmas meal for the last three years. At the back of Charlotte's mind was the worry of having to pay the bills, the rent and the next monthly bus fee of €150 for two of her children to travel to school in Riace.

* * *

Joseph in Riace wished his close friend Ibrahima was still around. He had met Ibrahima a year earlier when taking a walk by the sea in Riace Marina. He had a lot of time on his hands as there was no work. From then on, they became close. Ibrahima used to come and visit him in Riace and spending time together helped Joseph deal with the depression of not having work or a future here. But suddenly, Ibrahima was transferred out of the area. Worse still, he was sent to the notorious Sant'Anna CARA camp near Crotone.

Sant'Anna was like the state's dumping ground for the undesirable and unwanted: the site had the CARA camp for asylum seekers on one side and a prison on the other. In previous years, just under 2,000 asylum seekers were kept there each year. In early 2019, more than 1,000 were there, most having been for two or three years. Ibrahima took a bus from Crotone to arrive at this military-guarded camp on the motorway eleven kilometres away. The airport, with a large spherical radar dome, stood on the opposite side of the motorway. This was where African (from Nigeria, Somalia, Ghana, Eritrea, and other countries) and Asian migrants who were transferred from Lampedusa would be landing. Two thirds of the residents in this CARA had been transferred from Lampedusa. The others were mainly Afghans and Iraqis who had travelled from Greece. In all, there were more than forty nationalities there.

Inside the Sant'Anna camp, Ibrahima shared a small room with three others. Not only was the indefinite wait for his asylum decision unbearable, the camp managers had never allocated any allowances from the state to the residents at all. Instead, they were given a packet of cigarettes per week. This had been the norm for years. Even after the exposure of the corruption and arrests in 2017, nothing much had changed. Alsane, the Senegalese worker, was sent by the police authorities to Sant'Anna in late 2018 and witnessed the same conditions. He described it as an 'open prison.'

With so much time on their hands and no cash to send home, most people simply searched for work in the surrounding area. Group after group of African men would walk from the camp, along the busy, dusty motorway, for two miles, towards the coast, to the nearest town Isola di Capo Rizzuto. There, they would go and stand at various recruitment points to wait for farmers to come select their workers. People had to get to the town by 6:00 am to be able to be selected for the day's work. But the Sant'Anna camp only opened its gate at 8:00 am, and therefore people stayed out and slept overnight on the streets in the town.

Alsane and others had slept rough on street corners in Isola di Capo Rizzuto countless times in the middle of winter, to be at the recruitment point in the early morning, ready to work in the fennel fields. Alsane had never tasted fennel but knew that it was a popular vegetable that people used with salami in Italy. He learned how to harvest it from more experienced workers. If selected in the morning, he would be driven to the farm and work the whole day for €10–€30, depending on the employers. Sometimes, he did not get paid at all. Alsane knew he was a 'zero' to the local community. There was nowhere and no one to turn to for help.

With so many people having been in the Sant'Anna camp for years, some still waiting for their Commission decision, it was as if the bureaucratic delays were aimed at supplying the regional agriculture with the cheapest labour. In this sense, Sant'Anna resembled a forced labour camp. People were fed, housed and kept alive to work for next to nothing—and sometimes for absolutely nothing—for the benefit of the local economy. After living here for a while, you found your sense of being distorted as the system deprived you of your humanity.

Most people wanted to run away and discussed where to go and how to get there. As many of them were still waiting for their documents, they had to stay in the area. Isola di Capo Rizzuto was the nearest option, although the town with a population of 15,000 people had little to offer. There was one main street with several shops and cafés and a SPRAR that only opened for half the week. Time seemed to matter little in Isola di Capo Rizzuto. Even the buses were often more than an hour late and queuing passengers didn't seem to care. The town looked shut off from the outside world. You wondered about its past, the piazza named after the murdered prosecutors Giovanni Falcone and Paolo Borsellino, and the town's reputation of being penetrated by the local mafia.

'Don't come to join me,' Ibrahima told Joseph on the phone after weeks of being in Sant'Anna and having seen the surrounding area. Eventually, Ibrahima ran away from Sant'Anna, or 'escaped the hell of Sant'Anna', as he put it to Joseph. However, he went from one hell to another, ending up in the *tendopoli* of San Ferdinando.

16

WINTER SURVIVAL IN THE CALABRIAN TENT CITY

Here in the *tendopoli* of San Ferdinando, there was a 2,000-strong workforce, ready for the winter orange harvest. At the entrance, Malik, a man from Senegal with short spiked dreadlocks, was sitting in front of his makeshift stall displaying shoes, clothing, high-vis vests, and all manner of cooking utensils on a plastic sheet on the floor. He had collected these from various dumpsters in town. He shouted out loud, touting some plastic toy tennis rackets to passers-by. These weren't an easy item to sell here as there were no children. He was also trying to sell an old, petrol-powered generator for €70. But as he was too honest in explaining the repairs it needed, no one wanted to buy it.

Malik called himself 'Black Shine,' proud of 'being the blackest man around here,' 'so black that it shines,' as he held up his arms to show everyone. He was eccentric and well-liked, and his stall was popular. Malik had scars on his forehead, which came from the torture he went through during his eight months in Libya. He also suffered a broken rib when he was hit with the butt of a rifle in an attack in Tripoli; he was left with a permanent lump on his chest. During that journey, he also caught Hepatitis B. He was always showing people a bank note he had brought from Libya, with the picture of Gaddafi's son on it. Recounting the memories of his time in Libya made his voice crack.

Malik had been placed in an asylum shelter in Amantea, 105 kilometres away from San Ferdinando. The management and staff there could not care less about what he did with his time, so Malik had the freedom to go out as long as he wanted, and find work on the farms nearby. He couldn't cope with living inside the *tendopoli* every day like the others as he was still unwell and on medication. 'If you get too stressed, your head will crack,' he kept saying. A bike accident caused by a failed brake meant that he could no longer stand for a long time and therefore was no good for farm work. He decided to run a store instead and had been selling his gear here from 7:00 am to 7:00 pm each day, for the entire winter. His income was higher than an agricultural wage. Since then, Malik slept over in the *tendopoli* a couple of nights a week.

* * *

Michael, an athletic Nigerian man in his thirties, was standing in Malik's store, talking with friends. He was a familiar face to Malik, having been here for nearly a year. People would remember him as the one who called out to Salvini and asked whether he would live here when he visited the *tendopoli* back in the summer. Michael had arrived in Italy back in 2011 and was sent to a reception camp in Lamezia, a couple of hours away from San Ferdinando. There, the camp had his name on their books for seven years but didn't care whether he was actually there or not. During these years, he found work on the farms and joined his friends to sleep over in the *tendopoli*. At one point, he also left Italy looking for better-paid work. He went to Paris where a friend helped him find a night-shift job at McDonalds.

Eventually Michael had to return to Calabria because his documents were being processed there. Then he came to join his friends back in the fields again. By then, he already had his documents and would need to renew his residence permit every two years. When he arrived in the *tendopoli* on 12 January 2018, he decided to move into the 'official tents' area opposite, to be away from the notorious safety risks in the main makeshift camp. Michael still spent most of his time in the main encampment, as that was where most of his friends were and work arrangements made. In the early morning from Monday to Friday, he would go and wait at a pick-up point inside the *tendopoli* and follow fellow workers to be driven by the *caporali* to work on a farm from 7:00 am to 3:00 pm. He never earned more than €27 per day. One euro for one crate of oranges. He was charged a €10 fee for the *caporali*, and on top of that, a transport fee of €3 per day. Not much was left of his daily wages after these deductions. However, he was relatively new and had to rely on *caporali* to get him work.

Michael had met Becky Moses, the Nigerian woman who tragically died in a fire in late January not long after his arrival. To any newcomer to the winter harvest, Michael would say, 'Welcome, welcome to the land of racists.' He was referring to the system that perpetuated racism and kept Africans in appallingly unsafe conditions and in extremely exploitative employment. He was always calm when he eloquently expressed his frustration and anger. It was his eyes that revealed the deepest sadness.

His friend Isaac was emotional. It was hard to contain his long-suppressed anger. Isaac had been a builder in Nigeria and left home to improve his income to support his two children. He stood out as someone who had been 'toughened up' by hardship. He had intense, piercing brown eyes; he walked in a combative manner. He could never seem to wind down. Isaac had been through the worst: he had been in the miserable Sant'Anna CARA for a year, before escaping to come to San Ferdinando, where he had been living for two years.

As it happened, Isaac was walking around with a T-shirt saying 'Fuck off hipsters.' He had picked up from a skip in Rosarno, not knowing what 'hipsters' meant. 'Farmers' would have been a more suitable word. For two years, Isaac had always earned a low wage, of around €25 a day, harvesting oranges and lemons. This winter, with his residence permit, he obtained a work contract for three months, from November to January, with an orange processing factory. In the contract, the employer stated that he would be paid €39 per day. In reality, however, his pay was €27. Isaac was fuming with anger and requested an explanation from his employer, who then told him that they 'have got to pay tax.'

Isaac knew that harvesting and processing work alone could barely sustain his living here, let alone send money home. He had to find something else to bring in an income. He decided to follow others, and set up a food store with a café inside to cater for the Nigerian residents. He would be kept busy, for sure, as there were around 1,000 Nigerian men and women here. In the early evening, he would cycle to Rosarno and spend around €20 on foodstuffs from Mama Africa. After returning to his shack, with the help of a Nigerian friend, he prepared and cooked Nigerian stew with rice and sold it for €3 a plate. He sold the leftover food at lunchtime the next day, too. In his café at midday, many Nigerian women would come and dine. On the wall inside, hair extensions of different colours were hung on display as a female friend of his was trying to earn some cash making braids for women. All in all, Isaac was making €30 a day from his food stall and café— not much more than his wages in the orange-processing plant, but it was less strenuous. To top up his earnings, Isaac sometimes walked over to the town of San Ferdinando, a tourist area, and begged in the street. Sometimes tourists would spare him a few coins. A few offered him food.

* * *

Isaac knew of Surawa Jaithe, the eighteen-year-old Gambian boy who died in the fire at San Ferdinando in early December 2018. At the time of Surawa's visit to San Ferdinando, he was still waiting for the renewal of his residence permit. He had friends in the *tendopoli*. One of them, his close friend, was distraught that he didn't even get to see Surawa. He was away in Catania, Sicily, purchasing cheap bicycles to bring back to sell in the *tendopoli*.

That tragic night, the shack in which Surawa was sleeping caught fire, which caused a gas canister inside to explode, the flames then engulfing the shack. When the fierce fire woke people up, firefighters were called. However, even though they were stationed several hundred metres down the road, opposite the 'official tents', they arrived an hour after the fire broke out. By then, all that was left of Surawa was a charred, curled-up body with his arms across his chest, as if in a deep sleep.

Isaac saw the blackened wooden skeleton of the shack and believed that Surawa could have been saved if the fire service had arrived quickly. When Surawa's friend heard the news, he rushed back from Catania. He remained traumatised in the days that followed. He spoke about Surawa with tears in his eyes. He mumbled about the rapper

Tupac [Tupac Shakur], saying, 'I'm like him, I'm against the system that keeps us down.'

Malik, or 'Black Shine,' was a friend of Surawa's, too. Like many, he was deeply upset by his death. They used to chat and spend time together. Surawa liked him and had given him a ring, which Malik still wore. 'He was a really nice person,' Malik told everyone who asked.

The future looked grim for everyone. Isaac's residence permit was set to expire in March; he would have to travel to Crotone, where his lawyer was based, to renew it. He had no idea how tough it would be under the new decree. Africans had given this country their sweat and blood. 'In return, we received only racism,' he said to his friends. He wished he had confronted Salvini when he visited the *tendopoli* in the summer. Many people had wanted to beat him up.

On a Sunday, next to the camp entrance, the sound of energetic preaching and singing could be heard coming from the makeshift church. The mood was calmer. As the sun was out, more people came out and gathered, talking. There were still puddles from the rain of the previous evening. The paths between shacks were waterlogged and muddy. Isaac was busy with cutting up a lamb carcass. He and his friend laid the lamb out on a plastic sheet on the floor, threw the intestines into a bucket, and cut the meat into pieces, to refrigerate them. Following that, they started cooking lunch for the café.

One thing that stood out were the flags of workers' unions USB and CGIL that fluttered from several tents near the entrance. The USB's more proactive approach in organising collective action had won some trust here, whereas the CGIL's image was more one of a public authority, because it often only dealt with workers' documents and contracts and appeared not dissimilar to the police authorities (*questura*) in its role. According to Antonio Jiritano, the regional representative of the USB, around 90% of the *tendopoli* residents of San Ferdinando were members of the USB. The union didn't just assist workers in getting permits, dealing with the police and the prefecture, and giving assistance on labour contracts. Most importantly, it was always quick to organise demonstrations and other collective action in response to fires and the death of workers.

Opinions towards the unions, however, seemed to vary among workers here. Michael, who had been in and out of the encampment for the past few years, didn't believe that union officials had their interest at heart because 'they're Italians' and 'they're not interested in changing things for us.' Isaac had a different take to Michael and was more trusting of the unions and he identified with the activities that they organised on behalf of the African workers.

The USB activists came asking for two representatives from each nationality group in the *tendopoli* to go to Rome for a demonstration on 15 December, to protest against Salvini and his decree. Workers here were all for it, Isaac included. He saw it as a positive thing that African activists were representing their fellow workers. Antonio Jiritano of the USB said: 'The devastating effects of this [security decree] have already begun to manifest themselves: thousands of migrant citizens unable to obtain a humanitarian protection residence permit; a huge number of people expelled from reception centres due to a drastic reduction of funds; people becoming more and more trapped, without rights, unable to regularise their status...'

Jiritano believed that the significance of the December demonstration was that its leaders were many migrant activists who had been building and organising the mobilisation. It signalled the growth of a new generation of social and trade union activism— despite the political climate in Italy.

In this climate, Isaac's biggest fear was that the authorities would soon close down the encampment. 'Where are we going to go?' He desperately felt that everyone should act, to fight against such moves. Daniel, a USB member from Mali, said: 'What people want is to get out of this encampment and be offered proper housing. We've been denied this because we're black.' People gathered around him, nodding in agreement. Some started talking about slavery and its continuation in Italy. Daniel wanted people to get involved in the USB which he believed could unite all the nationalities here. The union pushed for a proposal that aimed to close down the model of emergency and focuses on providing suitable housing, given the huge availability of 35,000 empty houses in the region.

However, such an endeavour was not going to get a hearing in Rosarno or San Ferdinando. Local prejudice ran deep. Many local residents continued with their belief that 'Africans don't want to live in apartments or houses, and when they do, they don't pay the rent.'

This attitude contrasted with their different approach to white South European migrants from Romania and Bulgaria, who had always been able to rent places in town.

There had been three deaths in the *tendopoli* in 2018: Becky Moses, Soumaila Sacko, and Surawa Jaithe. The fires, the deaths, the racist murder, not to mention the *caporali* and the appalling working and living conditions. Michael desperately wanted to get out of the area. His Nigerian friend in Paris knew about his situation and invited him again to stay for a month. Without hesitation, Michael packed his bags and went by bus, via Rome, to Paris. There, he went back to the job at McDonalds. As he said to his friends, 'It's a low-paid job but there are no *caporali*.' At Christmas, Michael spent time with his friend and got to know many other Nigerians living in Paris. For the first time in a whole year, he felt he was fine.

On New Year's Eve, only one day after Michael's return from Paris, panicked screams were heard across the encampment. A fire had broken out in a shack at around 9:00 pm. The situation escalated fast, the flames spreading to other shacks within five minutes. Fortunately, Isaac was not near the fire, but as soon as he knew about it, he tried to help out by calling the fire service and shouting for everyone to get out of their shacks to be safe. In all, thirteen shacks were destroyed. One man was injured and taken to hospital. Isaac was relieved that no one died that night. Had the fire started later when people were sleeping, the consequences might have been very different.

17

END OF SEASON

As soon as the olive harvest ended and most seasonal workers had left Campobello, the *carabinieri* were, once again, on the backs of those who remained. This time, a deadline was given. They wanted the workers to leave the area by mid-January 2019. 'Not only do the police want to push us out of Campobello, they want to push us out of the whole region.' Sanji couldn't contain his fury. 'Maybe what they really want is to push us to suicide.'

The situation truly felt desperate, an endless hide-and-seek, and Benjamin feared that his group would be driven out of the farmhouse by force. They had been raided before the autumn harvest and their eviction was only deferred by the town's seasonal need for their labour. Now that this bargaining chip had gone, what could stop the *carabinieri* now? The insecurity and stress became so overwhelming that it gave Benjamin headaches. Trying to ignore it, his only defence mechanism was to shut down. He sat in the quiet, alone, saying nothing and responding to no one. No one could penetrate his thick wall of silence. This was something that he had resorted to in the hellish days in Tripoli.

When he could not take the stress anymore and the headaches became too much to bear, Benjamin went to a pharmacy in town and tried to explain to the staff what he needed. Unable to speak Italian, he pointed to his head, saying, 'stress, lots of stress,' and asked for medicine. They might or might not have understood him and he was given a herbal remedy cream which didn't help at all. His helpless situation finally compelled him to take action and start trying to find alternative housing—from anyone, anywhere, outside Campobello.

One afternoon, Benjamin decided to go looking for a room in Marsala, as he had heard about many Gambians living in the area. But he really had no clue how to start in a strange town like this. As he came out of the station, he simply walked around and stopped any African man in the street, asking, 'Brother, could you help me? I'm looking for a room here.' He stopped a dozen men. No one knew of a way to rent a room. No one had connections to a landlord.

Worse still, this year, the winter orange harvest had been delayed in Campobello due to poor weather conditions. Workers had to wait till mid-January. Before that happened, people could only pick up odd jobs here and there, to try to survive. At this moment, Sanji had only one local farmer, Piedro, to work for. Piedro's olive groves had all been harvested and now he needed a team of people to carry out the lopping of recently harvested olive branches, which would be turned into logs for woodstoves. The branches without olives were left to grow for next year. This was a fairly skilled job that required some experience with olive trees. Piedro and other olive farmers did not usually give this kind of post-harvest work to people who had just been on one harvest. Sanji had learned how to do this years before from watching Tunisian workers. Now he was among the selected few to do this job, alongside a team of Tunisians.

After the lopping job, Sanji was still desperate for work. Calls from farmers did not always guarantee actual work. A few times, a farmer promised work but didn't show up the next day to pick him up. It may well have been that he had found a 'cheaper' worker. 'Sometimes the Italians are like chameleons,' Sanji said to friends.

A few days later, Benjamin had some news. An old friend of his, Yugo, returned his call about finding a room. He said he had found a cheap one-bedroom flat in Trapani. He held a two-year residence permit which enabled him to rent a place, and after searching for a long while, he finally found a landlord who was renting out his whole building to non-Italians to cover the non-tourist season in Trapani when his apartments were left empty. With a 'yes' from the landlord,

Yugo was now looking for a couple of people to live with him to share the costs. To Benjamin, Yugo was like a brother. They had endured Libya together; survived the crossing and arrived in Italy together. Yugo had been there each time Benjamin was in need—the last time was in Germany, giving him a bed and finding him work. They felt they had shared the same destiny during all that time, until they were separated by events out of their control. Yugo had always cared and stayed in contact with his close friend. He had listened to Benjamin calling out for help ever since the makeshift camp of White Grass had been demolished in Campobello. At the time he had not been in a position to offer help. But now, the opportunity had arrived. 'Come and join me in Trapani,' he said to Benjamin.

This was what Benjamin had been waiting and hoping for throughout the year. He couldn't believe it and was thrilled at the prospect. He had saved up from the harvest work in the autumn and could contribute something towards the deposit. He had to rely on Yugo's help to meet the difference. It had been difficult to survive the winter in the disused farmhouse and Benjamin desperately needed to leave. The landlord in Trapani, however, knew the situation of the African men and wanted to exploit it. He charged them a massive deposit of €900 when the monthly rent was set at €100. The landlord, presumably, could invent an excuse to keep the deposit in the end, knowing that the African residents would have nowhere to seek recourse. But Benjamin was not deterred by this. He was determined to get out of Campobello to avoid the misery of winter without basic facilities and without work. At last, he had the opportunity to live under a roof in a normal building, like every Italian.

Benjamin wanted Alieu to come and stay with him in the apartment, but unfortunately, it could only take three people and Yugo had already found another person, Benjamin had to explain. Alieu did not want to hold him back. 'Go on,' he said, 'Go ahead and move to Trapani.' He said he would find other friends and try to move out of the area somehow. But Alieu knew that landlords did not normally let rooms to Africans and Benjamin had grabbed his chance when he had it. Now his two-year humanitarian protection documents were up for renewal, renting a room would be doubly difficult for him.

* * *

Sanji received tragic news a week before Christmas. His mother had passed away. She had been ill for a long time. Only a short time before she died, she had talked to Sanji on the phone and said, 'My son, I don't think I'll be able to see you again.' It saddened him so much to hear it. But he didn't expect her passing to be so sudden. He was devastated. His younger sister and daughter were all the family he now had and he knew he must do his best to make sure they were alright. He felt guilty that he was not able to send money home as there was so little work before the orange harvest started.

His mother's passing depressed him very much. He barely spoke to anyone for days. He needed to get away from the misery of Campobello, even just for an afternoon. One day, he jumped on the train to Marsala half an hour away and went to see his young friend Omar, the teenager who had recently turned eighteen and had been transferred to the former Acos Hotel camp in Marsala.

Things were not getting better for young Omar. In Marsala, he was no longer given any Italian language lessons as he had at the minors' shelter before. Inadequate though those lessons were, they were the only form of schooling that the teenagers in the reception system received. Not only was he not studying, but Omar's weekly allowance was delayed till the end of the month. Penniless, he would soon have to take up farm work like the others.

In Marsala, Sanji was also able to see his friend Adama, who shared the same room with Omar at the shelter. Also, coincidentally, one of Sanji's nephews had also ended up here, and was staying in the room next door. With the boys there, Sanji's visits to Acos became a social event for him, to relax and 'free his mind' of the troubles in Campobello.

Sanji spent the day walking around town with the boys. Simply being in a different environment made him feel a lot better. They walked through the historic centre of town to the Spanish-built, seventeenth-century Garibaldi Gate (*Porta Garibaldi*) which led them down to the seaside promenade. Along the coast they walked past a small white church sitting on the edge of the archaeological park where the old Roman city was buried. Further down on the headland, they could see disused wineries which used to export Marsala wine. And beyond the headland were small islands hazy in the distance. The gentle winter sunshine felt good on their faces.

They then strolled into a park next to North Gate (*Porta Nord*). Here, they still got some sunlight through the dense foliage. As they walked further in, they saw a peculiar pair of busts on marble plinths. They were Lieutenant Stefano Bilardello and Major Amerigo Fazio who had both died during Italy's invasion of Ethiopia in 1935, where a bloody genocide was conducted.

Before the Second World War, there had been a resurgence in the ideology of the Italian Empire. Following his rise to power, Benito Mussolini campaigned to expand Italian colonialism in the 1930s. During that time, Italy brutally secured its grip on Libya. Then, in October 1935, Mussolini invaded Ethiopia. Fascist troops entered Addis Ababa on 5 May 1936, and countless Ethiopians were murdered, many by the use of mustard gas. Mussolini announced victory four days later and declared the creation of the 'Italian Empire.' Italy then merged Eritrea, Italian Somalia, and the newly occupied Ethiopia into 'Italian East Africa'. Italian colonialism in Africa only formally ended with the collapse of Mussolini's fascist regime.

Here, on these busts, there was no mention of civilian deaths in Ethiopia and certainly not a word about the meaning of the war in the fascist era. That Italy's bloody colonial past was still commemorated in this way in a public space was an indication of how the country continued to look at the former colonies and colonised peoples after the Second World War.

Adama told Sanji what was hidden behind the apparent tranquillity of Marsala. Once again, the one thing that stood out was racism. Asylum seekers, including the children in the dozens of shelters, were in a society of their own, existing in parallel with the local community who made no effort towards their inclusion. It wasn't only about the visible hostility in the form of the swastikas sprayed on walls in the town centre. Many Africans, he said, had suffered aggression from local residents. In the worst cases, there was racial violence—something hard for a visitor to this quiet provincial place to imagine. A friend of Adama, an eighteen-year-old Gambian boy from the same camp, had become the latest victim of a car 'accident' when a racist local intentionally hit him while he was cycling on the outskirts of town and left him in a coma for a month. Adama shook his head, deeply upset. Vicious attacks like this had been happening to African boys on bicycles

227

all over Italy. When vehicles hit them, usually in the dark, they would turn off the car lights so that no one could see their number plates. There were never any police inquiries into these incidents.

* * *

Benjamin left the compound just two days before Christmas. He had lived there since March and had gone through a lot with his friends. It was emotional to leave them all behind, but he had to take his chance. Alieu wasn't feeling well when Benjamin was preparing to go and did not say much. 'Come to Trapani to stay with me for a few days,' said Benjamin. He knew Alieu needed to wind down from the stress of Campobello. But Alieu just sighed and didn't give him a definite answer.

The train pulled into Trapani station fifty minutes after Benjamin left Campobello. He carried most of his belongings with him in three plastic bags, mainly clothing. He had remembered Trapani as a soulless town. If it hadn't been for the people he met in the camp back then, he would not have survived. He had recently heard that his old notorious camp run by Badia Grande had closed down. He walked through the near-empty station, looking at an antique luggage trolley displayed at the top of the platform. There was a sadness to this once bustling station that resembled a scene from a spaghetti Western.

Yugo came to meet Benjamin and they greeted each other warmly. 'It's been a while, brother!' said Benjamin, reassured at Yugo's presence. He looked as thin as ever, though. He had never stopped working hard. He led Benjamin through a park, then turned a few lanes towards the old town centre. When Yugo finally stopped at the front door of an apartment building in a narrow alley, Benjamin couldn't help letting out a sigh of relief. He was here, finally outside an apartment. He looked up at the solid-looking exterior. 'Arabs live upstairs,' said Yugo. It looked a quiet and safe neighbourhood. Benjamin felt so fortunate, sudden and surreal though it was.

Yugo showed him into the ground-floor flat. The kitchen and sitting area were in one ten-square-metre room. There was a dining table and chairs in the middle. A dining table! Benjamin gasped. He did not expect that. Yugo and his other friend had taken the one bedroom—as Yugo had found the place, Benjamin thought it appropriate that they take the bedroom. He had the windowless box room, which was about three square metres, with which he was more than content: there was a proper single bed in it, with bedsheets and a pillow, something that he had never had since he left Gambia.

Benjamin had a good night's sleep on the first night. He was exhausted by the move and all the emotion. The following nights, however, it seemed to have got colder. But no one could afford to switch on the heating. So he did what his two flatmates did—piled all his winter clothing on top of the bed and kept the box room door shut. But heating was not their most pressing problem; money for the rent was. In the winter, there was less work to be had and Benjamin knew only a few farmers in the Trapani area. One of them was a tomato farmer for whom he used to work. But there was no luck there. Yugo then introduced him to work on a farm harvesting small flat onions (*cipollini*).

Since Benjamin had left, Alieu had not been to visit him, and when asked why, he would mutter about the cost of the train fare, 'more than €3.' Alieu had the farmhouse main room to himself now that Benjamin had departed. He had also tidied up the front yard. Plastic chairs were put out for friends from other farmhouses when they visited. Sanji came over to spend time and have food with Alieu and others more often now. Che, the Gambian man who always used to wear a Che Guevara beret at White Grass, and who had been living in the cement factory site down the road this autumn, often came over to see everyone too. At Christmas, the remaining six of them in Alieu's compound, joined by Sanji and Che, put together their cash and got themselves some lamb to cook a stew. They were all Muslim but decided that they would have a celebration, too. Back in Gambia, some Muslims joined in Christmas celebrations.

They made *domoda*. They cooked a huge amount of rice; it always helped because it filled you up. Then they sat around the large plastic bowl full of rice, with the lamb stew on top, and ate together scooping handfuls from the same bowl. They chatted about work and the lack of it. Sanji said several friends of his who were based in Syracuse were talking about tomato harvesting work in Ragusa. He was wondering whether he should join them. Sanji also suggested organising a protest right outside the Campobello town hall, if the police pushed further with the evictions. No one responded with much enthusiasm. They

229

barely had enough to eat. Let alone worry about a protest. The leftover meat went into their meals for the following two or three days.

Benjamin carried on looking for more work. Yugo was not in much more of a favourable position because his two-year humanitarian protection documents were up for renewal in eight months' time. Discussion about 'buying a work contract' started among the three of them when they sat discussing their options. Under the security decree, many people whose humanitarian protection documents were due for renewal found themselves in an extremely uncertain situation. Many were feeling confused and anxious. In the midst of all this, profiteers had emerged, charging people €500–€600 each for a one-year work contract.

These work contracts would serve as proof to the authorities that migrants continued to have employment in this country. They would take these contracts to the authorities, which would then ensure the renewal of their residence permits. These contracts were obviously fake because they needed to be paid for and did not involve actual employment, but were then lodged in the system, which meant that more than a few people in the administration were taking a cut along the way. The profiteers could be anyone—from local crooks and businessmen to corrupt low-level civil servants. The man who was selling this sort of work contract to Yugo was a police officer in Trapani. There were more than a few police officers involved in this kind of forgery for profit. Every two years when someone needed to renew their documents, they could go to these profiteers to buy a work contract. In this way, the government's decree had managed not only to criminalise and marginalise migrants further, but also enabled the squeezing of the maximum amount of money out of them while fattening up the local operators.

At the same time, stop-and-search by the *carabinieri* seemed to have increased in the streets of Trapani. Benjamin's flatmates had all been stopped; they were let go, as they had documents. Benjamin himself was once stopped by an officer and had to take out the wrinkled piece of paper that he had received from his lawyer a year ago, which said he had been granted a two-year residence permit. However, he had yet to receive the actual permit card which every migrant needed to get a work contract. A Gambian acquaintance of his, who did not have any documents to show, was not so lucky when stopped. He was arrested and sent to a CPR in Milo, four kilometres southeast of Trapani, awaiting deportation. 'He didn't do anything wrong. He just didn't have those papers,' Benjamin said. This CPR was managed by Badia Grande until February 2020, when it was found unfit for purpose[1] and closed down.

A week into the New Year, Benjamin returned to Campobello to see Alieu and all his friends in the old compound. With little work around and it being freezing cold, they all stayed indoors. One of them wept when he saw Benjamin, 'It's so cold here, brother, things are bad.' Things never ceased to be bad in Campobello. Alieu told him enough times on the phone. He also told him that he had got a job as a shepherd in rural Mazara and would be going to work there. Alieu was surprised to see that Benjamin had changed his appearance—he had shaved his head, his clothes were clean, and even his shoes were polished. 'Look at you, brother,' said Alieu, 'You're a changed man! Even your face is shining.' Benjamin was now able to wash his face and get properly clean every day. He still felt guilty for leaving Alieu behind and never stopped inviting him to come to stay with him in Trapani. And Alieu never answered him straight.

Back in Trapani, Yugo ran out of patience searching for work, as his family was desperate for his support. Friends in Malta told him there was construction work to be had there. So to Malta he went, on a plane from Palermo. It would be four months before Benjamin would see him again.

18

'INTEGRATE' AND DISINTEGRATE

In January 2019, Lucano, the former mayor of Riace, held a press conference to launch a new initiative named '*È Stato il Vento*' ('There was wind'). He told journalists that the new initiative aimed to 'support integration projects for migrants in Riace' and rebuild what Riace had achieved. Among those attending the launch were Giuseppe Lavorato, the former mayor of Rosarno, who would serve as the new foundation's president, as well as Father Alex Zanotelli and Chiara Sasso, the author of *Riace, an Italian Story* (*Riace, una Storia Italiana*). Father Zanotelli said to the audience: 'It is important to raise funds to consolidate the foundation and the committee... At this moment it is important to resist and defend Riace, which is one of the beautiful realities of Calabria.'

However, the Africans who still remained in Riace heard nothing about the press conference and the new initiative. There were fifteen of them, including Joseph, the man from Togo who had been on the SPRAR project. Throughout the winter, they struggled to find casual work. Joseph got a few days' orange harvesting work per week. Soon enough, that work dried up when the orange season came to an end.

Joseph spent most of his time staying indoors in the winter if he wasn't working. The wind from the sea chilled you in minutes. Occasionally when the sun was out, he would come out to the square

233

for some fresh air. Most of his close friends who had been here before the winter had already gone. He felt completely alone.

He still had not received his long-awaited documents. He felt he had to think of alternatives. Germany? France? Being French-speaking, it would make sense to go to France. Perhaps he could try Marseilles, a good working city with well-established African communities. Meanwhile, he couldn't help thinking how much he despised Emmanuel Macron, who, for him, was an imperialist and a hypocrite. 'French colonialism impoverished Togo and Africa in general,' he said.

French and other European colonialism prevented Africa from developing its wealth and its industries and maintained Africa's subordinate position for the benefit of Europe.

'Europe has few natural resources but is rich. We Africans have so many natural resources and yet we are the poorest in the world… Africans need to unite,' he deeply believed that.

A fifteen-minute bus ride away in Camini, it looked as though the new year was bringing new opportunities for the SPRAR project. Those in management saw their main task as securing funding and looking for new partnerships. In February 2019, the Italian Lions Club was the recipient of their new pitch for funds. Men in suits, in BMWs, arrived in the village one day, and were given an impressive reception in the town hall. One of the ideas proposed to them was to set up a new restaurant with international cuisine and a related cookery school.

At the same time, while there were still sixty houses waiting for renovation, the number of people being placed on the project was steadily declining. Rosario Zurzolo of Jungi Mundu acknowledged that at the end of February 2019, the overall number of migrants on the project had decreased from 118 to eighty-nine. This was, first and foremost, due to the lack of employment prospects.

Charlotte, from Nigeria, had endured the entire winter with hardly any earnings from her workshop. After waiting so long for the renewal of her documents and yet still not being granted them, Charlotte decided enough was enough, that she had to do something to better support herself and her children. One early morning in late February 2019, Charlotte and her family left Camini. They got on a bus all the way to Naples. Within two weeks of arriving there, Charlotte and her family got on another bus and travelled north to Germany.

Ironically, this was where many young villagers from Camini had gone two decades ago. In Germany, Charlotte would re-apply for asylum, knowing that her case was already in the Italian system. This was her desperate act to escape destitution and obtain state support for her children—despite knowing that sooner or later she and her family would be 'Dublined' back to Italy.

By February 2019, only around ten migrants in Camini were in employment, all in low-paid part-time or casual work, out of the entire migrant population. The one family man who had regular work was Jemal, from Eritrea. He had worked on farms back in Eritrea, and was now given a job running allotments and building a greenhouse at the bottom of the village. Jemal's total monthly earnings were around €900, which he shared 50:50 with Jungi Mundu who managed his work. Some of this wage had to go towards paying the rent as he was no longer on the project. He was supporting two children who were going to school here.

Not only was there little work for young adults, there was also no continuous education or vocational training. A young Nigerian boy, the only Nigerian in Camini now that Charlotte had left, spent his time strolling around the steep lanes and sitting in the Jungi Mundu café with a second-hand guitar, having nothing to do. He looked like any abandoned youngster, idling his time away in rural Calabria.

One evening, inside the Jungi Mundu café, the staff showed visitors a promotional documentary film about the harvest, made the previous year. People of all backgrounds, migrants and locals, were shown playing their part in agricultural work, the lifeblood of the village. But the farm work was for the film only; no one was paid. Was the production supposed to convey the message of the 'shared destiny' of Camini? The stark reality of employment and future prospects for migrants there were sadly very different from the drone-filmed images of collective endeavour. To achieve a genuine sense of collectiveness and shared destiny, there needed to be equality first.

When the Lions Club guests visited Camini, the project organisers arranged a delicious Syrian lunch which everyone enjoyed. Apart from showcasing international cuisine as indicating a taste for 'diversity' and 'integration,' were the village authorities able to go beyond tokenistic gestures of cultural inclusion and move to acceptance of differences in cultural practices? John Hampson, the British volunteer, saw that the Muslim residents on the project had only been able to worship at home and were not able to practice their religion in a public space, like the Catholic villagers did. He made a request to the mayor to consider allowing the use of a room in the town hall as a prayer room for Muslims. His request was ignored. When he put forward the idea a second time, the mayor replied: 'We cannot just go ahead and do this without considering the local community… As a mayor, I need to make sure that equilibrium is maintained, and not disturb the balance.'

This said it all about the 'integration' placed at the forefront of the marketing of such projects. In Camini, whilst the project prided itself on having migrants 'living in the community' (rather than in segregated ghettoes like in the rest of Italy), certain basic rights still needed to be fought for so new arrivals could live like everyone else. In this case, basic religious needs were not recognised. How could people even begin to feel part of a society when their religious practices had to remain hidden?

In European societies, 'integration' is used as an instrument for the legitimisation of racism rather than alternative to it. 'If racism is the denial of equality, then integration is the credo that evacuates the issue of egalitarianism,' French essayist Pierre Tevanian and Algerian sociologist Saïd Bouamama have written.[1] Whenever you hear the word 'integration' being trumpeted, you can be sure that it will never be accompanied by the recognition of the colonial history and the need to challenge racism and fundamental injustices. As Tevanian and Bouamama pointed out, the vocabulary of 'integration' was used in the same way in colonial times as it is now in the postcolonial: working as a pushback against demands for equality.

If liberals are truly interested in enabling people to become part of society and fully immersed in the cultural and public life of the country— rather than becoming invisible—then they need to start thinking about racism, which is structural and institutional. It is time to stop covering up the ugly truth of racism with the fig leaf of 'integration.'

* * *

In 2018 and 2019, the number of reception camps and shelters began to shrink. Activist Alberto Biondo told me that eight reception centres had closed down in Palermo alone between December 2018 and February 2019. As for the sixty minors' reception centres based there, half had been closed by mid-2019. In 2020, the closure of more centres had led to an increase in homelessness.

Richard Brodie, a founder and organiser of Porco Rosso, a cultural association and migrant drop-in centre in Palermo, said to me that the closure of camps couldn't solely be attributed to Salvini. 'A lot of camps are also closing because the Minniti decree [2017] shortened appeal times to six months, meaning people who arrived in late 2016 onwards have much less time in the camps... There's a lot of talk about the Salvini decree, but really the big problems we're seeing at the moment (and the bigger picture) is all to do with the previous [PD] government.'

Meanwhile, the most visible part of the security decree had been the closure of the large CARA camps. CARA di Mineo, near Catania in west Sicily, one of the largest reception camps for asylum seekers in Europe, with 1,357 residents, had its first transfer out of fifty people in early February 2019. They were sent to smaller centres across Sicily. All the early transfers were of single men. Families with children remained at the CARA until 9 July 2019 when the whole camp closed down. This was a CARA that had been notorious for years of corrupt management and miserable conditions for migrants. In October 2018, Badia Grande, along with several other consortia, won the contract, worth €17 million, to provide administrative and healthcare services. Poor treatment of migrant residents had always been a feature of the camp, but some of the staff were also exploited. Non-payment of wages for the medical staff led to doctors and nurses going on strike for several hours in February 2019. In this context, breaking apart such a structure should have been a positive thing. However, under the decree, those migrants transferred to smaller centres would soon suffer the refusal[2] of humanitarian protection and be shown the door. The end result would be homelessness and destitution for them.

Apart from the substandard conditions that pushed people to leave, the Sant'Anna CARA also created large numbers of homeless migrants as a direct result of evictions over the years. The situation went from bad to worse between winter 2018 and spring 2019. In the centre of

Crotone, only two charities, Caritas and the Agora Social Coop, were there to offer help to homeless migrants.

Marco, a cultural mediator for Caritas in Crotone, who spoke English and Arabic, worked in the Sant'Anna camp between 2002 and 2012 when Caritas was still part of the management alongside Misericordia. He found the work mentally draining and eventually had to leave because of the toll it took on him. He was relieved that he had left before the corruption scandals made the news. His colleague, Ramzi Labidi, head of the Immigration Office of Caritas in Crotone, said that although there had always been people made homeless by eviction from the Sant'Anna CARA, the number of evictions had increased since the security decree came into effect. However, Agora's shelter capacity was small, only six people. Caritas could only accommodate around twenty people in its shelter, and therefore had to prioritise the most vulnerable, such as those with health problems.

The insufficient capacity of charity accommodation meant that homeless migrants had to find their own spaces and build makeshift housing. One such space was the encampment under the motorway bridge next to the train station at Crotone. In spring 2019, there were more than fifty evicted people, many from Gambia, Senegal and Mali, living there in tents and shacks, without water or electricity. They now survived by taking up casual odd jobs in the area and purchasing their food and water from the nearby market. At the train station, people who had been or were due to be evicted from Sant'Anna and could afford to leave town, were waiting for trains to take them to bigger cities like Reggio Calabria. Some of them would eventually end up crossing borders to Germany and France.

Alsane had been evicted from the Sant'Anna CARA in the middle of winter in January 2019. He got on a bus and came to Crotone. Once there, he walked to the train station, wondering about his next move. He started talking to someone else who had just left the camp who told him that the charity Caritas had a homeless shelter in town. Alsane felt so relieved. He followed the man into town, across the central square, the Piazza Pitagora, through the arcades, and onto the street where the Caritas office was located.

There, Alsane registered himself for a bed. He was then taken to a derelict building with elaborate graffiti painted across the front, behind the old fresh fruit and vegetable market. It was a two-storey structure with a giant metal front door. The third storey was half in ruins. The building had no windows nor a roof, just an awning. Alsane stayed and shared a space with five others, all evicted from the Sant'Anna camp. The Caritas shelter also housed homeless Italians from the city. It was dark inside, and people used the torches on their mobile phones for light. It was freezing cold at night without a roof; Alsane went to sleep wearing his thick jacket. When it rained, the plastic awning would be closed and they would at least have a roof of sorts then.

At 8:00 am everyone was asked to leave the shelter. They were only allowed to return to sleep there after 8:00 pm. The shelter was closed on Sunday. Then Alsane and others had no choice but to go to their friends who were living in the tents and shacks behind Crotone station. The encampment could only be reached by crossing the rail tracks on foot. It was an isolated space shielded from a hostile world. Alsane would always be welcome to stay there for the night.

Now the orange season was over and it was too late to go to Rosarno for the harvest, Alsane found himself facing a difficult gap before the next period of work started. In the middle of February, he wandered around Crotone aimlessly. Sometimes he would go and sit in the town's only African bar run by the Djiguiya Association which he called 'the immigrant place'. There were colourful portraits of Patti Smith and Antonio Gramsci, alongside maps of Africa on the wall. There was a mural of Clark Kent ripping his shirt open to reveal his superman outfit but with 'S' replaced with a hammer and sickle. On the other side of the room was the television with Nigerian music videos playing on YouTube. In there, people from all African countries would come and spend time. For Alsane, it was the safest and most peaceful place to be.

Sometimes when he was around the train station, he would come to sit on the benches in the waiting room when it was almost empty, to take a break from the stress out there. He just sat, exchanging WhatsApp messages with friends for hours. His friends were dotted around the province of Foggia and were messaging him. He started to plan a schedule, as he normally did at this time each year. They would be working in the asparagus fields and he joined them each March. There, he would normally go to work in the area of Rignano

Garganico for a couple of months, and then to San Severo for a similar period of time. Following that, he would decide whether to go north to pick apples in Turin or stay south and pick olives in Capino, or join the harvest in Campobello in Sicily. Before he knew it, the year would have gone, winter would be back, and he would return to Crotone. He had done this cycle for years.

Ultimately, a lack of housing and documents was what kept Alsane in the south. His dream was to escape this life of the ghetto and live like everyone in the 'normal world.'

* * *

In the *tendopoli* of San Ferdinando, a three-hour train ride away from Crotone, the mood was tense. In the first months of 2019, CGIL posters with the words 'Dignity, rights, legality' were hung outside the burnt-out shack where Surawa Jaithe stayed on the night he died. On 23 January, Surawa's body was sent back from Italy to Africa. Around ten people, including Isaac and Michael, attended a small rally for him. No local politicians paid their respects, no reporters nor cameras. Just co-workers who shared the pain of Surawa's family.

People were anxious. There was a constant feeling in the air that things would not stay as they were for much longer and the encampment might be closed down soon. But everyone stayed put. What choice did they have? They all had to stick it out until the end.

The policy direction of the state was clear: the dismantling of informal settlements of African workers and the reduction of their public visibility. The migrant presence would be 'diluted' by separating them into smaller groups and pushing them further underground. For the authorities, the best case scenario was that some of these workers would end up travelling to other European countries and no longer be a 'problem' for Italy.

In the *tendopoli*, tragedy struck again on 15 February 2019. A fire broke out around midnight and spread quickly because of the flammable building materials. Moussa Ba, a twenty-eight-year-old man from Senegal, was killed as he slept. He had had a residence permit until March 2018 when it had expired; he had not managed to renew it. Without documents, he couldn't find a place to live and ended up in the encampment.

Moussa Ba's death gave Salvini the perfect justification for closing the site. This was the ultimate propaganda eviction. African workers in the *tendopoli* knew that the tragedies in these encampments were the result of the racism of the state and society that had segregated them. Many of them had come from various CARA camps and CAS shelters because they had been failed by the corrupt reception system—they were either evicted or transferred at random or had waited indefinitely for their documents. They were then failed by the towns and the institutions. They ended up here as a result of segregation. Salvini's directive exacerbated a desperate situation that had already gone on for years.

People inside the *tendopoli* were shaken by Moussa Ba's death. Malik, also known as Black Shine, knew Moussa. His stall was just two tents down from Moussa's tent. The young man had the whole of his life in front of him. Malik was indignant, and, for once, lost for words.

That morning, the Prefect of Reggio Calabria, Michele di Bari, called for a meeting of the Provincial Committee for Public Order and Security in San Ferdinando. Transfer plans were agreed there. From the evening of the 17 February, groups of twenty people were transferred from the *tendopoli* to reception centres across the province of Vibo Valentia. Then, on 28 February, Andrea Tripodi, the mayor of San Ferdinando, issued the eviction order to *tendopoli* residents. The notice, printed on a single sheet of paper, was taped on the shack that was used by Malik as his shopfront.

In the days leading up to the demolition, there were visibly more people on bikes travelling to and from the *tendopoli* and Rosarno, busying themselves with organising their last few days here. Some were trying to find possible lodgings from friends and acquaintances, others were planning to leave the area altogether. An immigration processing tent was set up where people were asked to show their documents and declare their status. Isaac had a residence permit, but resented the controls being set up around the *tendopoli*. A well-connected friend of his who worked in the small port town of Gioia Tauro managed to find a room there for Isaac and several other friends from the *tendopoli*, sharing the costs between them. At last, Isaac was to have a real roof over his head, although he would have to work in the fields again, as he would no longer be able to earn cash from running his café.

That morning, Malik, Black Shine, still stood outside his stall at the *tendopoli* entrance, just like any other day. He had to try to sell off as many of his goods as he could. This was the last day for his business here. T-shirts, shoes, cooking pots; Malik lowered the price to get rid of them. He also gave away things to those without cash. He would have to return to live full-time in the asylum shelter when the *tendopoli* was gone. The prospect upset him.

A loud banging came from the shacks a few metres behind Malik's stall. People who would not leave the building materials of their shacks behind were now taking apart the corrugated sheets, nail by nail, piece by piece. They were going to take the sheets with them and re-build their shacks elsewhere in the countryside. The banging echoed around the fields for hours.

The mood was strained and thick all day. It was written on everyone's faces. A local scrap dealer was picking up old bikes and throwing them onto his truck. People stood and watched, without a word, yet the anger was palpable, deep and strong. A lone African man could not take it anymore and stormed around the truck shouting, alarming several Italian TV news reporters who were interviewing passers-by. 'All white! All white!' the man yelled. His words were a painful reminder of the racist attacks of Rosarno in 2010 where local residents wanted the town for 'whites only'. His words also pointed to a society where 'blacks' were the underclass. The CGIL union flags still hung inside the *tendopoli*. One flag was at half-mast right by the entrance, almost symbolic. Where were the union representatives, one day before the demolition? No one knew. 'Where are they now when we need them?' said Michael. 'We are alone.'

It became clear that people's future paths were being categorised according to their asylum and immigration status. Those with refugee status were to be sent to SPRARs in the region (for 'integration'); coaches were parked at the entrance of the 'official tents' to pick them up. Those with humanitarian protection status were asked to stay in the 'official tents' where Michael was staying—to carry on working. Hundreds of other people, with or without humanitarian protection status, had already left for other agricultural regions, to carry on working and to find places to sleep in other informal settlements. Alsane's friends in the *tendopoli* were in this situation. They had all left for the province of Foggia, to find shelter in the ghettoes of Borgo Mezzonone and Gran Ghetto.

The 'official tents' were reaching the limit of their capacity, with more than 1,000 people living in them. Michael was frustrated and exhausted watching all this going on around him. Injustice, fear, extreme uncertainty. He wanted to leave this all behind, move away and move on. He wanted to join his friend in Paris. But at this moment, he needed cash to be able to travel there. Farm work was scarcer in the early spring, so he had to be patient. There was some onion harvesting work around. He had to get it via the *caporali* and would earn €22 a day after the €3 deduction for transport.

Isaac returned to the *tendopoli* to pick up his belongings for his new place in Gioia Tauro. Although he no longer had the worry of finding a new place to live, he was concerned about friends and people he knew here. He was angry and upset with the way the Africans were being treated by the authorities. Isaac called it 'evil'. Ghettoising Africans in the *tendopoli* was evil. Eviction without offering alternative housing was also evil, he said. Isaac would never forgive Italy for inflicting this on his fellow Africans. 'We are suffering. We've been suffering for too long.'

Isaac stood outside his old shack and talked with people who had not had the fortune of finding a new place. Michael came over to see him. Isaac prepared lunch and they sat in the café and had their last meal in the *tendopoli* together. Tomorrow, Isaac's shack and café would be no more. They both felt too low to speak much. That night, Isaac stayed overnight in the *tendopoli* with his friends for the last time. This was a place where he shared the struggle with everyone. They endured the harsh living conditions and lived through the tragedies of losing friends and fellow workers. They also cultivated friendships and solidarity here. This was a place Isaac could never put behind him. He wanted to stay with everyone until the last minute.

At the same time as workers in the *tendopoli* were so distressed at their upcoming eviction and felt lost about their future, the town of Rosarno was holding the 'Fat Tuesday' (*Martedì Grasso*) carnival the day before Lent started. This was their last opportunity to eat well and have a good time. Children ran along in fancy dress; mothers were pushing prams decorated with streamers and balloons, their babies with painted faces. Judging from the joyful mood in Rosarno town centre, you would have thought that the townsfolk were oblivious to the situation in the *tendopoli*. But the opposite was true: everyone knew about the demolition of the *tendopoli* planned for the next day— the very day when townsfolk would start their six weeks of Lent, when they were supposed to help the poor and give alms.

19

THE REPEATED CYCLE OF DEMOLISH
AND RE-GHETTOISE

8:00 am. Demolition began in the *tendopoli* of San Ferdinando, where only around 300 people remained. The area was completely surrounded by 600 heavily armed police officers and all roads leading to the encampment were blocked. No one was allowed to enter the area except those with a press card. The road to the rear of the camp was lined with *carabinieri* vans on one side and ten coaches on the other. Helicopters circled the area and police drones were filming the whole thing.

All types of police officers had been brought into the area: *carabinieri* in riot gear with shields and batons, municipal police, finance police, and scientific police all lined up by the *tendopoli*. Reporters were kept in a press area at a junction overlooking the front of the site that was being flattened by military bulldozers operated by soldiers and army engineers. Located right at the entrance, Malik's shop was one of the first things destroyed. It was now a flattened piece of muddy ground. He was so saddened to see it that he couldn't say a word. He sat on the opposite side of the road, staring at the empty space that was once his stall and his source of livelihood. He could do nothing but pray. God was all that he had now. 'The Lord is great,' he murmured. 'The Lord will guide us.'

While the press busied themselves clicking cameras, African residents of the *tendopoli* sat on the side of the road, silently watching their shacks and tents destroyed in front of their eyes. Many had so much sadness in their eyes, others were filled with anger. Police officers were armed with pistols and many riot police had teargas launchers with bandoliers of tear gas cartridges across their chests. A brand-new water cannon was parked on site. The authorities had anticipated people resisting their eviction. The heavy police presence and the arms they carried showed that they were prepared to put down any resistance with overwhelming force. But every African here was, in fact, too sad to fight back.

Police officers behaved roughly. When Michael went up to ask for information, he was waved away. One of them said to him aggressively: 'Speak Italian. This is Italy.' Then the mayor arrived, with journalists rushing up to him to shake his hands and interview him on camera. On this day and the next, very few journalists bothered to talk to the Africans who had been evicted. Michael made sure that he filmed as much of what happened as possible, using his mobile phone, to put it on YouTube, for the world to see. The CGIL flag at the entrance still hung at half-mast in the background, behind rows of riot police.

Isaac had not been allowed by the police to come near the *tendopoli* on the first day of the demolition. He was upset that he couldn't see it before it was bulldozed. That night, those who remained in the area and who didn't know where to go, had gone back inside the remaining part of the *tendopoli* to find a corner to sleep. It was desperate. Behind the flattened area, dozens still managed to find their way back to any remaining tents and shacks to spend the very final night.

Among those bussed out of the *tendopoli*, some were sent to Caulonia, some to Reggio Calabria, five were sent to Camini. Were the authorities going to call this 'integration'? This was treating people like cargo, transported from place to place, and depositing them in remote areas, away from their communities and their work. There was no consideration for the individuals and their needs.

Michael believed that people would eventually return to the site of the *tendopoli* and rebuild it sometime in the future. He didn't think that the authorities wanted to get rid of it permanently, because they knew they needed Africans as the main labour force in agriculture. 'The demolition was a show,' he said.

* * *

That evening, forty-five-year-old Francesco Caruso sat in the farmers' association meeting in the town centre of Rosarno, listening to local farmers discussing matters that concerned them. He watched them, thinking how much they looked like 'the faces of exploitation.'

Caruso was a sociology professor at the University of Catanzaro in Calabria, but he also referred to himself as a social researcher and full-time subversive. He came from Benevento, in Campania, a region rich in the production of fruit, vegetables and greenhouse flowers. He left his hometown to study political science at the Oriental University Institute in the city of Naples, during which time he became politically active. He founded a social centre in Naples, and started the building of social centres across southern Italy.[1]

Caruso's activism against the G8 conference in Genoa in 2001 led to his arrest on charges of 'subversion, political conspiracy and attack on the constitutional organs of the state.' He was imprisoned for a month, and for three years was kept from leaving his hometown. Soon after that, Caruso was elected and served as an MP for the Communist Refoundation Party for two years.

As a life-long activist and the author of *The Politics of the Subalterns: Organisation and Struggles of Migrant Workers in Southern Europe*,[2] Caruso pointed out the truth about what really went on with encampments like San Ferdinando. He believed that the *tendopoli* and its demolition was a case of the 'ghetto regeneration cycle,' where the emergency approach of the local authorities in addressing the housing needs of migrant agricultural workers had resulted in a cycle of state-funded encampment, followed by deteriorating living conditions due to poor management and decreasing funding, leading to the growth of informal settlements, which, in turn, ended in them being demolished by the authorities.

Caruso pointed out that the demolition was more of a show. The region needed migrant workers and migrant workers would no doubt be back for the harvest—and the settlement would be rebuilt once again. The pattern had been repeated in other regions of Italy:

informal settlements being demolished and rebuilt. Caruso predicted that the 'official tents' near the demolished *tendopoli* of San Ferdinando would start to disintegrate, too, when the funding dried up in a couple of years. The fundamental cause of such a cycle was the lack of political will to find real solutions, which could only be explained, in the end, by the deep-seated structural racism that determined the emergency approach of the authorities and policy-makers. While these settlements were demolished and rebuilt in an endless cycle, apartments and buildings continued to lie empty in towns like Rosarno and San Ferdinando.

According to Francesco Caruso, what these interventions did was 'normalise the position of migrant agricultural workers and their precarious living arrangements and conditions in the countryside.' While doing so, these interventions also aimed to conceal the reality behind the image of 'Made in Italy.'

* * *

On the second day of the demolition in San Ferdinando, the police numbers reduced as things seemed under control. Two thirds of the *tendopoli* had been flattened. Several men from the Ivory Coast and Sierra Leone looked on helplessly by the side of the road. They had now been placed in the 'official tents' area as they had the two-year documents. Like many, they had come from the notorious Sant'Anna CARA two years ago. How things had not improved for them! Meanwhile, in front of them, a group of Italian reporters were being led into the demolished site, to take photographs and film reports. They walked around the bulldozed land wearing surgical masks, focusing their cameras on any pile of rubble that caught their eye.

Along a lane on one side of the site, abandoned bikes had been piled up. A man sat there alone for ages, his head in his hands, staring at the demolition. In front of him was a wasteland: broken cookers, plastic chairs, mattresses, old scooters. Michael walked over to take a look. He searched through the bikes, to see if there was a good one that he could have. The brakes on his old bike were broken and he couldn't use it anymore.

Isaac heard from Michael that the camp was almost all gone on the second day. There was no point in going back anymore. Isaac prayed in the morning when he woke up—under a roof. In his new place, at least he was safe and well. He prayed and thanked God that he was alive. He wanted to reset the course of his life.

Most of Isaac's fellow residents in the *tendopoli* did not have the means to reset their lives. Many had ended up in there as a result of the actions of the authorities, and yet now they were being evicted because of an order by the same authorities. A group of Gambian boys from the reception camp in the former Hotel Costa Bella in Briatico, not far from Rosarno, were in exactly this situation. In February 2019, their camp, accommodating 600 asylum seekers, was closed down, and they had no idea why. Those still awaiting documents were transferred to a place with poorer facilities while those with humanitarian protection status, including a twenty-two-year-old Gambian named Alex, were asked to leave the camp without transfer somewhere else. They had to leave without any resources, and ended up homeless. Some of them, Alex's friends, had to come to stay at the *tendopoli* which was nearby. Alex himself remembered the encampment as a miserable place. He had never wanted to sleep overnight there, even when his friends invited him over. 'Even seeing the place made me depressed,' he said. Alex's friends didn't expect that, a month later, the *tendopoli* would be bulldozed and they would be without a home, again. They felt that the authorities seemed to be playing a cruel game with them, evicting them out of reception centres without notice and driving them into rural ghettoes and then pushing them out of the ghettoes, either into the streets or back into asylum shelters again.

In retrospect, Alex felt that he was fortunate to have decided to stay put in the same town when evicted from the former Hotel Costa Bella camp. Some of the residents from that camp had given up trying to stay in Italy and went abroad, to France or Germany. Alex had no cash to travel far. He decided to stay in Briatico, and along with five others from the camp, found a tiny bedsit in town. In January and February, Alex knew of four reception camps that had closed down in the surrounding area. People were treated like cattle, moved from place to place. After all, for these reception camps as well as for the state, the transfer of asylum seekers was simply a business transaction.

Like his fellow residents in the camp, Alex made a living working on the onion farms. He had to work because he was the eldest son in the family and was given the responsibility of supporting his parents and four siblings. After deductions by the *caporali*, he was earning €20–€25 a day, when a local worker would earn €50 if they chose to do the same work, which most of them did not. Back home in Gambia, €25 could buy a seventy-kilogram bag of rice that would feed the entire family for a month. Alex sent home €100 each month, which ensured his family would survive. For this, he had to keep working. He didn't usually talk to his family about the actual work conditions in Calabria. 'No one believes you when you tell them how tough it is in Europe.'

From May onwards, Briatico became a tourist resort and restaurants would then need workers for the season. Alex knew someone who knew a local restaurant manager and was introduced into a job preparing salads, ten hours or more per day, for €25. It was rare for an African to be able to work in a restaurant, but they needed good, fast and low-paid workers—Alex was faster than the local workers and certainly the cheapest. He was the top choice for his employer. Who would accept that kind of money for such long hours? Alex knew well that he was being exploited but accepted it because he needed money to send home. Once, a police officer came to dine in the restaurant, and happened to ask Alex about his work hours. 'I work just two hours a day,' he said. He told a lie for the boss, so that the owner wouldn't get into trouble, and he could keep his job.

There were many seaside towns across the country in need of workers to fill the vacancies for the tourist season. Not every locality was able to find sufficient seasonal local labour to meet the need. At the same time, Italy's annual quotas for migrant workers remained ridiculously low: the 2018 and 2019 Immigration Quota Decree (*decreto flussi*) for non-EU workers from a set list of countries only allowed 18,000 work permits for seasonal workers in tourist and agricultural sectors. As local labour was unable to fill the catering jobs in tourism, a small number of employers began to accept informal job applications from African workers in the area. Although Italian restaurants and cafés didn't normally hire 'blacks' as waiters, a few such businesses started to employ Africans as kitchen workers on zero-hour pay.[3]

Alex received such an offer in an ancient seaside resort town called Pizzo in June 2019. He worked day and night, preparing salads for more than ten hours each day. The employer paid him only €30, not much more than his agricultural wage on onion farms. Again, African labour met the requirements for high seasonality and flexibility, and the workers didn't exist in the employers' bookkeeping and there was therefore no trace of exploitation. As it turned out, Alex often moved from agricultural work to zero-hour kitchen work in tourism and back to agricultural work again. A few months later in the autumn, he went back to Briatico to pick olives for €25 a day.

Back in the 'official tents' in San Ferdinando, Michael dragged himself through each day waiting and looking for farm work. The tents were getting fuller with people who had humanitarian protection documents and had been moved from the demolished site. It was clear to Michael that the overcrowding was not sustainable.

Then, late during the night of 21 March, he was woken by horrific screaming outside his tent. He ran out and saw a crowd around a burning blue tent a few steps away from his. Some people were crying, others stood, silent with shock. It was a horrible fire that had left another man dead. The blue plastic material of the tent was gone, and its metal frame—and the frames of beds—was all that was left. Michael saw a human form amongst the charred mess. He felt his heart beating fast and himself short of breath.

As Michael found out soon enough, the man who was killed was named Sylla Noumo, a thirty-two-year-old from Senegal. Only two weeks before, he had been transferred from the demolished *tendopoli*. There was no response from Caritas, the organisation currently managing the 'official tent' area. Nor was there any explanation from any authorities about the circumstances that caused the fire. Any news about Sylla Noumo's death disappeared from the newspapers after a day.

* * *

Alsane's friend kept calling to ask him to come join him in Foggia. With little work going on in Crotone in mid-March, Alsane decided to leave. He took a bus from Crotone to Bari one morning and then got on a train from Bari to Foggia. As usual, he had only his small rucksack and a shopping bag with him. He never seemed to have accumulated more than a few personal belongings since his arrival in this country in 2010.

On arrival in Foggia, Alsane squeezed himself onto a bus heading to Gran Ghetto, or 'the Ghetto' as his friends called it, twelve kilometres away. Buses for Gran Ghetto weren't frequent, running every two hours until 6:00 pm, except on Sunday when there was no service. Another bus stop on the opposite side of the road was also lined with people, going to another makeshift settlement, Borgo Mezanonone, known as 'Borgo.' African workers had arrived in Foggia from all parts of the country to head to these settlements in the rural heart of the province.

The bus was packed with young Africans. Some had luggage, as if they had just arrived; others were bringing packs of bottled drinking water from Foggia to use in the Ghetto, as there was no proper water supply except from a pipe nearby. Soon the bus turned out of the city and into the rural outskirts of town. Passengers swayed as the vehicle rattled and bumped along the uneven country lanes, everyone holding on tight to the poles and to each other. The bus drove deeper into the countryside, passing massive fields with all kinds of crops. At last, twenty-five minutes later, down a country lane, the bus stopped in the middle of nowhere, and everyone got out at once.

Alsane did the same. He was hit by a strong blast of cold wind. He had to lower his head and turned up his collar. He tried to walk behind people to shelter from the wind. They were all walking towards the Ghetto, out of sight, behind trees in the deep of the flat plain, hidden away. The vast flatness stretched out for miles in every direction, with mountains at the edge of the plain. It looked and felt like the vast flat plain surrounding the CARA di Mineo in Sicily. More than a few people in the group had been in that camp and would have felt a horrible sense of déjà vu arriving here. Several new arrivals could not manage the long walk against the wind and accepted a lift in the old car of a Senegalese man, who had actually come from the CARA di Mineo. He was one of the few here who could drive, and managed to get himself a used car, often offering lifts to people up and down the lanes, charging them a small taxi fee.

A few minutes down the heavily potholed road, Alsane turned a corner into a row of disused barns, while others carried on walking past into the distance to reach the Ghetto. This was where his friend was living—in one of the derelict barns that belonged to a farmer for whom he was working. Alsane had come to stay with him last year, too. He knocked on the door and went in before his friend opened it. It was pitch-dark inside as it had no electricity, but Alsane knew his way round. There was nowhere to sit down but the concrete floor. Gas bottles were placed next to an old, filthy cooker. A mattress was laid on the floor to the left, where he would be sleeping.

His friend finally came to greet him. They went outside the barn and chatted, looking over the vast wheat fields sprouting green in front of them. This was the 'bread basket of Italy': Puglia was known for producing 80% of the country's pasta. The region's culinary catchphrase was the 'cuisine of the poor,' *cucina povera*, which referred to the use of the simplest and freshest ingredients grown locally with traditional methods. Alsane and his friend were themselves living on this *cucina povera*, with ingredients picked by themselves in the fields, often during work, and brought home to use for dinner. Some farmers were quick to make profits from the concept of 'cuisine of the poor' with a twist of innovation. Opposite the barn where Alsane and his friend were living was an organic farm, Di Carlo Matteo, that produced asparagus, grapes, and cheese. It had attracted some agro-tourists.

Alsane and his friend were a tiny minority who had a roof over their heads here, albeit a leaking one. Most Africans lived in Gran Ghetto, a twenty minute' walk away. Because of a history of being built, demolished, and rebuilt, Gran Ghetto was well out of reach and out of sight in March 2019. You couldn't even see it on the vast, flat plain. It was occupied by 1,000 people. The entrance was marked by a USB flag hung upside-down, probably accidentally. Alongside the numerous shacks, there were many old caravans, each with a tarpaulin stretched over the top to prevent leaks in the rain.

Alsane's friends had just arrived in this Ghetto from the demolished *tendopoli* of San Ferdinando. Every so often in the early evening, Alsane would walk twenty minutes across the fields to go and see them there. They sat in the tent of a fellow Senegalese man who had picked up an old television from a dump in Foggia and watched it together. Sometimes Alsane would call his two brothers and sister on WhatsApp and have a chat. He was the youngest of the siblings, but after his parents passed away, he always tried to send cash home when he was able.

The harvest started late, in April. Asparagus, and then tomatoes and grapes—'just like salad,' Alsane joked.

One night, Alsane saw on television that the Chinese president Xi Jinping had just arrived in Rome to sign an agreement for Italy to become a member of China's Belt and Road Initiative (BRI). Italy's agreement with China was worth up to €7 billion and included a project that would open up the Italian ports of Trieste and Genoa to Chinese containers. Italy's opening of its ports to international capital had coincided with its closing of ports to the working-class and the poor from the Global South.

Xi's visit was orchestrated by Luigi di Maio, who had nurtured relations with China ever since the League–Five Star coalition government came into power. When Xi and his wife Peng Liyuan visited Palermo, Luigi di Maio celebrated the first fruits of his work: the transportation of Sicilian oranges by plane to China from 2 April 2019. 'This represents a small revolution for our "Made in Italy" products,' said Di Maio.

However, the 'Made in Italy' Sicilian oranges were hand-picked by African and other migrant workers. They were the product of systematic exploitation, institutional racism and segregation. Alsane was baffled but at the same time rather amused by the news. 'Xi ought to come and see our ghettoes here in Foggia, Rosarno, and Campobello,' he joked bitterly.

20

'HOW MUCH LONGER DO WE HAVE TO SUFFER?'

Back in San Ferdinando, Calabria, Michael had his mind made up about his next move on the day Salvini visited the 'official tents' on 18 April and stated that the tents would have to go by the end of his term. For Michael, it became a choice of either staying put to wait to become homeless or leaving and doing something about it. He decided to leave—not only leaving San Ferdinando but Calabria and Italy, for good.

What Salvini represented was no exception to the norm. African migrants in Italy had endured being criminalised, marginalised, and segregated from society for as long as they had been there. Their circumstances had, for years, compelled them to leave Italy—even when they knew that their next destination might not offer them anything more than a temporary stay and that they could be sent back to Italy sooner or later due to the Dublin rules.

Michael gathered all the cash he had and travelled from Rosarno by bus via Rome to join his friend in Paris. He then started working at McDonalds. Joseph had left Riace and headed to Karlsruhe in Germany where he claimed asylum and was at least fed and housed in a shelter. His plan was to find a job to support himself and his family for as long as he had a roof over his head.

Italy had been shutting its doors for years. Its successive governments—from the PD government to the League–Five Star coalition and then the PD–Five Star coalition—along with the EU, had played a central role in outsourcing border controls to countries outside of Europe. Throughout 2018 and 2019, Salvini had effected a broad criminalisation of the NGOs, putting rescue ship activists under investigation.[1] Salvini stepped up his efforts to end sea rescue by introducing a new security decree, *Decreto Sicurezza Bis*, which won parliamentary approval on 5 August 2019. It aimed to levy heavy fines on rescue ships entering Italian waters without permission: the commanders of such ships would face fines of up to €1 million and would have their vessels seized.

These policies directly led to a situation where migrants were left to die at sea. In 2019, only 11,471 people arrived in Italy by sea, according to the UN Refugee Agency. Over 10,000 people, most of them sub-Saharan Africans, had been intercepted and sent back to Libya. More than 1,000 people drowned in the Mediterranean in 2019.[2]

* * *

Salvini and his politics were making further electoral advances. In the European elections in late May 2019, the League won over 34% of the vote, cementing its position as Italy's most popular party. Even in the south and the islands, it gained around 23%. On Lampedusa, where anti-migrant propaganda had hit a nerve, the League won nearly 46% of the vote. In other places where right-wing parties had widely disseminated their propaganda, while the left had failed, the League did well too, such as in Riace where they won over 30%. In Riace, Antonio Trifoli, a former policeman, was elected as mayor. He was first on the independent Riace Reborn list, backed by the League. By then, almost all the asylum seekers had gone. As Joseph and many Africans who had left Riace had attested, the culture of the community had not caught up with the cash that the village had brought in to renovate itself. The soft sand foundations upon which the previous 'integration' initiatives were built had quickly collapsed into a support base for the hard-right.

As for Five Star, it remained strong only in parts of the south where unemployment was severe. In Campobello, 1,135 residents came out to vote for Five Star, making it 'the first political force' in the town, as councillor Tommaso di Maria put it once again. In a summer marked by the banning of sea rescues and arrests of captains, Di Maria continued to rail against 'illegal immigration.' 'In the past we had smugglers getting migrants into Italy. Now we have the NGOs,' he lamented on social media.

Overall, Salvini's wish to forge a strong far-right presence in the European parliament was partially realised, with the new alliance holding seventy-three of 751 seats, which made them the fifth largest group. Although the far-right parties did not defeat the centrists, substantial gains were made. In total, the Europe of Nations and Freedom group (ENF) in which the League and National Rally sat, secured fifty-eight seats in the European parliament. Salvini was ecstatic and celebrated his electoral victory, tweeting, 'A new Europe is born.' In June 2019, his alliance in the European parliament renamed itself Identity and Democracy (ID), which combined the ENF and several other hard-right parties such as Alternative for Germany (AfD).

Domestically, the system continued to keep migrant workers in their subordinated place, toiling for the 'civilised' society above ground. While many of them wanted to escape destitution by crossing borders northbound, many more remained trapped because they lacked the resources or networks to move on. Others were put off by increasing deportations from Germany and the toughening of policies in France.

Sanji was among those who stayed put. In Campobello, he and his friends carried on, living in the same shed where they had been holed up since last autumn, working odd jobs through the seasons. Meanwhile, after Benjamin's departure from the shared compound, Alieu had been working as a shepherd near Mazara, earning barely enough to live, let alone send cash home. He had no means to enable him to leave Sicily, let alone Italy.

Mohammad, seen by fellow Gambians as one of the fortunate few, had returned from visiting his family in Gambia in the spring of 2019. He was a changed man. Once back home, his family introduced him to a local woman whom he married. He had barely spent two months with his wife before having to leave home and return to Italy. She had to contend with the reality that he would be an absent breadwinner for a long, long time.

On his return to Campobello, Mohammad's eighty-year-old employer welcomed him back with open arms. He continued living in the same garage, owned by his boss' sisters, he had vacated months before. Despite having documents and being able to travel between his home country and Italy, he remained a transient migrant worker enjoying no rights or entitlements. His status was brutally demonstrated by this garage living space—indicating his use as a farming tool, parked alongside tractor and plough. Mohammad would have liked to have thought that his future wouldn't be confined to this one place—the garage, the town, the province. But right now, he knew he wasn't yet able to build up networks and settle elsewhere. For now, he knew he had to continue in Campobello and be a loyal provider for his family— even more so now, after storms in Gambia damaged the family house and much of his village.

In Marausa, a few miles south of Trapani, Benjamin had managed to find some work on onion and garlic farms in June, but merely enough to pay the rent and buy food. In order to find more regular work, he wanted to sort out his documents. His laywer in Mazara charged him yet another set of fees but soon stopped answering his calls. He had nowhere to turn. Then someone suggested that he contact a lawyer in Rome—apparently because he was on record with the police there from when he stayed with his friends after his bike accident and eviction from his shelter several years earlier. Now, on the phone, the Rome-based lawyer asked him to travel there for a meeting. Benjamin worked his hardest and saved up for a bus ticket. When he eventually got to the lawyer's office in Rome in mid-July, he was charged €150 but refused a meeting.

'Come back on 24 July,' said the lawyer. That would be nine days' time—and he knew full well that Benjamin had travelled from Sicily and would be unlikely to be able to afford a place to stay. There was nothing Benjamin could do but to walk away and wait nine days. He had to stop and ask every African he met in the street about a bed for a few days. It was desperate, and for the first couple of nights he slept on the street.

On the third day, Benjamin met a Gambian man and pleaded for help once again. The man took him to a disused farmhouse on the outskirts of Rome in which many Gambians were sheltering. The place was overcrowded with people who were either working on farms in the area or, like Benjamin, were visiting lawyers to sort out documents.

The conditions in the farmhouse reminded him of White Grass back in Campobello, which depressed him enormously. He found a corner to sleep in, but the stress of the day and the worries about the forthcoming meeting kept him awake until the early hours.

When the nine days were up, Benjamin took a bus into the city and returned to the lawyer's office. This time, he was given an instruction to go to an address for an interview the next day. The next day came and there was no interview. Instead, he was told that he should 'get a work contract' back in Sicily. This instruction meant that he would need to purchase a work contract, in order to get a residence permit.

Confusion upon confusion, Benjamin travelled all the way back to Trapani, having failed to achieve what he aimed to do. He returned to the flat and asked for advice from Yugo, who had just arrived back from Malta as his Italian residence permit had expired. They were now in the same situation of having to buy a fake work contract which would give no guarantee of work. Yugo called it a 'deal' that you had to make in order to get your residence permit renewed. If only this deal were straightforward. As Yugo and Benjamin already knew, it would cost them hundreds of euros to be able to buy one. 'A mafia country, through and through,' sighed Benjamin. He felt utterly defeated by the wasted effort in Rome and the continuously changing instructions from profiteers. Having spent every penny he had on the fare to Rome, he had no means to afford the work contract. What should he do now? First of all, he needed to earn some cash. He started looking around for work in the vineyards, without documents, even if it was only two or three days a week. So the cycle of misery continued.

* * *

Salvini was emboldened by the European elections and the stronger national polling results. In early August 2019, in the middle of parliament recess, he called for snap elections, with the aim of ending the coalition and consolidating power. However, he severely miscalculated the dynamics of the forces at play. Prime Minister Giuseppe Conte didn't just walk away. Instead, he gave a damning critique of Salvini for the first time, saying the snap election was solely in Salvini's own interest. In a further twist, Salvini had also not anticipated Five Star seeking an alliance with its traditional foe, the PD.

The then Five Star leader Luigi Di Maio set an uncompromising tone for the negotiations with the PD, requesting the inclusion of his party's programme points in the new coalition's programme as a precondition for working with them. Amongst the measures he outlined was the acceptance of the policy that aimed at clamping down on migrant sea rescues. 'No changes to the security decree,' said Di Maio, clearly appealing to Five Star's grassroots. Eventually, Di Miao managed to get 79% of his members to vote online in favour of forming a coalition government with the PD. With their need to hang on to power, the two parties made compromises on each other's policy points. The new government was sworn in on 5 September 2019.

There were Five Star members on the ground who disapproved of their party allying with the 'establishment party' against which Five Star was founded in the first place. Some of them were more hard-line about migration policy and leaned closer to the League. Tommaso di Maria in Campobello was one of these people. 'Not in my name,' he said of the new coalition.[3]

Whatever Di Maria thought, many of Salvini's anti-migrant policies remained intact after the new coalition came to power. The PD–Five Star alliance did not scrap the security decrees. After all, it was under the PD's Marco Minniti that Italy had worked fully with Libya and effected the largest reduction in the number of migrant crossings to Italy—more than 80%—in 2017. The PD–Five Star alliance was well prepared to work in the environment already fermented under Salvini, meaning the security decrees outlived his reign. The interior minister, Luciana Lamorgese, only hours after the government was sworn in, rejected Sea Eye's appeal for a port of safety for its rescue ship *Alan Kurdi* that had been refused permission to dock by Salvini. *Alan Kurdi* had rescued thirteen people on 31 August, including eight minors, and had been stranded between Italy and Malta. 'We inform you that the Decree No. 53/2019 is still valid,' the Interior Ministry said in its firm reply to Sea Eye. 'The new government in Rome is apparently sticking to its tough stance on civil rescue teams,' Sea Eye said in a tweet.

In September, Ocean Viking, a rescue ship operated by SOS Méditerranée and Médecins Sans Frontières (MSF), carrying eighty-two migrants including fifty-eight men, six women, seventeen minors and a one-year-old child, had been left at sea for six days without permission from the new Italian authorities to dock. A woman on board in her ninth month of pregnancy had to be sent to Malta on a helicopter. The ship's request to dock was only answered following a migrant redistribution agreement that Conte reached with the European Commission. Still, in Rome, there was no talk of scrapping Salvini's security decrees.

Maurice Stierl, of Alarm Phone,[4] reported on 20 September the desperate situation in the central Mediterranean in the fortnight post-Salvini: 'The so-called Libyan coastguards—funded, equipped, trained by Europe—are trying to abduct as many people as possible back to Libya… Right now, eighty people are reaching out to us from within the Maltese SAR zone… Yesterday, a migrant was shot and killed by the Libyan authorities after trying to run away after being returned to Libya… Two shipwrecks occurred this week off the coast of Tunisia… We have long ago surpassed the mark of 1,000 deaths. The new commissioner for migration will be called "Protecting the European way of life".[5] Sounds about right.'

Under the PD–Five Star government, it was business as usual in the central Mediterranean: the order of things that had been put in place between Italy and Libya carried on. In early October 2019, Di Maio presented a new decree to accelerate the expulsion of migrants 'who have no rights to be in the country'. Under the decree, the time to examine asylum requests of migrants who come from a list of 'thirteen safe countries'[6] would be reduced from ten years to four months. If the asylum request is rejected, the expulsion procedure will be immediately triggered. 'We are working to avoid the "pull factor",' Di Maio said. On 2 November, his government renewed the notorious 2017 multimillion-euro agreement with Libya.

In the midst of all this, Salvini and the League had not gone away. Donatella Tesei of the League, backed by Brothers of Italy and Berlusconi's Forza Italia, was elected regional president of Umbria after capturing 57% of the vote and defeating the PD–Five Star candidate on 27 October 2019.

* * *

Evidently, 'Italians first' continued to dominate the direction of policy, controlling the lives of migrant workers and maintaining their segregation.

Benjamin's brief relief that Salvini was gone from government was soon replaced by frustration and anger that the same policies remained. The review of humanitarian residence permits under Salvini was still in progress under this Red-Yellow coalition government. Benjamin's friend Yugo borrowed money to pay for a work contract while Benjamin himself still couldn't afford one and didn't want to borrow. Then he was told by the local police authorities that he had to take a commission interview to decide on his status.

He asked around again for advice, and this time, he was introduced to a Trapani-based lawyer who charged him €200 to sort out his documents 'once and for all.' The lawyer reassured him that there was hope.

In October, Benjamin took the train to Campobello, hoping to find work in the olive fields like he did last year. Yugo came along to pick olives too, because the work contract he bought could only guarantee a one-year residence permit and therefore he couldn't return to work in Malta. When the two reached the disused farmhouse where Benjamin used to live with Alieu and the team, they found that the place had been bricked up. The front gate of the compound had been sealed with stone blocks and concrete and no one could enter anymore. This was the work of local law enforcement. His former group had dispersed. Alieu hadn't returned from Mazara. Benjamin and Yugo had to follow others to shelter inside the cement factory site next door where the majority of migrant workers, between 600 and 1,000 of them, were staying.

As luck would have it, Benjamin ran into Alieu's half-brother who had also come to work in the olive fields. He was a builder and had managed to construct a temporary wooden shack large enough for three people. Benjamin and Yugo asked to stay with him. The three shared one salvaged double mattress and the single blanket Benjamin had brought with him from Trapani, not enough to keep them warm. What's more, the autumn rain leaked into the shack, waking them up throughout the night. Benjamin sat in the dark, soaked, wishing that he could return to Trapani. But the extra transport costs made him abandon the thought.

In the autumn, the prefecture and the institutions in Campobello involved in the 'management' of seasonal labour continued with the same rhetoric of legality and practice of immigration controls. This time, they excluded the associations from their roundtable discussions. In Campobello, discriminatory practices continued: the temporary Red Cross camp was set up on the Golden Fountain site, with a capacity of 240 people and only for those workers with residence permits.

2019 was an even worse year for olive cultivation in Campobello, and far fewer workers were needed for the harvest. Benjamin had no choice but to go back to the same farmer. He paid workers €3 per crate of olives; Benjamin was only able to pick around seven crates per day which earned him a meagre €21. By early November, as work was so scarce, he had only worked seven days in total.

As harvesting slowed and some workers started to leave Campobello in November, Mohammad received terrible news from home: his young wife had just died of a heart condition. Without any hesitation, he got on a plane to return to Gambia for her funeral. As devastating as it was for him, he knew he was still among the fortunate few Africans in Italy. The majority of migrant workers here were not in a position where they could just leave and visit home, even for a funeral, and then return to Italy again. Most of them wouldn't get to see their families for years.

During the summer, Sanji had discovered that he could get into an abandoned farmhouse a few metres from Benjamin's previous compound. The wooden gate appeared securely locked and few bothered to check further. Sanji put his hand through a gap in the door and found that he could slide open the latch. He got in and found a filthy, 100-square-metre yard, as well as the farmhouse, partitioned into two rooms, completely empty and derelict. He moved in. The group who had shared the shed with him before didn't want to join him at the farmhouse, fearing that it was more likely to draw attention from passing *carabinieri* patrol cars. They preferred to stay in the shed, set well back from the road, unnoticed by the authorities.

Sanji later found out that the disused farmhouse where he now lived was once the property of a local mafia man who ran a brothel there. It became such a popular venue with the men in Campobello that local wives made numerous complaints to the police, telling them that the prostitution business had stolen their husbands. Eventually, the whole operation was closed down by the police. The mafia owner went into hiding, and his assets, including the farmhouse, were confiscated.

The farmhouse had been abandoned ever since. After Sanji moved in, word spread and friends started calling him, recommending their newly arrived friends to come and live with him there. In order not to get too overcrowded, Sanji limited the number of housemates to five. They always had to lock the gate firmly shut to minimise any attention from the *carabinieri*.

Sanji and his new group gradually accumulated items from the town's dumps in their yard: old bikes, a microwave, and a pile of metal sheets with which to build shacks. They also collected an abandoned TV set that worked, although it didn't last more than a few weeks. Sanji found himself a double mattress from the dump and placed it in one corner of the main room. A broken sofa sat in the middle of the floor, providing a makeshift social space for the group.

There was no electricity or water inside the farmhouse, but Sanji used what he nicknamed 'mafia electricity': he tapped into the main electricity cable before the meter to provide lighting. Unfortunately, during heavy rain, water got into the wiring and it short-circuited, causing a small explosion and fire. Sanji put it out and waited for the wiring to dry. They had to live without electricity for the moment.

During this time, Sanji continued to struggle to find work without proper documents, his residence permit having expired. It was harder during the harvest season as controls and checks on workers' immigration status tightened. Farmers became more worried about getting caught and fined for hiring 'illegals'. For this reason, the olive farmer for whom Sanji worked this season was only able to give him a total of fifteen days of work.

Sanji continued living in the confiscated farmhouse. In the morning, he would take the path at the side of his yard to get to the small camp where Tunisian workers had stayed last year. The space was now occupied by Sudanese, Malian and Gambian workers who had built around fifty tents and shacks. Sanji would come to have coffee in the makeshift espresso stall, which consisted of a tiny espresso maker on top of an old gas cooker at the entrance of a Malian man's shack. 'Café express!' the man shouted out to people. Customers could see the man's mattress on the floor from where they stood at the door to buy 50-cent strong espressos. Sanji often stood with an espresso and chatted with people. Some of them were still here in late November, waiting for their wages owed from the harvest whilst hanging on for a bit more work. Others were talking about going to Rosarno for the orange harvest.

Meanwhile, outside Rosarno, in the open fields next to the site where the *tendopoli* once stood, the 'official tents' area had been reduced in size by the authorities to accommodate only 300 people, under tight police surveillance. No one could enter the area without being questioned and ID-checked. Many African workers who came here for the orange harvest this year had to look for disused barns and squat in small groups in the surrounding countryside.

In Campobello, a few steps away from Sanji's place, the cement factory site was still buzzing. Prayer mats and work boots were for sale on a stall at the entrance. The site was still filled with people, and of around 500 in late November, 400 were Senegalese. They always seemed to persevere. When others were leaving, the Senegalese kept on, right to the end of the harvest. When Sanji came into the site, he would talk with Gaye, a middle-aged man who had been here as long as Sanji himself. Gaye had been helping to organise the Senegalese area of the camp and ensure things ran smoothly.

Sanji waited for the harvest to end, as he would be given a lot more work when the immigration checks were loosened. From the second half of November, he started to get plenty of weeding and pruning work, as well as irrigation pipe maintenance and tidying, which he called 'donkey work.' There was also some lemon and mandarin picking to do in the winter. Although wages were as low as before, Sanji wasn't leaving the area just yet. He heard that Alieu had now gone to work in Syracuse and in theory he could join him in the tomato harvest there. But Sanji didn't want to be beholden to anyone. He was proud. He wanted to wait and prepare until he had sufficient resources to support himself in a new place before asking for any help.

Sanji had not stopped dreaming of going to a country where he could become a footballer. He had a friend in Sweden, which kept alive his idea of making a new life outside Italy. But he also knew that, apart from going through the asylum system there, which he heard was becoming more difficult, he would have little chance of starting anew. That thought held him back.

A few days before Benjamin's work came to an end in Campobello, he received the good news from Trapani that he had been issued with his two-year residence permit card. He had been waiting for two long years, enduring virtual extortion from lawyers, and the permit card had finally arrived. This was a time when many other Gambians were having their cases turned down. For Benjamin, it almost felt unreal.

The permit would make it possible for him to rent a room (if there was no racism to deal with) without having to rely on a friend with formal status. It would, along with an ID and *codice fiscale*, guarantee a work contract—although it would not guarantee rights to the agricultural minimum wage or standard working conditions. Like other African workers, he knew that he would be paid the same wage with or without these documents. In reality, this residence permit card, which would need renewing in two years' time, represented a temporary, formal status which did little for the holder's rights and entitlements.

The real advantage that this permit would bring, in the eyes of many migrant workers, was the right to travel and work across borders within the EU. However, with his meagre and irregular earnings, Benjamin did not have sufficient means to consider going anywhere at this stage. His current aim, first and foremost, was to survive and send some cash home. His horizons remained constrained.

As the olive harvest ended, Benjamin and Yugo packed their bags and returned to Trapani to brace themselves for the limited amount of garlic planting and other farm work that was available in the winter. As he dragged himself along the dusty road towards Campobello train station, with his old blanket around his shoulders, Benjamin felt as burdened and trapped as ever before.

It had been six years since Ousmane Diallo died, and nothing had changed for migrant workers. The *omertà* of suffering, which society keeps quiet and pretends not to see, had made all this pain normal. 'How much longer do we have to suffer?' Benjamin asked, looking out towards the olive fields in the distance.

AFTERWORD

Ever since the migration of non-Europeans became part of the consciousness of citizens of Europe, the narrative about migration has always been Eurocentric. The imagery used to depict those fleeing across borders ranges from flow to flood to crisis. The idea that the movement of people—'migrants' and 'refugees' as postcolonial subjects—into the European continent constitutes a crisis has always been embedded in this Eurocentric way of thinking. In political and media discourse, the framing of migration as a crisis reveals that the presence of the Other is regarded as a rupture in European everyday life, as Encarnación Gutiérrez Rodríguez has written.[1] For Europe, the Other challenges its 'way of being' in a fundamental manner, their presence alone reflecting Europe's past imperialism, upon which the continent's wealth was built. The arrival of the Other causes anxiety and fear in the European mind, as if Europe's colonial history is catching up with it.

There came a need to rationalise this European anxiety and fear. In Rodriguez's words: 'The rhetoric involved in the production of the "refugee crisis" [and "migrant crisis"] resurfaces within a specific conjuncture of racism in Europe... Colonial legacies of the construction of the racialised Other are reactivated and wrapped in a racist vocabulary, drawing on racist imagery combined with new forms of governing the racialised Other through migration control... The media and political rhetoric on the "crisis" illustrates the continuation of the coloniality of power.'

In Europe's narration, white Europeans have always been the ones to hold the microphone, notepad and pen, observing and documenting. The subjects of their narration are given the opportunity to speak while their voices are filtered, their discontent toned down, their experiences minimised by censors and gatekeepers. For a long time, the migrating person has only been talked and written *about*, portrayed as having little agency or capacity to take part in shaping their own destiny. In the best-case scenario, a migrant who survives their journey and overcomes hurdles presented by national borders is seen as a 'rescued person' in the 'refugee welcome' efforts. Whether they are labelled a refugee or a migrant, their story is still a white man's story.

This Eurocentric narration is part of the continent's colonial legacy. Frantz Fanon suggested through his work that the Black social being has been emptied of content and their agency immobilised. Marked by a permanent absence in a white supremacist society, their sense of non-existence exceeds the mere feeling of inferiority; it is how dehumanisation works day-to-day.

In European discourse, the 'migrant' is set up as a category distinct from the 'refugee.' A migrant freely chooses to leave home for economic reasons, while a refugee is forced to leave by political circumstances. This is despite the fact that, in the real world, migratory movements are driven by intertwined political and economic circumstances. Someone who leaves home to improve their livelihood does not have more choice than someone who must escape a hometown destroyed by war. The traumas in Libya that almost every sub-Saharan African migrant has endured are evidence that experiences cannot be divided between political and economic imperatives. 'Choice' is no choice.

To Europe, both 'migrants' and 'refugees' are seen as alien Others. In this hierarchy, the racialised Other is categorised as deserving or undeserving. The refugee, by their passive, political victimhood, can be granted a conditional place, whereas the migrant, being a 'free, economic agent' in European eyes, is undeserving until they earn their worth through substantial 'contribution' to their host society. The Eurocentric narration always omits the reality: there is a constant crossing-over and movement between 'refugees' and 'migrants'; the two are one. In Italy, the asylum reception system has clearly formed a symbiotic relationship with the underground world of migrant labour.

Europe's racial hierarchy places migrants (which has come to stand for so-called 'economic migrants') at the bottom of the pyramid, the category in which most Africans fall. They are the largest part of the subordinated class, building the Babylon of contemporary Europe.

What stood out throughout my research was the extent to which segregation exists and is still practised in twenty-first-century Italy. The categorisation and allocation of space according to race is evident across regions. Provincial towns are inhabited by white Italians while African workers are kept out and agrarianised. The colonial arrangement of space that Fanon described is still very much alive today; people from former colonies are being segregated in postcolonial Europe.

Such segregation, based on enduring racism rooted in colonialism, determines the lives of African workers in Italy. It keeps them in their subordinate place and drives them to work and live in desperate and often dangerous conditions. In many cases, segregation can kill them.

These facts became apparent to me soon after I visited camps in Italy in 2016, during my initial attempt to understand how the asylum reception system worked. I saw people kept in miserable conditions while their lives were put on hold indefinitely as they awaited their asylum decisions. Yet what lay beyond this visible misery was a mystery.

Back then, I stood on the hills in Corleone, Sicily, where an asylum reception camp was located, overlooking vast fields some distance away, when several boys from Gambia told me about their work on farms that they pointed out in the distance. This happened again and again, as people talked about the fields in which they toiled, far removed from the daily lives of the local populace. It was a world beyond the reception camps, with a vast, hidden layer of secrets and suffering, unknown to and unreachable by polite society.

When I went back to live in Italy in early 2018, things started to become even clearer as I immersed myself in the day-to-day lives of the people whom Italy was so keen to label and dehumanise. Living in west Sicily, I was surrounded by farming communities and was able to visit places where migrant workers congregated and built encampments and rural ghettoes. As I got to know many migrant workers, they gave me an insight into the lives they were leading and their place in the local community and society in general. Over several months, I found myself personally engaged in this segregated world of labour kept away from the public eye.

As a direct result of racism, agricultural work was the primary employment option for African workers in their first country of arrival in Europe. From February 2018 to December 2019, I followed in workers' footsteps moving from crop to crop, season to season, from Sicily to Calabria, and to Puglia, all major agricultural regions in Italy. To experience the physically demanding work and to get a real sense of the dynamic of worker–employer relationships, I asked a Gambian man to bring me to work in olive fields alongside him and his Gambian and Tunisian co-workers in west Sicily.

I saw the sacrifices these people were making in order to support their families back home. These workers are truly the hidden faces behind the image of 'Made in Italy.' Institutions, as well as society as a whole—from the years of the centrist administration to the fourteen-month-long far-right-led government that came into power in 2018, and now to the PD–Five Star coalition government—have all been guilty of enabling and maintaining these workers' exploitation and segregation. Under Matteo Salvini, the deputy prime minister and head of the Interior Ministry, whose government lasted until September 2019, these workers were being further criminalised and driven underground, their dignity as human beings stripped away. In 2020, the PD–Five Star coalition government showed no intention of ending Salvini's security decrees. Anti-migrant policies continued.

Ciao Ousmane flips the prevalent Eurocentric approach that paints a picture of migrant victimhood with the main protagonists being white saviours. This book gives an alternative, detailed account of how people rebel and resist, individually and collectively, against the indignities and injustices imposed on them. Throughout, they find ways to cope with their circumstances and fight back against the system that subjugates them. Benjamin, Sanji and Mohammad, three single dads, who were compelled by a variety of circumstances to leave home, found themselves seeking a livelihood in the olive fields surrounding a rural Sicilian town, Campobello. Their lives have been marked by their development of coping strategies to deal with appalling working and living conditions, evictions and frequent police raids, and by their fight against racism and racial violence.

Following Benjamin and many others who went to Rosarno and San Ferdinando in the Calabria region for the orange harvest in the winter, I witnessed a similar struggle in the rural ghettoes there. This is Matteo Salvini's constituency as a senator. Salvini has pointed the finger at migrant workers as the cause of the region's problems, instead of at the notorious Calabrian mafia, the 'Ndrangheta, which has controlled the recruitment of agricultural workers for years. The *tendopoli* to which Benjamin and his team headed one winter sat in large fields miles away from Rosarno and San Ferdinando, both of which had plenty of empty apartments. The townspeople did not want Africans in their midst. Not only did African workers have to deal with daily threats of racism and violence, but they were also living in an encampment in appalling conditions while their work was controlled by the local *caporali*. In between my visits, this Calabrian *tendopoli* saw the deaths of four workers, three in fires and one murdered by a local racist. Each time people lost their co-workers and comrades, they protested and went on strike. They did what they could to make their anger heard.

Becky Moses, a twenty-six-year-old Nigerian woman, was burnt to death during a fierce fire that swept through the *tendopoli* one night in January 2018. I traced her footsteps back to where she was placed in the reception system in Riace, a Calabrian village hailed as the model for 'integration.' I met with Becky's friends and looked into the employment aspect of the integration projects, in Riace and another small village nearby, Camini. I saw that the concept and practices of 'integration,' which have been treated as the common-sense approach in liberal circles, have always been based on a Eurocentric vision of history and pre-empted demands for equal rights by encouraging the passivity and invisibility of migrants and refugees. On the contrary, Becky's friends in Riace and Camini were not passive victims. They gave several years of their lives to these villages and tried living there, and when it didn't work, they took their destiny into their own hands and left for better opportunities elsewhere.

From 2018 to 2020, I witnessed a series of demolitions of informal encampments across the regions of Sicily, Calabria and Puglia.[2] No alternative housing was ever provided. Faced with political manoeuvring and emergency-based directives, many NGOs and local civil society groupings were complicit in their silence. Workers' unions were helpless in front of the bulldozers. Migrant workers were on their own. They fought their own battles with their own means and struggled to survive dehumanising working and living conditions in the midst of continuous police raids, crackdowns and evictions. Their working lives in Italy are characterised by this endless ghettoisation and high mobility—not by their own choice, but enabled by the state and its institutions.

In March 2020, whilst the Covid-19 pandemic swept across Italy,[3] neither local nor national governments offered a solution to workers' high-risk living environments. As Italians self-isolated in their homes, African workers remained crammed in tents and shacks, without regular water supply, let alone safety equipment such as face masks and disinfectants. Many of those without documents were unable to get access to medical help or be tested in hospitals if they fell ill. They remained on their own.

By May, the pandemic had created a shortage of between 250,000 and 270,000 agricultural workers in Italy.[4] Not only were Romanian and other southeastern European workers not arriving to harvest the crops, but the internal lockdown also meant that African workers couldn't always access farm work. Forty per cent of the crops risked rotting in the fields. In this context, the regularisation of migrant workers emerged as a national debate once again. The minister of agriculture, Teresa Bellanova, who left the PD to join Matteo Renzi's Italia Viva party, called for partial regularisation of undocumented workers 'in order to get the economy moving again.' In mid-May, having come to a compromise with Five Star, who had opposed regularisation from the start, the coalition government came up with a regularisation scheme that excluded the majority of African workers.[5]

'We contest that the regularisation is only reserved for those who have residence permits which have expired since October 2019, effectively excluding most of the victims of the security decrees still in force,' USB activist Aboubakar Soumahoro, who organised a one-day strike, said in a press statement.[6] 'We are invisible to the government, and so on 21 May we will be invisible in the fields.'[7]

Whilst industries and society were in urgent need of African workers' labour during the pandemic, they continued to bargain over its worth. As harvests carried on, with the cheapest and most flexible labour, capitalists and the political elite continued to demand that the majority of this workforce be 'out of sight, out of mind.' African workers who had been abandoned during the pandemic continued to work in asparagus fields, then picking tomatoes for €2–€3 per hour. To date, many have remained unable to change their irregular status.

This is truly the despicable nature of racial capitalism. For Europe, the 'necessary outcasts' are not removed, but kept well segregated and hidden, serving the needs of capital.

How do workers keep living and working in such circumstances of immense suffering and injustice? I often wonder how they have the strength to carry on. Ultimately, it is those regular phone calls from home, kids calling out to their mum or dad on the other end of the line, that keeps their hearts strong and ensures their resilience.

Ciao Ousmane is a tribute to the workers who cross borders to change their fates and the fates of their families. It is, at the same time, an exposé of the gravest, ugliest oppression forming the basis of much of Europe's wealth. Eventually, through the lived experience of racial alienation, the subordinated class becomes conscious of its place and emerges to confront its racialised existence and seeks to change it, like the hundreds of Gilets Noirs ('Black Vest') activists who stormed the Panthéon in Paris on 12 July 2019, demanding regularisation of their immigration status. 'We are not just fighting for papers [to be regularised] but against the whole system that produces *sans-papiers*,' said activist Houssam. 'We want to destroy all the actors in the racist system, or at least go on the attack against them.'[8] There were also the Sardine Nere ('Black Sardines'),[9] who went onto the streets of Naples in December 2019, protesting against their limbo status and demanding an immediate end to the continuation of Salvini's security decree under the PD–Five Star government.[10] 'Our lives cannot wait any longer,' they shouted out. Since June 2020, the Black Lives Matter movement that has flourished following the killing of George Floyd in the US has sparked further self-organisation and activism among African workers across Italy. They are not only demanding papers for all but also working towards the dismantling of a white supremacist society.

When members of this subordinated class take up their fight, they transform themselves from the object of the Eurocentric narrative into the subject of their own destiny. The object in-itself becomes a subject for-itself. As Fanon described, they then begin to realise themselves through the struggle for self-determination. In this struggle, the social relations that embody the 'race' and racialisation experienced by the subordinated class are disrupted and challenged. The eventual overthrow of these relations brings about the opportunity for self-emancipation and the hope of creating conditions for a universal humanity.

NOTES

FOREWORD

1. *Homo Sacer. Sovereign Power and Bare Life*, translated by Daniel-Heller Roazen, Stanford University Press, 1995.
2. See *We Are All Fast-Food Workers Now: The Global Uprising Against Poverty Wages*, Annelise Orleck, Beacon Press, 2018.
3. See 'A Raw Deal: Abuse of Thai Workers in Israel's Agricultural Sector', Human Rights Watch, 2015.
4. Ben Doherty, 'Hungry, Poor, Exploited: Alarm Over Australia's Import of Farm Workers', *The Guardian,* 2 August 2017. https://www.theguardian.com/global-development/2017/aug/03/hungry-poor-exploited-alarm-over-australias-import-of-farm-workers, last accessed 15 July 2020.
5. Cited in *The Black Man's Burden: Africa and the Curse of the Nation-State*, James Currey, 1992.
6. See 'Italian Fascist War Crimes in Ethiopia: a History of Their Discussion, from the League of Nations to the United Nations (1936-1949)', Richard Pankhurst, *Northeast African Studies, New Series*, Vol. 6, pp. 83-140, 1999.
7. Cited in *A History of Bombing*, Sven Lindqvist, Granta Books, 2000.

OMERTÀ

1. According to ISTAT, 2013.
2. In Sicily, there is a great variety of olives—currently, there are more than twenty-five cultivars.
3. According to ISTAT, 2013.

4. It was named after its architects Umberto Bossi, leader of the-then Northern League (*Lega Nord*), and Gianfranco Fini, the deputy prime minister and head of the National Alliance (*Alleanza Nazionale*, AN). The AN was a successor of the post-fascist Italian Social Movement and its members later founded Go Italy (*Forza Italia*) and Brothers of Italy (*Fratelli d'Italia* or FDL).

5. It was known as the *Centri di Permanenza Temporanea e Assistenza* (CPTA).

6. It was punishable by a fine of €5,000 to €10,000. It also became possible to detain migrants up to 180 days in Identification and Expulsion Centres (CIE).

7. The authorities set quotas for migrant workers in all categories of work, in an annual government decree (known as the *decreto flussi*).

8. https://home.kpmg/xx/en/home/insights/2019/04/flash-alert-2019-078.html

1. OLIVE COUNTRY

1. Loïc Wacquant is a sociologist of urban poverty and racial inequality and is currently a professor at University of California, Berkeley.

2. Quoted in an interview with Emily Eakin, 'A Professor Who Refuses to Pull His Punches', *New York Times*, 8 November 2003. https://www.nytimes.com/2003/11/08/books/a-professor-who-refuses-to-pull-his-punches.html, last accessed 15 July 2020.

3. The housing rights of migrant workers are set out by the Office of the United Nations High Commissioner for Human Rights (UN-OHCHR) in the Right to Adequate Housing, which has been recognised in many national constitutions and in the Universal Declaration of Human Rights.

4. Hand harvesting makes it possible to have an olive oil with low free acidity essential for extra virgin olive oil. The hand-picked olives are pressed after a maximum of twelve hours.

2. BUILDING BABYLON

1. 'Unionism of Migrant Farm Workers. The Sindicato Obreros del Campo (SOC) in Andalusia, Spain', Francesco Saverio Caruso, pp. 277-292 in *Migration and Agriculture: Mobility and Change in the Mediterranean Area*, ed. Alessandra Corrado, Carlos de Castro and Domenico Perrotta, Abingdon: Routledge, 2017, p. 280.

2. On the unfair practices imposed by large retailers to set prices, see Oxfam's June 2018 report, 'Human Suffering in Italy's Agricultural Value Chain'.

3.   Antonello Mangano is the founder of the investigative research platform terrelibere.org.

3. FIRES AND A MODEL WORKER

1.   Published in the journal *Sociologia Urbana e Rurale*, 117, 2018, pp. 12-36.
2.   Ibid., p. 23.

4. IN AND OUT OF CAMPS

1.   Martina Lo Cascio and Valeria Piro, "Dal Ghetto al Campo", p. 17.
2.   Apart from seasonal workers, Alcamo had more than 1,000 non-Sicilians residents here: over 700 Romanians, 200 Tunisians, and around 60 Albanians.
3.   See Martina Lo Cascio and Valeria Piro, "Dal Ghetto al Campo", pp. 10-11.
4.   Sergio Bonanzinga is an academic in the Department of Culture and Society, University of Palermo.
5.   Carolien Lubberhuizen, 'Bargaining Identity & Difference: The Construction of Local Identity at the Historical Marketplace of Ballarò, Palermo,' Utrecht University, 2017.

5. YOUNG LABOUR AND 'INTEGRATION'

1.   *Il Sistema di Protezione per Richiedenti Asilo e Rifugiati*, or the Protection System for Asylum Seekers and Refugees, a secondary reception centre.
2.   This is a shared theme of discussion in their work. See *La Mécanique Raciste*, Paris: Dilecta, 2008.
3.   See 'Can We Speak of a Postcolonial Racism?' by Pierre Tevanian and Saïd Bouamama, in *Colonial Culture in France since the Revolution,* ed. Pascal Blanchard, Sandrine Lemaire, Nicolas Bancel, Dominic Thomas, trans. Alexis Pernsteiner, pp. 527-535. Bloomington: Indiana University Press, 2014.
4.   'Italy Unveils Plan to Better Integrate Fewer Migrants', https://www.thelocal.it/20170209/italy-unveils-plan-to-better-integrate-fewer-migrants, 9 February 2017, last accessed 15 July 2020.

6. JOINING THE HARVEST IN CALABRIA

1.   Organised crime in Italy generated a turnover of €21.8 billion from agriculture in 2017, according to Coldiretti. See https://www.coldiretti.

it/economia/mafia-business-254-mld-euro-tavola, last accessed 15 July 2020.

2. It is the third highest in Europe, following the Spanish enclaves of Ceuta and Melilla in North Africa, according to Eurostat.

3. Michele Semprebon, Roberta Marzorati, Anna Mary Garrapa, *International Migration*, 55 (6), 2017, pp. 200-215.

4. See https://migration.ucdavis.edu/cf/more.php?id=40, last accessed 15 July 2020.

7. BECKY AND THE 'INTEGRATION' VILLAGES

1. 'Immigration to Italy is Falling for the First Time since 2014', thelocal.it, https://www.thelocal.it/20191216/immigration-to italy-is-falling-for-the-first-time-since-2014, last accessed 15 July 2020.

11. SALVINI AND A RACIST MURDER

1. 'Governo, Salvini: "Per i clandestini è finita la pacchia. Le ong? No a vicescafisti nei porti"', *La Repubblica*, 2 June 2018. https://www.repubblica.it/politica/2018/06/02/news/governo_salvini_lega_migranti-198005208/, last accessed 15 July 2020.

2. Catania is on the east coast of Sicily; Ragusa is in the southeast.

12. 'TELL ME, MINISTER, WOULD YOU YOURSELF LIVE IN A PLACE LIKE THIS?'

1. CARA: *Centri di Accoglienza per Richiedenti Asilo*, hosting centre for asylum seekers; CAS: *Centro di Accoglienza Straordinaria,* extraordinary reception centre.

2. See https://www.asylumineurope.org/reports/country/italy/content-international-protection/housing

3. See above.

4. According to Martina Lo Cascio and Valeria Piro, in their report 'Ghettos and Camps: The Institutional Production of Marginality in Sicilian Rural Areas' (*'Dal Ghetto al Campo: La Produzione Istituzionale di Marginalità Abitativa nelle Campagne Siciliane'*), *Sociologia Urbana e Rurale*, p. 26.

5. Ibid., p. 27.

6. Ibid., p. 27.

7. Ibid., p. 27.

13. OLIVE SEASON ONCE AGAIN

1. *Sistema di Protezione per Richiedenti Asilo e Rifugiati*, Protection System for Asylum Seekers and Refugees, a secondary reception centre.
2. Martina Lo Cascio and Valeria Piro, 'Ghettos and Camps: The Institutional Production of Marginality in Sicilian Rural Areas' ('Dal Ghetto al Campo: La Produzione Istituzionale di Marginalità Abitativa nelle Campagne Siciliane'), *Sociologia Urbana e Rurale,* p. 28.
3. Ibid., p. 28.
4. According to Professor Riccardo Valentini, a director of the Euro-Mediterranean Centre for climate change.

14. OUT OF SIGHT, OUT OF MIND

1. According to ISTAT. Also see https://www.cairn.info/journal-autrepart-2011-1-page-215.htm#, last accessed 19 July 2020.
2. Or a Social Security card in the United States.

17. END OF SEASON

1. Migrants set fire to the centre protesting about poor conditions, while employees were not paid wages for four months.

18. 'INTEGRATE' AND DISINTEGRATE

1. See 'Can We Speak of a Postcolonial Racism?' by Pierre Tevanian and Saïd Bouamama, in *Colonial Culture in France since the Revolution* (2014), Bloomington: Indiana University Press, p. 2.
2. More than 7,000 people were refused humanitarian protection status between October 2018 and February 2019, according to the Institute for International Political Studies (ISPI). https://www.theguardian.com/world/2019/feb/14/italy-rejects-record-number-of-asylum-applications

19. THE REPEATED CYCLE OF DEMOLISH AND RE-GHETTOISE

1. Italy had one of the strongest social centre movements in Europe. They first appeared in the 1970s and were the focus of radical urban movements in the country. They were subsequently transformed—with their formalisation and legalisation in the late 1980s and early 1990s, when they became leased by local councils, which changed their organisational structure.

2. *La Politica dei Subalterni: Organizzazione e Lotte del Bracciantato Migrante nel Sud Europa*, Rome: DeriveApprodi, 2015.
3. That is to say, no hours of work were guaranteed and therefore the employee could be dismissed or hired on the whim of the employer.

20. 'HOW MUCH LONGER DO WE HAVE TO SUFFER?'

1. These included crew members of the Luventa, from the German NGO Jugend Rettet (Youth Rescue); Open Arms, Aquarius, run by Médecins sans Frontières (MSF) and SOS Mediterranée; and Mare Jonio (Ionian Sea), operated by Italian NGO Mediterranea and sponsored by Sea Watch.
2. According to the IOM, by 9 October, 76,558 migrants reached Europe by all sea routes in 2019.
3. The pressure from the grassroots, especially after Five Star lost more than twenty MPs, eventually led to Di Maio's resignation as party leader in January 2020.
4. Alarm Phone is an activist collective that runs an emergency number to support rescue operations. It is formally known as WatchTheMed Alarm Phone, launched in autumn 2014. See https://movements-journal.org/issues/02.kaempfe/13.stierl--watchthemed-alarmphone.html.
5. The new president of the European Commission, Ursula von der Leyen, described in September 2019 the new role of vice-president in charge of migration as 'protecting the European way of life'.
6. The thirteen countries listed in the repatriation program are: Algeria, Morocco, Tunisia, Albania, Bosnia, Cape Verde, Ghana, Kosovo, North Macedonia, Montenegro, Senegal, Serbia and Ukraine.

AFTERWORD

1. See 'The Coloniality of Migration and the "Refugee Crisis": On the Asylum-Migration Nexus, the Transatlantic White European Settler Colonialism-Migration and Racial Capitalism,' *Refuge* 34 (1), 2018, pp. 16-28. Dr Encarnación Gutiérrez Rodríguez is Chair of Sociology at the University of Giessen, Germany.
2. Following a fire in the encampment of Borgo Mezzanone in April 2019 when a twenty-six-year-old Gambian man was killed, two hundred *carabinieri* and soldiers arrived on 11 July 2019 and demolished seventy-four shacks and evicted 130 people. However, the high-risk living environment created more fatal fires: one on 4 February 2020 that killed a thirty-one-year-old Nigerian woman, and then on 12 June,

one that took the life of Mohamed Ben Ali, a thirty-seven-year-old Senegalese worker.

3. In March, the Italian government set up a new decree and declared the country's ports "unsafe" for ships carrying migrants rescued at sea. The decree lasted till 31 July, and since then, migrants, including minors (coming into the country as well as many already living in reception centres) have been sent to overcrowded, poorly managed quarantine ships.

4. According to Minister of Agriculture Teresa Bellanova.

5. Regularisation occurs through two channels: 1) Employers who have previously hired undocumented workers can come forward and apply for work contracts for their employees (who had been identified by photo-signing before 8 March 2020), in which case the employer pays €400 for each worker; 2) A worker who has a residence permit that has expired since 31 October 2019 and who hasn't left the country before 8 March 2020 can apply for a temporary resident permit, which costs €160, to look for a job. The permit can last from three to six months. Soon enough, it became clear that most farmers didn't want the burden of regularising workers. Moreover, the rules didn't consider those affected by the security decree under the previous Salvini-led administration. Only those who were irregular since 31 October 2019 could hope for the six-month 'job search permit'.

6. See https://www.radiopopolare.it/sciopero-degli-invisibili-21-maggio-intervista-a-aboubakar-soumahoro/ last accessed 19 Jul 2020.

7. In mid-July 2020, the majority of Italy's agricultural migrant workers were still being kept out of the government's regularisation scheme. According to data from the interior ministry, only about 80,000 migrant workers have applied so far. Eighty-eight per cent of applications are unrelated to agriculture. In mid-October, the interior ministry announced that 220,000 migrants have applied for temporary documents – the majority of them not in agriculture.

8. See 'The Gilets Noirs Are in the Building', https://www.jacobinmag.com/2019/07/gilets-noirs-france-protesters-sans-papiers?fbclid=IwAR2hmTCS1TriuhRxQld5rXttTJJrvB3Kenl6WEAcjXptSpUC5ASFNyf3xSk

9. The Sardines, a grassroots political movement against Salvini, began in Italy in November 2019. The 'Black Sardines' (*Le Sardine Nere*) was formed by migrants in Naples who wanted their voices heard and had not been able to do so at the Sardines protests. Later, the Black Sardines changed its name to 'Migrant Movement' (*Movimento Migranti*).

10. Salvini's security decrees were amended by a government decree approved by the cabinet on the 5th of October 2020, despite opposition from some Five-Star politicians. Rescue boats which violate official orders in carrying out their activity will now face lighter fines of up to $59,000. The new decree will also ban repatriation that would put the repatriated person at risk of torture.

BIBLIOGRAPHY

Amnesty International, 'Exploited Labour: Migrant Workers in Italy's Agricultural Sector', London, 18 December 2012.

Blanchard, Pascal, Sandrine Lemaire, and Nicolas Bancel (eds), *Colonial Culture in France Since the Revolution*, Bloomington: Indiana University Press, 2014.

Caruso, Francesco, *La Politica dei Subalterni: Organizzazione e Lotte del Bracciantato Migrante nel Sud Europa*, Rome: DeriveApprodi, 2015.

Corrado, Alessandra, Carlos de Castro, and Domenico Perrotta (eds), *Migration and Agriculture: Mobility and Change in the Mediterranean Area*, London: Routledge, 2017.

Fanon, Frantz, *Black Skin, White Masks*, tr. Charles Lam Markmann, London: Pluto, 1991.

———, *The Wretched of the Earth*, tr. Constance Farrington, London: Penguin, 2001.

Garau, Eva, *Politics of National Identity in Italy*, London: Routledge, 2015.

International Migration, Vol. 51, No. 3, September 2017.

Oxfam, 'Human Suffering in Italy's Agricultural Value Chain', Oxford, 21 June 2018.

Refuge: Canada's Journal on Refugees, Vol. 34, No. 1, 2018.

Sociologia Urbana e Rurale, No. 118, January 2018.

Soumahoro, Aboubakar, *Umanità in Rivolta: La Nostra Lotta per il Lavoro e il Diritto alla Felicità*, Rome: Feltrinelli Editore, 2019.

Tevanian, Pierre, *La Mécanique Raciste*, Paris: Éditions Dilecta, 2008.

ACKNOWLEDGEMENTS

I am so grateful to all of you who opened your hearts and shared your stories with me. You let me walk into your life and see your suffering and pain. You gave me your friendship and spent time with me. You wanted your situation to be known to the outside world. You've wanted change. *Ciao Ousmane* is for you and for your struggle. I truly hope that it will contribute, even in a small way, towards that change.

I'd like to give my warmest thanks to Michael Dwyer, my publisher at Hurst, and my editor Farhaana Arefin, for choosing to bring out this book. Thank you so much for giving space to a subject from which many in the publishing industry tend to shy away. Thank you for giving a platform for these voices to be heard. Thank you so much for your hard work in producing this.

Warmest thanks to Liz Fekete, director of the Institute of Race Relations (IRR), for kindly giving feedback on the manuscript and for writing the brilliant foreword. Thank you so much, Liz, for your very kind encouragement and support!

My sincere thanks go to sociologist Francesco Caruso in Benevento. You gave me advice and enriched my understanding of Italian agriculture and its labour. I learned a great deal from our meetings in Rosarno and your hometown Benevento. I'm so grateful to Alberto Biondo of Borderline Sicilia—you shared your insights especially on the asylum reception system and kindly introduced me to your local contacts.

Thank you, Salvatore Inguì, Anna Maria Alagna and colleagues for welcoming me at the Sappusi social centre in Marsala and talking to me about social anti-mafia activism. Many thanks, John Hampson, for your great help and company in Camini—I couldn't have done this without you!

Many, many thanks to Patrick Ward for editing the first few chapters. Big thanks to Philip Grant, my copyeditor, for being so thorough and brilliant! Also, huge thanks to Daisy Leitch, Production Director, for looking after the book from proof to print. Thank you all very much for your professionalism.

I want to thank my partner, Dave Barkway, especially, for your consistent, loving support throughout. You are the person who makes sure the day-to-day is fine, which has enabled me to carry on with the research. You were the one to talk to after a difficult day and you were the sounding board. At the end of the project when I was ill, you were always there for me, no matter how difficult it became. My big thanks also goes to your brother Michael for his kind support and help throughout. Thank you all so much.